Pomp and Circumstances

Also by Claire Mowat
The Outport People (1983)

CLAIRE MOWAT

Pomp and Circumstances

Includes a 16-page section
of photographs

M&S

Canadian Cataloguing in Publication Data

Mowat, Claire
Pomp and Circumstances

ISBN 0-7710-6548-5

1. Mowat, Claire. 2. Governors general—Canada.
3. Scandinavia—Description and travel.
4. Schreyer, Edward, 1935- . 5. Ladies-in-waiting—Canada—Biography. I. Title.

FC626.M6A3 1989   971.064'4'0924   C89-093645-5
F1034.3.M6A3 1989

All photos in the 16-page picture insert courtesy of Peter Bregg of *Canadian Press*, with the exception of those taken by the author.

Cover Design: Pronk&Associates

Printed and bound in Canada

McClelland & Stewart Inc.
The Canadian Publishers
481 University Avenue
Toronto, Ontario
M5G 2E9

for Ed and Lily Schreyer

Acknowledgements

My thanks to Lily Poritz Miller for her editorial assistance, to Mary Elliott who not only typed the manuscript many times but gave me valuable advice as well, to Peter Bregg who generously gave me photographs, to Robin Long who provided me with a place to work, and to Farley for his never-ending encouragement. I am most grateful to Lily Schreyer who invited me to join this journey, and to the many members of the governor general's household and staff who were always helpful and who shared their trade secrets with me.

Contents

What infinite heart's ease
Must kings neglect that private men enjoy!
And what have kings that privates have not too,
Save ceremony, save general ceremony?
And what art thou, thou idol ceremony?
What kind of god art thou, that suffer'st more
Of mortal griefs than do thy worshippers?
What are thy rents? what are thy comings-in?
O ceremony! show me but thy worth.

Shakespeare
KING HENRY V

Cast of Characters

ED: a political *wunderkind* who was once the youngest member of the Manitoba legislature, then the youngest premier of Manitoba, and ultimately the youngest governor general of Canada in this century. He is married to

LILY: an effervescent, red-haired people-person who has cheerfully shared and assisted this amazing career while managing to maintain her sense of humour.

CLAIRE: an author who shares with Lily that peculiar mixture of joys and problems which results from being married to a dynamo. She is married to

FARLEY: another author who once, long ago, beseeched the young premier of Manitoba to halt the slaughter of whales in Hudson Bay. By the time this was accomplished they had become pals for life.

THE CAST ALSO INCLUDES: aides-de-camp, butlers, chamberlains, diplomats, equerries, footmen, generals, horses, interpreters, judges, kings, ladies-in-waiting, mounties, noblemen, officers, photographers, queens . . . and many others.

THE TIME IS SPRING 1981.

The Beginning

*I*t all began with a phone call one December morning in 1978.

"Heard the news?" asked a long-time friend.

"No. What's up?"

"Your pal, Ed Schreyer, has just been named governor general of Canada!"

"Ed? Governor general? You've got to be kidding."

"I just heard it on CBC. They interrupted 'Morningside' to announce it."

"I can't believe it," I said, and sat down.

As the news slowly sank in I floated an inch off my chair. Could this actually be? Could someone we *knew* have been appointed to the most exalted office in Canada? I made a pot of tea and called Farley away from his typewriter to share the excitement.

Ed's appointment defied the previous guidelines for selecting a governor general. For one thing, he was, relatively, very young — only forty-two years old, whereas the previous four Canadian governors general had all been about sixty when they were

11

appointed. There had been, Farley and I dimly recalled, some youngish men — dukes and earls — back in the nineteenth century, who had been dispatched from Britain to keep the colonials in line. However, since 1952 our governors general have all been born in Canada and the office has been held alternately by men of British and French ancestry, but Ed was neither. He was of Austrian-German extraction, the grandson of farmers who had left eastern Europe in the 1890s to settle in Manitoba. Perhaps even more astonishing was Ed's political background. Far from being a pillar of either the Liberal or the Tory establishment, he was a social democrat. Most of the previous incumbents had been so Tory blue they had been indistinguishable from the colour of the vice-regal flag.

"This makes sense, you know," said Farley as we mulled over the amazing development. "Stop and think. It's an English speaker's turn at the job, but Ed's appointment isn't going to antagonize Quebec quite as much as another Toronto Tory would. *And* he's from the West. It might appease the westerners' alienation once they have one of their own sitting on the throne."

"And he knows so many languages," I remembered. "German, Ukrainian, and Polish, as well as French and English."

"Gets better and better," Farley agreed.

"Still, he's so young."

"So why should the governor general's job be reserved for senior citizens?"

Why indeed?

That afternoon I bought a copy of every newspaper available at our local variety store. There it was in bold headlines. Buckingham Palace had announced that Edward Richard Schreyer was going to be Canada's twenty-second governor general. Ed and his wife Lily, my vivacious friend, were about to become *Their Excellencies*.

The circumstances that had brought the four of us together were far-removed from the realm of protocol. It was an ecological matter that prompted Farley to call on the then-premier of Manitoba in 1973. He went to Winnipeg to protest the proposal of a tourist-lodge operator in Churchill, Manitoba, who planned to take boatloads of tourists out into Hudson Bay to experience the dubious pleasure of shooting a white whale.

''This is dreadful and I'm asking you to use your power to prevent it,'' proclaimed Farley with righteous indignation.

Premier Schreyer deliberated with the cabinet minister responsible for northern development and, together with the innkeeper, they turned the project around in a matter of days. Tourists would now be taken out in boats to *look* at the beluga whales and biology students would be hired to explain the life cycle of the whale.

Every participant went away from those negotiations with a smile. After that Ed and Farley discovered that they were on the same wavelength on many issues. Lily and I liked one another and we all became friends.

On a January morning seven weeks after that memorable phone call, Farley and I were among the hundreds of people who sat in the Senate Chamber in Ottawa to witness the ceremonious installation of a new governor general. Choirs sang; regiments marched; cannons fired a 21-gun salute across the snowy expanse of Parliament Hill; and I wept with joy. When it was over, an open, horse-drawn landau

13

whisked the Schreyers away to Rideau Hall in wintry splendour that rivalled the cinematic magic of *Doctor Zhivago*.

There was a magnificent banquet that evening in the ballroom of Rideau Hall, the rambling mansion that has housed our governors general since the time of Charles Stanley, Lord Monck, and that would house the Schreyer family for the next five years. One-hundred-and-twenty overjoyed friends and relatives had gathered to celebrate an event which none of us could ever have foreseen. If my participation in Ed and Lily's new life had never gone beyond that one triumphant evening, I would have been quite content. But that evening turned out to be only the beginning.

Farley and I have gone to considerable lengths to know our complicated country well and it is our good fortune that we are both comfortable meeting strangers. Because of this we were among the many friends of Ed and Lily who were occasionally invited to be present at Government House events. We were able to help with the pleasant task of putting guests at their ease. Most of the people who are formally invited to Rideau Hall to receive an award or attend a banquet will probably only be there once in their lives. If they speak to the governor general, it will only be for a minute or two. Another hour or two will be spent in the company of the other guests and with various members of the governor general's household, family and friends who do their best to make sure everyone has a memorable time.

I enjoyed doing this. I can chat easily about a range of trivial subjects. I usually remember people's names, dance well, and find it easy to smile. I had a lot to smile about. How many people ever find themselves being summoned to the summit to help the sovereign — or the nearest approximation we'll ever have in egalitarian, post-colonial Canada?

We had always known that Ed and Lily were tireless travellers. Lily likes to soak up the scenery and architecture, savour new cuisine and absorb the ambience of an interesting place, which is also the way I like to travel. Ed, on the other hand, becomes curious about the physical realities — geography, geophysics, and geothermal energy all fascinate him — in fact, everything that begins with the Greek prefix *geo-*, of the earth, is grist to his mill. Had his mother foreseen his future, she might well have named him George. Ed pores over maps the way some people gobble up novels.

A state visit is a highly structured series of events whereby one country pays a visit to another. The central figures are the two people who wear the mantle of the head of their respective states. In a monarchy it is the monarch. In a republic it is the president. In Canada it is the governor general. Ed Schreyer was the governor general of Canada from 1979 to 1984.

Canada doesn't have an entrenched tradition of sending governors general abroad on state visits. We only began to do this with Governor General Roland Michener during the 1960s. However, contrary to the nature of the word, traditions are always changing. The governor general's role, while it may seem to be suspended in lucite, is evolving. Every governor general of Canada has some latitude in how he or she may interpret the functions of head of state. And Ed, in the tradition of Roland Michener and Jules Léger, strongly believed that one of those functions should be to carry Canada's national presence to other countries.

It was in January of 1981, two years after Ed and

Lily and their children had settled into a life of pomp and ceremony, that a state visit abroad was first discussed in our presence. I sat snugly in front of one of Rideau Hall's many fireplaces one evening and listened with a mixture of awe and envy while Ed outlined their itinerary. They would travel to the five nations known to the world as the Nordic countries: Sweden, Finland, Norway, Denmark, and Iceland.

"I find it quite interesting," explained Ed, "that three of those five have monarchies and the other two have presidents. They all have their own flags and each has a parliamentary government of its own. Yet there's a peculiar alliance among them. For instance, when our protocol people enquired which one of the five we should visit first, they all agreed it should be Sweden. No jockeying for precedence, apparently."

I have had an absorbing interest in Europe's northernmost nations for years. As an art student, I looked to those countries for inspiration when I grew bored with the avalanche of mediocrity that assaulted me every day from the one nation which mesmerizes Canadians — the United States. As far as I was concerned, the Scandinavians did things right. They designed with imagination and manufactured with precision — whether it was Danish jewellery, Swedish cars, or Norwegian cheese. Icelanders knitted the world's best sweaters. And Finnish architecture was in a class by itself.

Farley had long been interested in Norse history. He spent five years writing *Westviking*, a book about the westward voyages of the ancient Scandinavians. At the drop of a hat, he can talk up a storm about the migrations of the tenth-century people who left Norway for Iceland and then later sailed from Greenland to Canada. Fortunately, he rarely does.

16

"You really ought to come with us," Ed said unexpectedly.

"Yes, why don't you?" Lily urged. "Then we'll at least have someone to talk to."

I laughed. "But Lily, you're not going to be travelling by yourselves. You'll have all those External Affairs people as well as your household. I doubt if there would even be room for us."

"Of course there's room. And besides, I have to choose a lady-in-waiting. That's it! Claire, I want you for my lady-in-waiting."

"Me? Lady-in-waiting?" I was stunned. "Well, I . . . I don't have any experience. I wouldn't know what to do. Well, not exactly."

"You don't need experience. All you have to do is be charming. And get all dressed up," Lily said mirthfully.

Lady-in-waiting. Such a marvellous medieval title. To me it belonged in Shakespearian dramas. The lady-in-waiting always seemed to be sitting on stage in an Elizabethan chair, daintily doing embroidery while the action swirled around some princess and her lover. But this was the 1980s. What were ladies-in-waiting doing now that the age of chivalry had passed?

I was thrilled to be asked to take part, but apprehensive. Just where was I going to learn what would be expected of me? We don't have a "court" tradition in Canada. It was easy to be the charming hostess when I was on familiar turf, but it would be another matter to know what to do and say in a court setting presided over by a monarch and bound by a multitude of ancient rites and rituals. Nevertheless my trepidation was overruled by my enthusiasm.

"Farley will come too, of course," Lily insisted.

"As what?" Farley asked. "The husband-in-waiting to the lady-in-waiting?"

"No, not at all," said Ed. "You could come along as part of the press entourage."

"But Farley would have to sleep in a hotel somewhere while Claire got stuck in a palace," Lily protested.

"Like Rapunzel," Farley mused. "Claire can stand at the window and let her hair down while I climb up and sneak into her room."

"I have a better idea," Ed continued. "You can be the artistic presence, my advisor on cultural matters. Besides, don't they publish your books in those countries?"

They do. Farley is one of a handful of Canadian authors whose work has been translated into Swedish, Finnish, Danish, and Norwegian. Only Iceland had not published any of his work but even there his short stories have been read on their radio network.

"I can create a new role," said Ed firmly. "Not an advisor. After all, External Affairs gives me more than enough advice. You can be . . . companion. That ought to cover a multitude of functions. Companion to the governor general. That way you'll be part of the Accompanying Party. Otherwise we'd seldom see you."

"Well, I've played a lot of roles," Farley mused, "but never one like that. However . . . there are those who find me companionable—in my way . . ." he grinned.

"You mean you *will* come?" Lily exclaimed.

Farley caught my eye. "If I turn this down, Claire will never forgive me."

"You realize that you'll have to buy Claire a whole new wardrobe," Lily said, a little apprehensively.

No doubt about that. Although the invitation was

sudden, this was no spur-of-the-moment journey of the sort we had usually undertaken on our own. This expedition would involve more planning than any I had ever known before. Our names would be needed immediately for diplomatic travel documents, invitations, accommodation and seating plans. I would need a lot of clothes of the sort I do not usually wear. Evening gowns, to start with. And hats. And shoes and handbags that matched each other and everything else. In an expansive mood, Farley declared that the least he could do for Canada was to outfit me in a manner that would do our country proud. But, though he didn't give it much thought at the time, he was also going to need a few new clothes himself.

For example, Farley would be obliged to buy something he had never owned, a three-piece, pinstriped suit. In fact, he didn't even own a two-piece suit. His wardrobe was a modest array of comfortable sweaters and slacks, with jackets made of tweed or corduroy. His only quasi-formal outfit was his Scots regalia: kilt, velvet jacket, sporran and shoes with silver buckles. But that ethnic costume would not satisfy protocol.

We live in a small Ontario town which is not noted for its haute couture, and spend our summers on a farm in Nova Scotia. Only rarely do either of us attend events that can be described as "formal." One or two new outfits a year usually meet my needs. Now that had to change, and in a hurry. I suddenly began haunting the dress salons of Toronto and Ottawa.

I had always imagined that this kind of shopping spree would be pure delight, an act of self-indulgence as gluttonous as eating a whole box of chocolates by myself. I soon learned something only a few women ever have the chance to discover. For those who *must* dress well, whether they be princesses, prime ministers or the wives of prime ministers, shopping soon becomes a chore, time-consuming, and hard on the feet as well. Unless she has her own couturier and a clothing budget that rivals that of the wife of a South American dictator, a high-profile woman in our culture is faced with endless hours of tiresome shopping over the course of such a career if she hopes to look presentable, at least, and interesting at best.

By the time the search was all over—if, indeed, a woman's search for clothes is ever over — I never wanted to see another dress shop. I vowed I would wear my spring 1981 wardrobe forever. But, I must confess, it's a vow I haven't kept.

Lily Schreyer always had a flair for clothes. She could look flamboyant, solemn, colourful or casual —whatever the occasion demanded. And she had to do it at her husband's personal expense. In Canada the wife of the governor general does not receive a clothing allowance.

"Men have it easy," Lily observed on the weekend in March when I arrived in Ottawa to plan our wardrobes for the grand tour. "Ed can get by with two dark blue suits and one formal dinner suit. That's basically all he needs to cover every eventuality. Can you imagine how it would go over if I tried to dress like that?"

She was right, but the psychology of it still puzzles me. Why are we enchanted by the sight of the Princess of Wales in her latest dress and hat, while we barely notice the new suit her husband may be wearing?

"Bring *every*thing with you," advised Thelma Francoeur, the shy, industrious woman who was Lily's dresser. "Better to have too much than not enough. You won't be carrying your own bags, you know.''

Thelma looked after Lily's clothes, and it was a full-time task. Lily's daily schedule often demanded three or four changes. On an average Ottawa day there might be a reception in the morning, then a luncheon, followed by a visit to some worthy institution, with perhaps a formal event in the evening. To make matters even more complicated, the daily agenda often involved events in other cities and towns. The amount of time required for packing and unpacking, pressing, sewing on the odd button, as well as dispatching things to the cleaners, and putting everything away so it could all be found again in a hurry was formidable. But Thelma was up to it. She had already served the wives of two governors general—Nora Michener and Gaby Léger—and few people in Canada knew as much about the mechanics of maintaining the image as did the self-effacing Thelma.

Among her responsibilities was keeping a record of what Lily wore to every event. This is the same procedure used by Queen Elizabeth's dresser and, presumably, those of every other queen, so that their ladies will not appear at some annual event wearing the same dress they wore the year before. Lily attended an average of four-hundred-and-fifty events a year and it was impossible to remember what she wore unless it was written down. For some reason people are insulted if Number One comes back a second time wearing that same blue velvet dress, no matter how beautiful it might be. Thrift is not a quality admired in high-profile ladies; showmanship is.

For two solid days, Lily, Thelma and I huddled together in the sitting-room of the Byng Suite in

21

Rideau Hall and pored over the official program. Lily and I had to decide, well in advance, every single thing we were going to wear to every event for nineteen days. We ploughed through page after page of an itinerary prepared by the Department of External Affairs and the governor general's household which told us, in general terms, what kind of clothes were required for women and men for each event. "Afternoon dress", "hat", "dark suit", "evening dress", "white tie", "decorations," or sometimes that curious category known as "lounge suit" appeared beside the name of the occasion. In my mind, "lounge suit" always conjures up images of a velvet smoking jacket, but what it means is that the men wear business suits, or blazers and trousers. They must still wear shirts and ties, of course.

The clothes plan also ensured that Lily and I would not appear together in similar outfits. The governor general's wife had to be the woman to stand out in a crowd or in a photograph. It would be confusing if we stepped onto the tarmac looking like two flight attendants from the same airline. Tarmac? No, we wouldn't be stepping onto the tarmac. We would be walking on carpets, red ones at that.

The itinerary was bewildering—a whirl of luncheons, dinners, layings of wreaths and visits to hospitals — peppered with place names we had never heard of and could barely pronounce: Kouvola, Rovaniemi, Århus, Thingvellir. Often we simply had to guess when we were going to need low-heeled shoes, or raincoats, or hatpins. Would a wool suit be warm enough in Rovaniemi in the north of Finland in May? Would a coat be needed for an evening event in Bodø, Norway? What sort of weather should we expect in Iceland in June? Once in a while, when I wasn't pondering weighty problems such as whether my bone-coloured shoes would look all right with my yellow dress, I actually gave a thought to the people who lived in those exotic places, people who would now be busy making complicated arrangements to receive us. Just what was I going to *say* to them?

I speak rudimentary French and I know a handful of Icelandic words, but not a syllable of Swedish, Finnish, Norwegian, or Danish. There wouldn't be time to learn. Even Ed, with his fluency in five languages, didn't speak a Scandinavian tongue. The language problem could be resolved through the use of interpreters but I still had the jitters. How was I going to project a sufficient aura of sophistication among those formidable people who had full-time careers in that rarified world of protocol and palaces?

At Canadian Forces Air Base in Ottawa on the May morning of our departure, I got my first taste of what was to come. We were driven from Rideau Hall to the airport in a column of black limousines and police cars. As our chauffeurs pulled up sedately to the front door of the air terminal, I glanced across the runway at the waiting Canadian Forces 707 jet. This was a weekly flight which originated at the air base in Trenton, Ontario and flew first to Ottawa, then on to the Canadian Forces base in Lahr, West Germany. Both crew and passengers were waiting—just for us. No one on that plane was going anywhere until we did.

Inside the terminal building we did not have to listen to departure announcements, and no one asked for tickets or passports. We were ushered into the VIP lounge where there was coffee, and the ambassadors of the five Nordic countries. Together with their spouses, they had come to see us off, for this is the protocol when one head of state is departing to pay a visit to another's country—a final reassurance that all is well between them. We chatted amiably, mainly about the weather, until one of our aides-de-camp caught my eye and inclined his head in the direction of the aircraft. It was time to leave, time to take on the world. Well, part of the world anyway.

When the governor general flies with the military, the forward section of the aircraft is partitioned off to create a private cabin fitted with two tables, each flanked by four first-class-width seats. Behind that there are two divans on which it is possible to stretch out full-length and sleep. There were even fresh flowers at Ed and Lily's table in a small vase that was fastened down with masking tape so it wouldn't slide into their laps during take-off.

This drawing-room was ours exclusively during the seven-hour flight to West Germany. Ten of us— Ed and Lily, their thirteen-year-old son Jason, two aides-de-camp, an RCMP inspector, Esmond Butler, Léopold Amyot, and Farley and I shared this elite space.

Tall, impeccable Esmond Butler held the august position of Secretary to the Governor General—the Canadian equivalent of court chamberlain. Esmond had served every Canadian governor general since Vincent Massey. Jaunty Léopold Amyot, a career diplomat with much Gallic charm and boundless energy, was then the Chief of Protocol for Canada, a job that comes under the jurisdiction of the Department of External Affairs. These two men, and their staffs, were responsible for the painstaking business of stage-managing epic tours like ours. They were the director and producer of the show.

"Good morning, sir," the captain said crisply to the governor general, as we buckled our seat-belts. "This is our route today," he added, handing him an aerial chart with each leg of our transatlantic journey carefully plotted. Ed always wanted to see flight plans. The captain immediately returned to the cockpit, the aircraft door was firmly bolted, the engines roared, and we were off.

A strict dress code obtains for everyone, military or civilian, travelling on board a Canadian military flight. Jeans are not permitted. Males must wear ties, and that includes boys travelling with their parents. Tidy people create a better impression when they're seen disembarking at foreign airports. If one is travelling with the military, tidiness is a matter to be taken seriously. No alcohol is served on military flights, not that I would have wanted any at nine o'clock in the morning. After take-off I sat contentedly with my cup of instant coffee, served in a Royal Doulton cup and saucer, watching the landmass of eastern Canada slip by below.

Lily, Jason and ADC David John had settled down to a game on Lily's portable Scrabble board. Farley was deep in a book about a new archaeological discovery in Denmark. Ed was busy writing something —a speech most likely. Esmond Butler, Léopold Amyot, and ADC Bernie St. Laurent were all engrossed in piles of paper dealing with final adjustments to our schedule—changes to be added to the briefing-book each of us carried.

These books were to be our Bibles for the next three weeks. There would be scant time to read anything else. From the pages of each pocket-size, three-ring notebook our master plan unfolded. Every moment was plotted. Every event and every participant was listed. Each doorway through which we were to pass was duly noted, as was every pause for an official photograph. The number of minutes it took to get out of an automobile or to walk from the front door to the dining-room or to say a gracious farewell was precisely calculated and noted according to the twenty-four-hour clock. There were diagrams of war memorials charting the correct way to approach them. Every car in which we were to ride was numbered. Nothing was left to chance. It takes from six months to a year to organize the infinite details of a state visit.

For an hour or more I studied my briefing-book as intently as if preparing for an examination. I soon got bogged down in all its minutiae and long lists of unpronounceable names. At lunchtime I was rescued by Captain St. Laurent, who realized how bewildered I was.

"Never try to take in more than one day at a time," he suggested, a bit of advice that ought to apply equally to everyday life.

Bernie St. Laurent of the Royal Twenty-Second Regiment—the historic Vandoos—had been an ADC to the governor general for a year and a half, and a career military man for seven years before that. He knew what it was to live by the book. A compact, dark-eyed twenty-seven-year-old from Baie Comeau, Quebec, Bernie had an impish smile and a sense of humour that would relieve a few desperate situations in the days ahead. After lunch, I gratefully put my briefing-book away, then read nothing heavier than a fashion magazine.

When we landed at the Canadian base in Lahr it was midnight, local time. We were quickly dispatched to various small hotels in this picturesque corner of the Black Forest region of southern West Germany. We spent two days in Lahr, mainly so that we could sleep away our jet lag. We had also to wait for the arrival of Mark MacGuigan, the Canadian Minister of External Affairs, and several members of his staff who would be travelling on to Sweden with us.

Lahr is almost a Canadian colony in the middle of western Europe. Its economy revolves around the presence of the Canadian military. Along the main street, many of the shops display small Canadian flags in the window to indicate that the merchants speak English and French and welcome Canadian customers.

Even though I'm an incurable tourist, I didn't see very much of the place. A sense of self-preservation told me I should conserve my energy for the marathon ahead. My principal recollection of Lahr is one of sleeping for twelve hours at a stretch and waking up to the springtime songs of birds.

Rested, but not entirely relaxed, we took off for Stockholm on a Monday morning that smelled of lilacs. The thirty-five Canadians on board our Armed Forces Boeing 707 had the plane to themselves. We shared a mood of high excitement for this was the real beginning of our odyssey and it was also the first time we were seeing one another in full finery. All dressed up, we really did have somewhere to go. Even Farley, who has traditionally taken a perverse pride in being one of Canada's worst-dressed men, looked newly respectable in his pin-striped suit.

Sweden

Monday, May 18, 1981
Stockholm Arrival
Dress: Dark Suit
    Afternoon Dress
    with Hat and Gloves

I read the list of those who would be at Arlanda air-port to greet us: the Canadian ambassador to Swe-den, the Swedish ambassador to Canada (who had nipped smartly off to Sweden as soon as he had said farewell to us in Ottawa), the Swedish Minister of Foreign Affairs, the Swedish Chief of Protocol. On and on it went. How was I going to keep track of all these people?

And Sweden. What did I know about it anyway? Just the dull stuff of school essays. When I actually tried to imagine the place I saw only green fields dotted with wild strawberries; sombre clergymen dressed in black; and tousle-haired virgins plucking chickens on fourteenth-century farms. Most of my images of Sweden had come from the films of Ingmar Bergman.

Still, it was incongruous that my first glimpse of anything Swedish should have been a fighter air-craft. In fact, there were three of them — menacing, needle-nosed little planes that darted out of the blue and flew a parallel course barely beyond our wing-tips. I have seen it happen on television but in real life I did not expect to find masked men looking in at me while I was five miles up in the air. The pilots wore oxygen masks but they were near enough to us that we could see their eyes as they turned to face us. I sat there, safely buckled into my seat, hypno-tized by a display of military aerobatics that seemed too close for comfort to me. We were not in peril. It was Sweden's salute to us, to thirty-five diverse play-ers who were fast approaching the moment when the curtain would go up on act one of our pageant.

Sweden was hidden by clouds as we flew across the border but the stunning arrival of the Swedish Air Force shocked me out of my reverie. While most of our group scurried from side to side of the cabin for a better view of the fighter planes as they circled around us like figure skaters, Ed had to watch calmly from his seat. A head of state does not stand up to take a salute inside an aircraft, even though that might seem like the appropriate response. The Swed-ish pilots kept their faces toward us for a minute or so, the way soldiers respond to an ''eyes right'' in a military parade. Then, once we began to descend into a bank of cumulus clouds, the three little planes tilted, turned and, with the precision of sanderlings, vanished into the mist.

We were now only minutes away from our arrival. Lily and I started fussing with our hats and those antiquated devices I hadn't seen anyone use since my grandmother's time: hatpins. Ladies' hats, we had been advised, tend to blow off at airports. Ed touched up his morning shave with a portable razor. Captain Bernie St. Laurent buttoned his spectacular red tunic. Up to this point he had been travelling in his undershirt. His dress jacket, made of heavy wool serge, was not designed for the era of jet travel. Nor was his hat, a towering black fur busby of the sort worn by the guards outside Buckingham Palace. He couldn't wear it until he was about to leave the aircraft because if he put it on inside the plane he wouldn't be able to stand up straight.

The seat-belt signal flashed and we emerged from the clouds above a patchwork of green fields. Suddenly I thought of a dozen more questions I wanted to ask Léopold Amyot, our protocol expert, but the wheels had touched the runway and it was too late to plead for help. The lady-in-waiting was on her own.

The 707 halted in front of one of the long, low buildings of Bromma airport. The second that the engines died, Léopold came bounding down the aisle. He was the first out of his seat since it was his job to ensure that the rest of us left the plane in the correct sequence. The first person to appear at the top of the portable aluminum airport steps would be Ed, followed by Lily and Jason and then by aide-de-camp Captain St. Laurent. As the door swung open Bernie donned his tall hat. He had to bend forward at a 45-degree angle to do this, and then charge out through the opening like a matador. He snapped to attention at the top of the steps and there the four of them stood solemnly at attention while a band struck up "O Canada," immediately followed by the Swedish national anthem. As the last note sounded, Léopold hustled the rest of us out of the aircraft like well-regulated school children. Mark MacGuigan led the way, followed by the Canadian ambassador to Sweden and then me. It was the first time in our marriage that I had ever outranked my renowned husband! It was also the first time in my life that I had walked off an airplane carrying nothing but my purse. No totebag. No magazine. No raincoat over my arm. One does not make a grand entrance laden with such mundane paraphernalia, so all our hand luggage was left on board for Jean Nadon to deal with. M. Nadon was the maître d' at Rideau Hall but, since Ed did not employ a full-time valet, he had invited Jean to join this expedition as his personal assistant. Getting all our bits and pieces to our destination was his responsibility. Ours was a different one.

I was overwhelmed as I took in the scene spread before me. Directly in front of us an entire regiment of soldiers in colourful uniforms stood at attention, while a military band flanked them on one side, and a column of glistening black limousines stood immobile on the other. A forest of red and white Canadian flags snapped in the breeze, intermingled with the blue and yellow of the Swedish flags. Plainclothes policemen were all over the place. And there, at the bottom of the steps, was the ceremonial red carpet. I took a deep breath and started down.

The reception committee consisted of a long line of impeccably dressed men and women headed by a tall, soldierly gentleman with silver hair, wearing full military regalia and a plumed hat. This was Prince Bertil, the Duke of Halland and the king's uncle.

One by one, we shook hands with the duke and with his English wife, Princess Lillian, and then with all the other dignitaries. Our objective was to keep moving briskly. A smile, a handshake, and a quick ''good morning'' were all any of us had time for. Every beat counted, like a musical score.

The duke and duchess, and Ed and Lily were then escorted to the longest of the limousines while the rest of us hurried, elegantly of course, towards the other cars. A row of chauffeurs stood rigidly at attention beside a line of open doors.

Panic hit me as I realized I had forgotten which car I was supposed to ride in. Everyone—Canadians and Swedes—had been issued with a booklet titled ''The Order of the Cars.'' Frantic, I fumbled mine out of my handbag. Car Number 6, thank God! Breathless, I sidled in beside Jason and a Swedish protocol officer just as the chauffeur snapped the door shut. Within seconds the entire motorcade was off. My heart was pounding at the thought of what would have happened if I had failed to make it. I would have been left behind in a strange airport amid the Swedish military, trying to explain that I was, like the frog prince, really supposed to be in the Royal Palace.

Once clear of the airport, our cavalcade divided. Our governor general and his wife were to join the king and queen for a triumphant parade through the city, while the rest of us rushed ahead to the palace to be on hand to greet them. Our cars picked up speed. We whizzed into the suburbs of Stockholm as if this were a game of cops and robbers. Traffic had been halted to let us pass, no small feat in a city of a million people. The traffic lights had been turned off and police were holding back all vehicles at every intersection. Even cars and trucks in the opposite lanes of the divided highway had been brought to a standstill. At one point we passed a line of halted vehicles a mile long. Quite a few of their drivers had seized the moment to step out, stretch their legs and feel the sunshine. They stared as we zoomed by. It was heady stuff for me although our captive audience was probably cursing us for delaying them. I'm sure they wondered who we were. At that point I was beginning to wonder who *I* was myself.

We sped on into the labyrinth of city streets until finally a bona fide palace loomed before us. It was immense, covering two blocks right in the downtown heart of the city, the largest palace in all of Europe. About five storeys high, it was a massive fortress of dark masonry which would have kept any seventeenth-century enemy at bay by its sheer volume.

The cars slowed as we rolled past a detachment of policemen and turned through an archway in the façade into a vast interior courtyard. We scrambled out so that Léopold could get us all lined up again in the right order. A glum, fair-haired Swedish detective issued each of us with a large security badge. I struggled ineffectually to pin mine to my coat lapel. It seemed an inelegant touch, especially since I had given so much thought to every accessory that accompanied my peach-coloured coat and the pale straw hat with the peach-coloured flower in the band. A tag pinned on a coat always puts me in mind of sad, refugee children being dispatched somewhere without their mothers.

"Tuck it in your pocket," advised Esmond Butler conspiratorily. "I always do. They look all wrong on an occasion like this."

I did as he suggested. But these days style has to compete with security. We live in an imperfect world where even the guests of the king of a peaceable kingdom have to be clearly identified.

The distant sound of a marching band warned us the parade was approaching. Waiting for it in that magnificent courtyard on such a glorious spring

34

morning was no hardship. A real courtyard: not one of those open spaces that modern architects build into the middle of new office buildings. This was an ancient quadrangle paved with cobblestones, at least a couple of acres in extent and entirely surrounded by the palace. In the centre the stones had been arranged in a mosaic to form a huge, geometric star. In every corner and doorway guards dressed in their toy-soldier uniforms stood rigidly at attention.

The sound of the band grew nearer and nearer until we knew that the parade was just beyond the palace walls. For a second I had a childish impulse to run out through the archway past the sentries and the detectives to see it go by. But I didn't dare move. Finally the mounted escort came swinging through the portals ahead of two very ornate, horse-drawn landaus. The first bore King Carl XVI Gustav of Sweden and the Governor General of Canada. The second carried Queen Silvia and Lily. The festooned horses clippity-clopped into the courtyard and stopped precisely in the centre of the cobblestone star.

Officers of the Royal Swedish Guards, wearing uniforms that I swear I had seen in some operetta, helped their majesties and excellencies step down. An officer shouted a command. The crimson-clad soldiers presented arms with thunderous synchronization. The band struck up a solemn anthem. Side by side, Ed and the king walked slowly toward a cenotaph in the far quadrant of the courtyard. An aide-de-camp handed a wreath to Ed and, with a bearing that would have convinced anyone he had been born to the manor, he gently set it down in tribute to some long-gone Swedish warriors.

What a moment of splendid theatre this was — a spectacle far more moving than any Grey Cup parade. I wanted to shout, "Hey, look at us every-body! Canada! Ed and Lily!" I wanted the whole world, not just this handful of diplomats and aris-tocrats, to see how well we had carried this off. Nat-urally we had to stand still in respectful silence while the band played the Swedish national anthem. There is no call for cheerleaders in the world of protocol. I realized that I had no idea at all who the soldiers and sailors were who were being remembered in this moving ceremony. Sweden hadn't been involved in combat in either the First or Second World Wars, those horrible catastrophes that are commemorated on every Canadian war memorial.

I kept my eye on Lily and the queen who had waited together, a discreet distance behind their hus-bands. Two women of about the same height and weight, one with red hair and one with black, they looked so beautiful standing there in the gentle light of Swedish spring. If Lily had any doubts about whether she had chosen an appropriate outfit, the sight of the queen of Sweden must have put her mind at rest. Both of them were wearing white wool coats and white hats over dresses of dotted white silk. Only the colour of the dots was different. It was ironic that after all the planning Lily and I had done to avoid looking as if we had been to the same sale, she and the queen of Sweden should end up looking like trendy twins. As the visiting wife of a head of state, Lily had the first choice of the colour of whichever dress she wanted to wear to a formal evening event. The hosting queen would select a complementary one. However, that guideline wasn't applied to day-time clothes.

Once the wreath-laying ceremony was over, the king and queen walked across the courtyard to wel-come us. I had never met a king or a queen before.

The king, wearing the imposing uniform of Commander-in-Chief of the Swedish military, shook my hand, looked me in the eye and almost managed a smile. The queen followed him down the line of impressed Canadians greeting each one of us with a beatific Mona Lisa expression. She was gorgeous. King Carl XVI Gustav and Queen Silvia, both in their mid-thirties, were a handsome couple. But very quiet. Neither uttered a word. Eye contact. Hand contact. Perhaps that's what people remember on such an occasion more than words.

Finally the moment had arrived to enter the palace. We followed the king and queen at a polite distance across the courtyard and through a pillared doorway into a cavernous, gilded rotunda. The space was as big as an average Canadian church and entirely floored with marble. There were also marble walls, archways, pillars and a broad, rococo stairway that led to some Valhalla far above us. A platoon of Grenadier Guardsmen dressed in Napoleonic uniforms flanked the stairway, each man holding a long brass trumpet of the sort you see being tooted by angels on Christmas cards. I looked up to the lofty heights and wondered if this was what an indoor heaven was supposed to look like.

My reverie didn't last long. Suddenly there was an almightly blast from the chorus of trumpets. This was the signal for the king and queen to lead the procession of Swedes and Canadians up the Cecil B. DeMille stairway. I floated upward and onward with the others, past enormous mirrors and graceful statues, while the trumpets continued their fanfare. Would anyone back home ever believe this? It was the kind of welcome that might have been organized for a medieval pope.

The stairway ended at the third floor where we

were ushered into yet another enormous, high-ceilinged room. A pair of heavy doors was closed discreetly behind us by two uniformed footmen and — presto — there we were with only the Schreyers, the king, the queen, the prince, the princess, and a couple of photographers. Everyone else had been left out in the hall.

We were in the drawing-room of the Royal Guest Apartments. "Apartments" was hardly the word. These were four vast rooms, each more opulent than the last, set aside for the accommodation of visiting monarchs, presidents, maharajas — and, for the first time ever — a Canadian governor general. Every corner and cornice was gilded and fluted and the walls were hung with elaborate tapestries the size of bedspreads. This was the sort of place I used to pay money to look at, back in my student days, in the palace of some defunct Italian duke. This time, I could not help reflecting smugly, I was getting in for free.

It was time for the next rite to take place, the giving and receiving of gifts. The origins of the exchange of gifts between guests and hosts are buried in prehistory and anthropologists have much to say about the significance of this timeless ritual. Kings and queens seldom have any unfulfilled material needs, but official visitors always arrive bearing gifts and receive gifts in return. The protocol staff usually decides what gifts will be given. Months in advance of a state visit enquiries are made about the personal tastes of the heads of state and their families.

"It's a tricky business, choosing the right gift," Vaughan Martin, our soft-spoken assistant protocol chief, told me later, "because the gifts given and the gifts received should be of about the same value."

Everyone who has ever exchanged Christmas

presents understands the difficulty. The problem of balance isn't any different between the high and mighty. No one wants to be embarrassed by a gift that is either too extravagant or too stingy.

"Oddly enough, it's the Third World that embarrasses us with riches," Vaughan added. "Sometimes with gifts of gold, silver, and jewels. Canada can't reciprocate: we don't have the budget."

Fortunately for Canada, the king and queen of Sweden enjoy winter sports, which is to be expected in the land where skiing was invented. They received matching parkas made in the Canadian Arctic by Inuit craftspeople. In turn, they presented Ed and Lily with two glorious pieces of Swedish crystal: prismatic vases that reflected the morning light and looked as if they belonged in that magnificent room much more than the parkas.

The ritual was followed by a newer one, the group photograph. It must be a rare day in the life of a royal family when they are not photographed. Everywhere they go, the camera follows: even when they stay at home to entertain, official photographs are always part of the ceremony. Perhaps the only way they could escape this invasion of the technological age would be to stay in bed and pull the covers over their heads. There must be days when they wish they could.

After the photographers were finished, the royal family departed to some private corner of their regal domain. That left us more or less alone, and free to explore this storehouse of eighteenth-century treasures.

"Do I *really* get to sleep in this?" asked Jason, bouncing on the edge of a canopied bed that could have come from the set of a Strindberg play. Thirteen-going-on-thirty was the way I thought of Jason.

He not only looked older than his thirteen years; he also acted it most of the time. Perceptive and reserved, he could still switch to boyish enthusiasm to balance his premature wisdom. "This is neat," he said, inspecting the heavy folds of drapery which could close off the bed like a berth in a Pullman car.

The bed may have been two hundred years old, but the mattress, fortunately, was modern. Nevertheless, it was hard to believe that anyone actually slept in rooms like these. All around us were enormous mirrors and paintings in heavy, ornamented frames; underfoot were carpets woven in Persia centuries ago, and the walnut tables and cabinets were inlaid with intricate designs in ivory and rare woods. The whole place felt like a museum and I half expected a guard to appear and scold us for touching the displays. While Lily and I cautiously ogled our palatial surroundings, Jason fulfilled every boy's dream of opening each door to see what lay behind it.

The Schreyers included their children in their travels whenever they could, but the timing of this tour, from the middle of May to early June, found their two oldest children, Lisa and Karmel, immersed in their studies for exams in the final years of high school. Toban, aged six, was too young to come so that left only Jason who could be released from the bondage of final exams.

What he discovered behind those mysterious doors were some closets as big as most people's bedrooms, a couple of very modern bathrooms and, at the back of the suite, a concealed corridor with a separate stairway for the servants. Here a footman was unloading luggage from a trolley and nearby, in a small, dim room, Thelma was already at work setting up the iron and the ironing-board. This was reality.

"Know what?" I said to Lily, "I don't think Farley

and I are supposed to be staying here.'' I had observed that all the luggage belonged to the Schreyer family and there was no trace of any of ours.

"Oh, why *don't* you stay?'' offered Lily hospitably. "We've got all kinds of room!''

We both burst out laughing. There was, indeed, room for the entire Canadian delegation in this enormous suite, and the palace contained 596 additional rooms of one sort or another. However, only twelve of us were to stay in the palace. The rest of our retinue had been assigned to the Grand Hotel, a couple of blocks away.

The king, queen, and their three young children don't live in the Royal Palace. Their home is Drottningholm, a smaller and, I can only assume, cosier palace situated on one of the fourteen islands which form the city of Stockholm. The Royal Palace is used primarily for state events such as our visit.

We circled back to the drawing-room, and heard someone knocking on the mammoth entrance door. Jason answered it.

"Ah, Mrs. Mowat. And Mr. Mowat. I have lost you,'' said my counterpart, the queen's lady-in-waiting, as she spotted us. Mrs. Cecilia Herman-Nilsson was a smiling, dark-haired beauty who spoke commanding English with a lilting Swedish accent.

"Please come with me now. I will take you to your apartment,'' she insisted.

Our apartment turned out to be on the opposite side of the palace, a good city block away. We were led smartly to it through a seemingly endless succession of marbled halls, hung with row upon row of portraits of bygone nobility. I tried to take it all in but there was no time to linger. Mrs. Herman-Nilsson moved at a military clip. No doubt it was all as familiar to her as an old wallpaper pattern but I could have

spent the entire day happily browsing around looking at everything.

Our quarters consisted of a drawing-room, two
bedrooms and a bathroom, and even though much
smaller than the Royal Guest Apartments, they were
still as large as the executive suite in one of the better
Canadian hotels. There the similarity ended. Here
were oriental rugs on the floor, centuries-old paintings in heavy frames on every wall, and dark,
wooden furniture in the style I know as Queen Anne
(although in Sweden it may be named after another
queen). The two bedrooms each contained a single
bed. Evidently Farley and I were intended to sleep
apart.

On a marble-topped table stood a big bouquet of
spring flowers and a generous array of gifts. There
were half a dozen picture-books about Sweden, several tins of candies and biscuits, a bowl of fruit, and
six bottles of assorted wine and liquor. There was also
an "official" gift from the king, a little crystal bowl
with the royal insignia etched on it. Traditionally
each member of the Accompanying Party received a
gift from every head of state. Canada, in turn, provided gifts for every member of our host's household
who assisted us, from the court chamberlain to the
chauffeurs. These gifts ranged from Eskimo carvings
on down to letter-openers bearing the Canadian coat
of arms—objects that had been selected according to
the rank of the recipient.

The drawing-room furniture was upholstered in
sumptuous ruby-red damask, but there was no
opportunity to sit down and savour it. We had less
than ten minutes until luncheon, which left us barely
time to wash our hands and find our combs. I seized
a couple of minutes to extricate our evening clothes
from their garment bags. I could only hope that the

wrinkles would disappear before the state dinner that evening. I couldn't imagine how we would ever find our way back to Thelma and the iron.

Our immediate concern was to find our way through all those corridors to the place where luncheon was to be served. Along with all the picture-books, we had been provided with a map of the palace. It was almost as complicated as the map of a small town and the names were in Swedish. As we stood there studying it we heard voices out in the hall, reassuring Canadian voices. They belonged to Colin Sangster and Esmond Butler who were quartered nearby. I darted into the hall, as happy to see them as if I were a marooned sailor and they were the rescue ship.

"Don't go without us," I called desperately, pleading for one more minute to restore my lipstick.

"You'd better be quick," Colin snapped. A handsome devil sporting a clipped military moustache, Major Sangster was a career army officer "on loan" to Government House where he served as the governor general's travel officer. Colin knew that when the Swedish court states that lunch is at one o'clock, you had better be there, ready and waiting, at twelve fifty-nine. The palace household was just as precise about the timing of events as the Swedish fighter pilots.

These details had all been worked out during an advance visit known as the "dry run," a dress rehearsal of the entire tour conducted six weeks in advance of the real thing. Several members of the governor general's household, at least one aide-de-camp, one police inspector, and three or four people from the Department of External Affairs had paced through every footstep. By the time "H.E." (the verbal shorthand members of the household use among themselves when they are referring to His Excellency) arrived on the scene, his senior staff people had made sure — well, almost sure — that there would be no horrendous surprises.

Among the many matters to be considered when a head of state or a prime minister travels are such things as what foods he or she dislikes; does he have more energy in the morning or in the afternoon; does she need a lot of sleep or only a little; does he like a rest after lunch; does she have any allergies or medical problems? *Everything* from security arrangements to flower arrangements is planned and checked, and checked again.

The household had really done their homework and so were familiar with the layout of every palace, hotel, or ship in which we were to be housed. Ed and Lily were always shepherded from one event to another, but Farley and I were expected to find our own way, and to get to our destinations on time.

That first day was especially unnerving and we had already made one blunder without even being aware of it. Somewhat later, Colin tactfully told us that we should not have been present at the official exchange of gifts. In our innocence we had simply followed our friends into the Royal Guest Apartments since no one had told us to go anywhere else. It amuses me to think that somewhere in the Royal Swedish archives there is now a photograph of Farley and me standing with the Schreyers alongside the royal family. The royals had been far too polite to send us away.

We dashed down a flight of unfamiliar back stairs but lost track of Colin and Esmond by the time we reached the ground floor. Imagine our relief when we saw Ed and Lily walking down the hall. We blithely pranced along behind them and were just about to follow them up a narrow stairway to the royal family's private quarters when Mrs. Herman-Nilsson suddenly materialized and nicely, but firmly, redirected us to our proper destination.

We had almost done it again. We had failed to understand that there were *two* luncheons—a private gathering for the royal family and Ed and Lily, and a separate one for the forty people who made up the Swedish and Canadian households.

We were ushered down a corridor and into an antechamber containing an escritoire on which there was a detailed chart of the dining-room table. It bore the names of all the guests in their designated locations. At palace luncheons, one does not amble around nonchalantly looking for a place-card with one's name on it.

The dining-room was huge, with silk brocade-covered walls hung with many portraits of once-crowned heads. I had been assigned a place between two unsmiling gentlemen who held senior positions in the court. Although both spoke fluent English, neither of them had much to say. But by then food interested me more than polite chit-chat. Breakfast had been six hours earlier in Lahr, and I now had an appetite as big as a Canadian lumberjack's. Abandoning the royal rule of thumb that you should eat just half of everything that's put in front of you, I vigorously attacked my plate of smoked salmon and ate it all, right down to the last caper. It wasn't until I had finished that I sat back and scrutinized the other diners.

Smiling Léopold Amyot was sitting across the table from me, deep in conversation with his opposite number, the Swedish Chief of Protocol. They were out of earshot but I was mildly curious to know what they were talking about. Did they speak about such ponderous matters as the changing concepts in formal clothes? Did they commiserate with each other about the long hours of work? Or dared they disclose the idiosyncrasies of their respective majesties and excellencies?

As we awaited our main course, the Swedish Chief of Protocol suddenly switched his gaze across the table, stared me squarely in the eye, raised his wine glass and uttered one word, "Skol."

Pleased to be noticed, I smiled, raised my wine glass, took a sip and merrily replied, "Cheers!"

"Ah, Claire," said Léopold in the restrained tone of a kindly teacher with a slow student, "in Sweden they have a charming custom for making a toast. Let me show you . . ."

He demonstrated. A gentleman raises his glass, looks deeply into the eyes of a nearby lady, and says, without any inflection in his voice, "skol." The lady responds by returning his look with equal intensity while raising her glass and repeating the salutation. After that they both take a sip, still staring raptly into one another's eyes. "Skol" is not bandied casually back and forth in the convivial "down the hatch" manner we use in Canada. In the court of Sweden, it is a private acknowledgement between a gentleman and a lady.

"It is a fine custom," said the taciturn palace official on my right. "It gives us a chance to flirt a little." Whereupon he raised his glass, turned towards me and without a glimmer of a smile, looked me in the eye and solemnly pronounced, "Skol."

"Skol," I replied as earnestly, turning to gaze into his grey eyes. I felt like Eliza Doolittle as I finished off the last of the Château Coutet 1976 in my glass. "Well," I thought, "if palace protocol isn't any more difficult than this, I'll soon have it down pat."

"I have been to Canada," announced the same gentleman, evidently ready to talk to me now that we had observed the ritual salutation.

"How nice. I hope you enjoyed your visit."

"I was not long there. A few hours only," he replied.

"And where were you?"

"Gander. I believe it is in Newfoundland."

Gander airport, buried in the Newfoundland forests, a long-ago obligatory refuelling stop for transatlantic flights in the days before jet travel, is almost redundant now.

"Gander is . . . ah . . . well, it's a pleasant, small community, but I wouldn't say it is exactly typical of Canada," I replied diplomatically.

"I did not see much," he said. "It was the middle of the night. Snow was falling."

"Perhaps you will visit Canada another time," I suggested hopefully, "and see more of it."

"Perhaps," he said unenthusiastically and returned to his food.

So much for witty conversation at the palace table. I was dallying over my dessert, a marvellous concoction of cream and meringue, when everyone abruptly stood up. At some signal which only the initiated heard or saw, the diners all shoved back their chairs and filed out of the room. I hastily grabbed my handbag and gloves from my lap and hurried to keep up. We proceeded into an adjoining salon where excellent coffee was served in demitasses. At formal events, and even informal ones throughout the Nordic countries, coffee after a meal is always served in another room. It's an agreeable procedure because then you have a chance to talk with someone other than those who sat beside you during the meal.

Twenty minutes were allowed for coffee and conversation and then we were ushered down a flight of stairs to a room resembling a university lecture-theatre. Here the king and queen and our own vice-regals rejoined us while we watched a film about contemporary Sweden. As the lights were lowered I feared the worst, some dreary documentary full of statistics guaranteed to put anyone to sleep. But what we saw was an imaginative short film illuminated by panoramic vistas of the Swedish countryside and peppered with tidbits of social and economic information. I might have guessed that the Swedes would never produce a dull film.

Having been briefed on the realities of present-day Sweden, we now descended—literally—into the past for a tour of the Royal Armoury. Housed in the labyrinth of cellars beneath the palace, the Armoury is a museum of military hardware. Led by the king, we sauntered through subterranean chambers over-flowing with swords, shields, suits of armour and guns of every description. Several rooms were filled with military uniforms dating back three centuries. One Swedish king had died during a battle in Poland in the seventeenth century and the faithful horse on which he died had been preserved. There was one gruesome exhibit of a cocked hat with a hole in it, the dried blood still surrounding the spot where a bullet had entered the head of a king who had been killed while attempting to conquer Norway. Another exhibit showed the fancy costume worn by yet one more unlucky monarch who had been assassinated at a costume ball. Being the king of Sweden three hundred years earlier had been a career fraught with occupational hazards.

I began to revise my image of Sweden as an exemplary kingdom. I wish I had been bold enough to ask the mild-mannered Carl Gustav how he really felt about his aggressive predecessors who had died in battles waged against nations with whom the Swedes now live amicably as neighbours. Was he proud of them or ashamed? But that first day I wouldn't have dared to ask a king what he thought about anything. I followed along, keeping my own thoughts about the evanescent nature of defeat and victory to myself. King Carl Gustav will certainly never ride a horse leading a cavalry charge, but he may not be remembered as vividly as his ancestor with the hole in his hat who died trying to conquer the Norwegians.

In 1973, when he inherited the throne of Sweden upon the death of his grandfather (his father had died in an airplane crash when Carl Gustav was a baby), King Carl XVI Gustav was only twenty-seven years of age. He became one of the world's youngest kings and he was already one of the world's most eligible bachelors.

He first met his dark-eyed future queen at the Olympic Games in Munich in 1972. Silvia Sommerlath was a commoner, the daughter of a Brazilian mother and a German father, who had grown up both in Brazil and in Germany. Fluent in several languages, she was working as a hostess at the Games when she captured the eye and the heart of the king. Nonetheless they didn't become officially engaged until four years later. What took them so long? Was someone putting pressure on the king to marry a woman with a pedigree?

Perhaps there had been overtones of the fate of his controversial uncle, Prince Bertil. The prince had remained a bachelor until he was in his sixties because the love of his life had originally been his housekeeper and the late king wouldn't tolerate the idea of their marriage. But when King Gustavus VI finally died in 1973, Bertil married Lillian after a betrothal of nearly thirty years and made her a princess. And Carl Gustav married Silvia and made her a queen.

If there had been any doubts about Silvia's ability to rise to the occasion, these had long since been dispelled. Beautiful and confident, she looked even more comfortable doing her regal job than did her shy husband. Farley walked beside her most of the time we toured the Armoury. Her smile was as measured as that of a flight attendant — in first class, of course. Royal people do not have to be effusive or even entertaining to be noticed. Apart from a couple of references to her children and a few comments relevant to the military history of Sweden, she expressed no opinions and gave away nothing of herself.

The role of the Swedish monarch, like that of the governor general of Canada, is mainly ceremonial. Heads of state are the touchstones of the rituals of government: the opening of parliament, the presentation of ambassadorial credentials, the state visits, the presentation of awards, and innumerable luncheons and dinners. In Sweden, the king holds the highest military rank, and though he can never legally assume command, he *can* stand in the way of any attempt to establish a military dictatorship. That ace up his sleeve must cheer him on days when his life seems humdrum. Mainly he lends his presence to great events and worthy endeavours and shakes an awful lot of hands. Monarchs do not voice unpopular opinions — at least not in public. And if they crack a joke they have to be sure that it is not at anyone's expense. It is not a life for anyone who is easily bored, aggressive or short-tempered. It must be excruciating for anyone who has some driving ambition of his or her own.

The tour of the Armoury ended and I had twenty-five minutes to get dressed for the next event. Ten of the twenty-five were taken up just finding my way back to our apartment. With the speed of a fireman I donned yet another pastel afternoon dress and then set off resolutely through another maze of stately halls in search of a suite that bore the romantic name of the Rooms of Chivalry. There I was to attend Lily at a reception for the diplomatic corps.

During a state visit, the visiting head of state receives all foreign ambassadors who have been posted to that country. This ritual hour of diplomatic small talk takes place so that the rest of the world will be assured that, in this case, Sweden and Canada are on good terms. It's a protocol that reminded me of the etiquette of the outports of Newfoundland, where visitors from "away" have to be shared with the neighbours.

My role at these afternoon receptions was to take some of the pressure off Lily by circulating among members of the "Dip" corps, as the household fondly referred to them. For fifty-five minutes I exchanged inconsequential banter with the heads of diplomatic posts from such diverse places as Romania, Japan, and the United States. Then it was my task to find Lily and let her know, in an unobtrusive way, that she had to leave in exactly five minutes. An ADC would give Ed the same signal. This made it possible for them to gracefully wind down conversations and not have to depart abruptly. A head of state is never to be seen looking at his or her watch.

"Oooff. I am weary," I said when I returned to our apartment and finally sank into the red silk upholstery.

"Did those diplomats give you a hard time?" asked Farley.

"No, no. It's just . . . well, a day full of strangers can be hard work."

"I know. Why don't I fill up that big bathtub for you?"

"Super idea."

One of the best restoratives I know of is a long, luxurious soak in a tub full of hot water. And even a short soak is better than none.

I believed I had ample time to get dressed for the state banquet that evening—over an hour. I methodically laid out all the bits and pieces of my evening finery. As I fiddled with a pair of gold chains that had become hopelessly knotted in my jewellery box, it dawned on me what an enormous proportion of our time was going to be spent dressing, undressing, and getting dressed again. There wouldn't even be time to launder pantyhose, underwear or socks, and leave them to dry on the shower rail, as was my travel routine. There would be no time to keep a diary, which had always been another of my rituals. Time was clearly going to be more precious than all the gold-leaf rosettes in the palace. There would be no chance to have anything dry-cleaned. If I happened to spill béarnaise sauce on my dress, well that was game over for that dress until I got back to Canada. No wonder Thelma had told me to bring so many clothes. My finely honed skills of assembling a clever, small, travel wardrobe to see me through any occasion was useless in this situation.

Farley took a long time fidgeting with the unfamiliar frippery of his rented white tie and tails: the cummerbund, the cufflinks, and the bow tie. When he finally got the whole thing together he pinned on his nine miniature medals and looked very distinguished. I had never imagined that the scruffy character whom I first encountered wearing paint-splattered clothes as he worked on his leaky old schooner could ever look so dapper.

We met one another in the French colony of St. Pierre et Miquelon where I was taking a summer course in French and where Farley had hauled his Newfoundland schooner ashore on the slipway for repairs. He was dressed in the most raggedy old pants imaginable and a shirt that was filthy dirty as well as dotted with green paint. The idea that I might some day see him wearing full evening dress, and even embellished with medals, certainly never crossed my mind that day in 1960.

"Farley," I exclaimed. "I love you in that outfit! You should dress that way every night. Just think, if you were a concert musician instead of an author . . ."

"Alas, love, I can't play a note. Would you settle for maître d'?"

"Sure. We'll open a classy restaurant."

At that moment Colin Sangster stuck his head through the doorway.

"Five minutes. How're you doing?"

"Five!" I shrieked.

"Due to arrive at nineteen-three-o," he stated with military exactitude.

"But I thought the book said twenty-hundred hours!" I argued.

"That," he said, "is for His Ex and Her Ex. Everyone else ready and waiting thirty minutes in advance."

There was one mad scramble in our suite as I grabbed my earrings, rings, evening-bag, and somehow applied my mascara and lipstick, while Farley did his best to fasten the tiny little hook and eye at the back of the neck of my beaded chiffon evening-gown. When we dashed out of our baroque bedrooms to chase down the hallway, the suite looked as if it had been trashed by a pair of burglars. I was appalled to think that the palace servants, who would undoubtedly be coming around to turn down the beds, were going to behold the tangled mess of damp towels, rumpled shirts, and scattered shoes. What would they think of Canadians? But there was nothing to be done. The show had to go on.

We galloped down the stairway in an unregal hurry, oblivious of the statues, the paintings, and all the showcases full of priceless porcelain, then we burst out through the arched doorway into the courtyard. It was a heavenly evening, still and cloudless and the surrounding palace walls had taken on a bronze-coloured glow in the northern twilight. The panic of the previous moments ebbed away as we caught up with the others and our glittering group strolled across the cobblestones. We looked as if we belonged in one of those slick advertisements for a Rolls-Royce. If only someone had made a film of me as I went tripping across that stupendous courtyard wearing the most expensive dress I had ever owned.

"Are you managing all right?" Esmond asked me. I was the only one of us who had to negotiate the bumpy surface of the courtyard in high-heeled shoes.

"I'm O.K., thanks," I said, "as long as I'm walking in the gutter."

"Which is just where I found her!" Farley quipped. "And look at her now!"

"Hey, wait up!" called Jason breathlessly. He came running across the courtyard behind us. He had come even closer than we had to being late. In his white tie and tails, he looked like a cross between a musical prodigy and a footman-in-training.

When we reached the doorway on the opposite side of the palace, I had to lift my gown an inch or two so I wouldn't trip on the marble steps. That was when I noticed the wide run in my stocking from the toe on upward. This was only a small misfortune, since no one would see it under a long dress beneath a banquet table, but I also discovered that in my haste I had broken a fingernail and the jagged edge had caught in the filmy material of my gown. I shook it loose and tried to keep my right hand out of harm's way for the rest of the evening. How I longed for a nail file, but even if I had remembered to tuck one into my beaded evening bag, there wouldn't have been a chance to use it. During the rest of the evening we would be "on parade" at all times and woe betide anyone who even had to go to the bathroom.

With a courtly wave, a tall footman pointed to a stairway leading to a stately drawing-room lined with mirrors and capped with a magnificent chandelier. Here all the guests were required to await, in a single line around the perimeter, the arrival of the crowned heads. I was glad of the chance to stand still for a few minutes and just to watch the other guests as they filed in. However, Jason assumed that this frieze of guests must be a receiving-line. Back in Ottawa it would have been. So he dutifully began working his way along it, shaking every hand and occasionally stopping to introduce himself to some startled Swede. It wasn't until he was two-thirds of the way around the room that he chanced to look back and discovered he was the only person engaged in this chummy activity. He stopped in his tracks and sought refuge beside the first Canadian he could find.

At exactly eight o'clock the court chamberlain rapped his ceremonial rod on the marble floor three times, the signal for everyone to freeze. The king and queen entered the room, followed by Ed and Lily. The dignified quartet moved across the room with slow and measured tread so that everyone could look at them, and also so that the photographers (who were allowed only five minutes to do their job at the beginning of an evening event) could record this theatrical procession for the next day's newspapers.

The king looked impeccable in his white tie and tails, bedecked with sash and medals. However, it was the queen everyone wanted to look at. It always is. How bizarre it must be to live out a lifetime knowing that, for ever and a day, every detail of your appearance will be exhaustively scrutinized. Did Queen Silvia ever have second thoughts, wishing she had married some ordinary chap back home? She smiled her enigmatic smile as she crossed the room wearing a diamond tiara and a sleek yellow evening-gown draped with a blue sash and several state decorations.

It isn't easy for a woman to make a noteworthy appearance when she has to share the limelight with a queen in full regalia, but Lily did it. She has classic good looks, arresting red hair, and her terracotta-coloured silk gown was every bit as regal as the queen's. She looked just marvellous.

Ed, who is substantially bigger than the king, looked positively monarchical in his formal clothes. Who on earth could have invented this flattering if uncomfortable garb for men? It's a fashion that has been declining in popularity, even among concert musicians, but it remains *de rigueur* for all court events in Sweden. And that too seemed out of character. How ironic that people with such progressive

notions about everything, from environmental protection to nuclear energy, should be such absolute
sticklers for formality.

The royals and vice-royals led the procession into
the banquet hall. This room, the largest in the palace,
is called Karl XI's Gallery. It is long, narrow, and
seemingly endless and is the most extravagant dining-room I have ever been in. Amid the Corinthian
columns and cornices, there must have been half an
acre of Renaissance paintings covering the walls and
even the lofty ceiling. An art historian could spend
months just studying the details of all those paintings, and enumerating the architectural frills. The
single dining-table, which must have been as long as
two, or maybe three, railway cars, seated one
hundred and fifty people, seventy-five to a side. A
forest of spring flowers in tall silver vases reached
towards infinity at the far end of the table. A regiment
of monumental silver candelabra advanced, like prairie telephone poles, to the horizon. Flickering can-
dlelight danced on the facets of five hundred cut-
glass goblets while countless tiny lights from a score
of crystal chandeliers shone above us like stars. One
hundred and fifty Louis Quinze side chairs waited to
support us as soon as the king and queen sat down.
Not even Hollywood in its heyday could have
invented anything quite like this.

I was five seats to the right of the queen, well
above the proverbial salt, and outranked only by Ed,
Princess Lillian, the Canadian Minister of External
Affairs, and the court chamberlain. On my right sat
the governor of one of the Swedish provinces. Once
we were seated, an unseen orchestra high up in the
minstrels' gallery above us began to play. Immediately a battalion of footmen dressed in white ties and

tails — and white gloves — marched into the enormous hall to serve the soup.

As I took it all in I wished, I must confess, that everyone who had ever put me down could have seen me then. I'll bet you regret that you didn't invite me to your coffee party back in Grade Eleven. I'm sure you wish you'd never broken our engagement and married What's-her-name. You must be sorry you fired me from that crummy job. Petty stuff. But I just couldn't resist wallowing in the sin of pride, until my soup was served.

A small menu card embossed in gold with the royal coat of arms, and printed in French, stood in front of each diner. French is the common language for dining in the diplomatic world but I couldn't identify everything that was listed. The epicurean delights of the court of Sweden had not been included in the vocabulary of any of the French courses I had ever studied. But that didn't hinder me from devouring my *crème d'oseille mousseuse*. It was delicious, whatever it was.

My curiosity about what an *oseille* might be sparked a conversation with the governor.

"It is a plant which grows in the fields," he told me. "I am sure it must grow in Canada also. It is a wild plant, a weed, you might say."

I racked my brain in vain to try and think of any Canadian weed which might form the basis of this delectable soup. The governor apologized that he only knew how to translate *oseille* from French into Swedish, Danish, or German. That didn't help me.

I could at least figure out what the next course was: *Queues de langoustine au citron vert*. And only in Atlantic Canada have I tasted lobster that compared with this. But when the main course arrived—*soufflé de gelinotte*—I was stumped again. What in heaven's name was a *gelinotte*?

"It is a big bird, a wild bird, living usually in the north of our country. I am sure that you eat this bird in Canada also," the governor speculated.

"Some sort of duck?" I suggested.

"No, not those. It is a bird which is often reserved for special occasions."

"A turkey?"

"No."

This linguistic obstacle was to recur regularly at banquets in the days ahead. Wild birds and plants are often ingredients in the cuisine of the privileged, yet their names are probably the last things we encounter when we study a foreign language. Back in Canada, I looked up *gelinotte* and learned that it is a species of grouse. *Oseille* turned out to be sorrel.

While we ate our dessert, *fraises des bois Chantilly*, wild strawberries that brought to mind Ingmar Bergman's Swedish countryside in its springtime sublimity, the court chamberlain asked me how long I had served as lady-in-waiting.

"It isn't a permanent position in Canada," I explained. "The wife of the governor general invites someone to fill the role whenever it's required. It can be a friend, a family member, perhaps the wife of some member of the household."

"I see," he said, without further comment. I couldn't tell if he approved of this quasi-republican state of affairs or not. After all, he was accustomed to dining with career ladies-in-waiting, not with patriotic amateurs like myself. Our conversation languished, and fortunately it was soon time to move on to yet another colossal hall for coffee.

Farley rejoined me on the way in.

"How did it go with you?" I asked, conspiratorily. "Meet anyone interesting?"

"Well, I had a countess on one side who was slightly dotty. And the countess on the other side was *really* dotty. But the grub was great," he conceded.

In the great mirrored hall in which we now found ourselves, footmen moved around passing out cigarettes and cigars. Smoking is tolerated in European courts, but only after dinner. It is considered bad form to smoke between courses. At coffee time a surprisingly large number of guests lit up. However, the air did not grow smoky. That's the advantage of rooms with ceilings as high as those of a cathedral. Nevertheless, looking up at the murals covering the ceiling, I couldn't help but wonder what all the smoke might do to them. Would those gilded medallions become grimy and the painted pink cherubs turn to a nondescript shade of putty? But then, if it is a palace and you are a king, what does it matter? You can have the paintings restored and the cornices re-gilded any time you feel like it.

The king, queen, Ed and Lily were seated at one end of this rectangular, rococo room on a semi-circle of brocaded settees. They had no choice but to be content with one another's company because the rest of us were not allowed to go near them. We were herded to the other end and kept at bay by a stern, gold-encrusted court marshal armed with a swagger-stick. He stood guard over an invisible boundary line between the regal quartet and the hundred and more lesser mortals.

The only person who had the temerity to risk an encounter with the marshal was Bernie St. Laurent. As the governor general's aide-de-camp, it was his duty at all events to remain in close proximity to him and he took his job seriously. Three times he tried to cross the unseen line, but each time he was rebuffed by the vigilant marshal who, without a word, poked him sharply in the stomach with that bullying swagger-stick. After the third rebuff Bernie admitted defeat.

"That guy isn't fooling," he said. "If he'd been using a bayonet, it would have gone right through me!"

In Sweden, it was abundantly clear, nobody—but nobody — was permitted to intrude upon the after-dinner conversation of the king.

The evening was not especially convivial even if the surroundings were divine, the service impeccable, and the coffee and liqueurs abundant. The Swedish guests didn't mingle much with us and so we Canadians inevitably gravitated towards one another. I spent most of my time talking with our trusty policeman, Inspector Mike Thivièrge.

When Mike left New Brunswick to join the Mounties fourteen years earlier, he could hardly have expected to wind up sipping liqueurs in a royal palace, but the surroundings didn't faze him a bit. During the preceding two and a half years Mike had been in twenty-nine countries doing his job. He told me he never got more than four or five hours' sleep on any night during a tour. A big man with a large moustache, curly hair, and a sense of humour, Mike was a member of the elite VIP security section of the Royal Canadian Mounted Police, a hand-picked unit responsible for the protection of the governor general, the prime minister and the leader of the opposition. On any tour abroad, it was his job to make sure that the local police protection for our prime minister or our governor general matched the standards that were enforced back home.

Officers seconded to this unit serve in it for only

three years. Perhaps more than three years of pâté de fois gras and Château St. Germain might distract a man from the hard-nosed business of being a policeman. More realistically, three years is probably the longest that anyone can stand the pace.

"What worries me the most are the nuts who think they have some kind of divine mission," he said when I questioned him about the risks. "They figure they can prove something by knocking out the leader. Just look, already this year they've had a go at the pope and at the president of the United States."

"So you just never know who might be lurking," I concluded, looking across this wide ballroom at a row of recessed doorways and a sea of unfamiliar faces.

"Most of the time, no. But sometimes we do. Police films taken during the visit of President Nixon to Canada showed a guy in the crowd who also showed up in films of a crowd surrounding George Wallace down in the States. You memorize faces like that."

"Mike, how does someone get chosen for this kind of job?"

"Well, stamina, for starters," he said as he placed his empty glass on a silver tray. "And flexibility. And, of course, the ability to assess a threat," he added purposefully.

I would add another qualification: a certain panache. VIP police officers have to travel in close proximity to Number One. Sometimes they eat together. They often ride in the same car. They come to know the family of the protected person too. These men have to be able to deal comfortably with the social intricacies of all kinds of domestic and foreign situations. They have to know how to dress for everything from a pope's funeral to a canoe trip. They must be able to sense when to be a friend to those they protect, yet still know when to keep their distance. It's a tall order.

By eleven-thirty I was ready to call it a day. However, it is a horrendous breach of etiquette to leave before royalty does, and the regal party appeared to be taking their time. I was longing to get back to our cosy flat over in the east wing, but it was nearly midnight before the king and queen decided to make their gracious exit. Then we were finally free to find our way back across that haunting courtyard. It was even lovelier after dark in the cool night air with the moon overhead. I could cheerfully have spent the night out there in a sleeping-bag, dreaming incredible dreams. But the prospect of the next arduous day propelled me back into the tapestried halls.

As we were climbing the stairway to our suite, it occurred to Farley that we hadn't the vaguest idea where we were supposed to go for breakfast. In which faraway corner of this immense labyrinth would we find a cup of coffee? We looked up and down the echoing corridors for a familiar Canadian face but saw none. Finally, a courtly older man dressed in an antique uniform with many large medals on his chest passed us with a polite nod.

"Excuse me," Farley enquired, "but could you kindly tell me how to find tomorrow's breakfast?"

"Breakfast? Dear Sir and Madame, it will be my pleasure to take care of you myself. I shall bring it to your suite. What would you like? Coffee? With milk? With cream? Some croissants with preserves?"

"Sounds splendid," Farley replied.

"It will be in your drawing-room at seven o'clock. Good night, Sir. Good night, Madame." He bowed and disappeared.

"That guy is right out of a Noel Coward play!" whispered Farley as we closed our door. In fact, he virtually was. We later learned that he was a retired stage actor who now served the Swedish royal family.

"I *might* just get used to this," I thought.

But could I? It took me another hour to fix my hair, pack my evening clothes, untangle my jewellery and pack it again, file my nails, remove my make-up, and lay out all the clothes for the next day. By the time I tumbled into my solitary bed, I was utterly exhausted. And this was only the first day. Was I going to last the course?

The major-domo, his medals clanking, arrived brightly at seven the next morning bearing a silver tray loaded with coffee and croissants. Still sleepy, I padded into the drawing-room where the morning sunshine was filtering through the curtains, illuminating the dim interior like a room in a Rembrandt painting. I went over to the window and spent a few minutes just looking down at the tranquil courtyard where the palace guards were standing at attention at their posts. I still wasn't used to being on the inside of a palace, unaccustomed to the fact that those soldiers out there were intended to fend off the multitudes beyond the walls.

A phone call at 7:30 ended the only peaceful interlude we would know that day.

"Good morning!" said the brisk Mrs. Herman-Nilsson. "Would you please advise Her Excellency that we will be walking on cobblestones this morning and that she should wear shoes with not high heels."

"Thank you," I mumbled while urgently scanning a specially printed telephone directory that was supposed to contain the number of every Canadian staying in the palace. We were all listed *except* Ed and Lily. I considered the possibility of jogging over to their suite, but the likelihood of not finding my way there, or back again, changed my mind.

I admitted defeat. "I'm sorry. No one has provided me with Her Excellency's telephone number."

"I shall try Miss Thelma then, shall I?" the queen's lady-in-waiting replied smoothly. I sensed that, as a novice lady-in-waiting, I had just been awarded one demerit point.

There were to be two separate expeditions that morning, one for His Excellency and one for Her Excellency. This is a usual procedure when a visiting leader brings a spouse. For one thing, it gives the visitors double exposure and, for another, it gives each a chance to pursue his or her own interests. So Ed, whose fascination with all forms of energy production is endless, was to accompany the king on a tour of a power plant which somehow heated one entire city district of Stockholm. Glad that I didn't have to endure a morning of staring at incomprehensible machinery, I looked forward to the prospect of joining the queen and Lily on a tour of the suburb of Kista, a model working-class community.

A motorcade with the inevitable police escort whisked us out to Kista. The cars slowed as we approached a shopping plaza and a clutch of stores and apartment blocks that looked depressingly like the kind we build in the suburbs in Canada. A crowd had gathered on the sidewalk to watch our arrival for we had the star attraction of Sweden with us. On Monday, Queen Silvia had shared the limelight with the king. On Tuesday, she held centre stage, with a gaggle of Canadians playing supporting roles. Swedes have taken Silvia to their hearts with a passion. That morning she was hounded by the media at every turn. A horde of photographers recorded her every step.

The Director of City Planning and the Chairman of the Stockholm City Council escorted us around a complex that had been constructed about fifteen years earlier to meet the needs of low-income people who lived and worked in the city. Our first stop was a day-care centre in the midst of a complex of beige buildings. Here we learned that a staff of trained workers provided care for children twenty-four hours a day, seven days a week, any time their parents needed it. In Sweden parents pay only ten per cent of the actual cost of day-care, and single parents receiving social assistance pay nothing. All around us we saw children with big brown eyes and olive skins, children of a Mediterranean heritage in the land of blue-eyed Vikings. Of the eight million Swedes (approximately the same number of people who live in Ontario), close to one million are recent immigrants from such places as North Africa and southern Italy. The multi-national mosaic is now the trend in most of the industrial world.

The Swedes have attempted to provide elementary education for these immigrant children in their original language as well as in Swedish, so that they won't become alienated from their parents and their ancestral cultures. Such consideration impressed me. It must be an awesomely expensive task setting up classrooms and curricula in languages such as Turkish and Greek.

"My compliments," I said to the council chairman, "on your enlightened attitude."

"We try such things," he said modestly. "We have sometimes made mistakes."

Not too many mistakes, I thought. I didn't tell him that in parts of Canada we still argue, like children ourselves, about whether the offspring of Italian and Inuit parents should be educated in English or French.

Everywhere we went, hordes of children tagged along after us. The bolder ones approached the queen to give her handfuls of flowers. Mostly these were wildflowers snatched from ditches, but some were pansies and geraniums nabbed from window boxes. Queen Silvia managed to hold all these motley bouquets and still look eminently regal.

Security detectives dressed in three-piece suits were all around us. They have the same haircuts and wear the same sort of clothes all over the world. In that neighbourhood, where all the local men had left for work, they stood out like lawn ornaments. I admit their presence initially made me feel quite important but I suspect that is a reaction which would quickly pall for the handful of people like Queen Silvia who must be guarded all their lives.

Kista looked like a decent place to live, even if it was a little frayed around the edges. It wasn't beautiful; but is there a working-class suburb anywhere that is? At least it had excellent rail connections with the downtown area so that the automobile, the biggest financial drain as well as the greatest social disruption ever visited upon mankind, was much less in evidence than it would have been in a similar Canadian suburb.

Who can resist that ultimate seduction, the automobile? Although I despair about what it has done to society, I am not immune to its charms. Being whisked about Stockholm just one car behind the lead limousine with the royal standard fluttering from the fender was intoxicating. Leaving Kista, we sailed directly to our next event in the city centre, unimpeded by speed limits or parking problems. Of

all the luxuries available for the rich and the powerful, there is only one I covet — the services of a
chauffeur.

The old quarter of Stockholm has been undergo-
ing a massive restoration. Decrepit little shops that
once housed blacksmiths and harness-makers have
new fronts, new signs, and new occupants. They are
now the domain of art galleries, artisans, studios,
and cosy restaurants. Lily had requested visits to pot-
ters, weavers, and jewellery designers because she
was in the process of setting up an umbrella organization in Canada to promote the work of our own
artisans.

A youthful, bearded man who held the post of
city antiquarian greeted his queen and her Canadian
visitors and led us on a walking tour of the refur-
bished "Old" Stockholm. We cautiously picked our
way along the cobbled streets in our semi-sensible
shoes. Broad-heeled jogging shoes would have been
ideal here, but when you are Number One, or even
Two or Three, on display parade you can't dress as
comfortably as that. Photographers continued to run
after and ahead of us like a pack of anxious dogs,
while the detectives made sure they maintained a
polite distance. It was only when we entered one of
the ateliers to watch some silversmith or wood-carver
at work that we got any respite from the flashbulbs.

Unfortunately there was barely time to admire the
work being done, and none left over to do any actual
shopping. Our timetable was relentless and I was
feeling a little cheated that we had to hurry back to
the palace. There was just enough time to change
into afternoon dresses before we were carried off to
a luncheon being given in Canada's honour by the
City of Stockholm.

The interior of the City Hall was wondrous, especially to one accustomed to Canadian municipal edifices. The Golden Hall, where we dined, was as long and as high as the concourse of Toronto's Union Station, but with every inch of the walls covered with mosaics of gold leaf. They formed immense, odd murals in a style that I can only describe as a blend of the Byzantine with the Bauhaus. This is the room in which winners of the Nobel Prize are fêted. The building was built between 1919 and 1923, an unheralded era of architecture when the rest of Europe was digging itself out from the rubble of the First World War. The cost must have been staggering.

There was ample elbow room for the two-hundred-and-fifty guests. Our first course was avocado stuffed with caviar, followed by fillet of reindeer. Reindeer is a very popular delicacy in Europe. In Canada wild reindeer, which we call caribou, is not available commercially, which is a pity. During luncheon, a band played from a gallery above us — light classical waltzes, marches, and sonatas — music distant enough that it didn't intrude into our conversations. The selections were listed on a gilt-edged card placed in front of each diner. How strange to find that all the music was by composers I had never heard of — Sköld, Hannsson, Sjöberg, Korling, Wennerberg — despite the fact that I have been a devotee of classical music all my life.

I was seated between two city councillors, one of whom attempted to explain to me how municipal government works in Sweden. He did not represent one section of the city the way a councillor in Canada would. He had been elected because he belonged to a specific party. The vote was as much for the party as it was for the candidate. He described himself as a left-wing conservative, presumably something akin to being a Canadian Red Tory.

He paused during his lesson to raise his wine-glass, look me in the eye, and soulfully offer me the obligatory "skol."

In late afternoon it was Canada's turn to entertain. To help us do so the Canadian military had provided a formidable chunk of Canadian territory. The destroyer, HMCS *Huron*, had preceded us across the Atlantic and was now moored alongside a pier in Stockholm harbour.

Warships are not inherently beautiful vessels, but it is possible to dress them up. Hundreds of yards of red and white bunting had been draped all around the helicopter flight deck. Above that the governor general's blue-and-gold standard fluttered majestically in the afternoon breeze. Flags and banners are instant decorations, the added touch that makes a gathering anywhere look joyful. In Canada only gas stations and car lots seem to deck themselves out in banners and pennants, signalling some gala event that never happens.

The *Huron* is over 400 feet long and her large helicopter deck turned out to be an ideal place to hold a party. A boisterous gathering was already in progress when our limousines pulled up at the pier. We clambered up the gangway to be greeted by the brass of Canada's modest navy: Commodore Stanley Riddell, commander of the entire Canadian fleet, and Commander James Spalding, the ship's captain. Suddenly we were back in Canada.

The people invited to this reception were Swedes with Canadian connections through business, diplomatic and academic circles, together with some Canadians living in Sweden. They were not a particularly imposing bunch and it was relatively easy for me to act the role of a gracious hostess. All I needed was a lot of stamina because these shipboard gatherings were scheduled at the cocktail hour late in the afternoon when my energy lagged and I hadn't quite got my second wind.

"Hi. Remember me?" A young Canadian navy lieutenant had appeared in front of me, smiling broadly.

I courteously smiled back, thinking he had mistaken me for someone else. He wore his last name on a small tab on his uniform, so I could see that his name was "Gear." It didn't help.

"I'm from Port Hope," he said.

Gear. Port Hope. Then it dawned on me.

"You can't be Harold Gear?"

"Right."

The last time I had seen Harold Gear, he was a skinny fourteen-year-old being scolded to do his homework. In a space of time that felt to me like overnight he had become a tall, handsome helicopter pilot. We talked about mutual friends back home and about his career in the forces. The boy had become a man, full of purpose and enthusiasm, a somewhat rare metamorphosis for twenty-one-year-olds in this bewildering world. Harold introduced two of his friends to me, polite young men who both exuded the same air of confidence.

"Harold, you've got to meet the governor general. You'll love him," I insisted. "Follow me."

We edged our way through the crowd, past *Huron*'s own four-piece dance band, which was energetically playing Broadway hit tunes, and over to a corner of the deck where Ed was engrossed in a conversation with a Swedish couple. ADC Captain Dave John was standing a few feet away. He saw me approaching and held up one wrist, pointing at his

71

watch. This was the signal that we were now into the countdown. I quickly introduced Harold and his pals to Ed and then hurried off to disengage Lily.

One little-known advantage of being a head of state is the ease with which that person can depart from a large gathering. No one dares to buttonhole a governor general and insist that it's too early to leave. No one presses him to come home for coffee. No one backs him into a corner to finish a long drawn-out conversation. The ADC gently propels His Excellency in the direction of the door. The good-byes and thank-yous are promptly said and the governor general leaves. Would that it were so simple for all of us.

Our day was far from over. Back at the palace there was another frenzied interlude in which to shed our afternoon clothes and get into our evening wear. Just time for a shower, I calculated, but not for a shampoo. Thank heaven for curling irons and hair spray.

Canadian state visits normally include two major banquets. The first is given by the host country, the second by the guest country. I am not the only one who questions the wisdom of staging two mammoth dinner parties on consecutive evenings which are attended, for the most part, by the same people, but that's protocol. You ate with us. Now we'll come and eat with you. The rite of sharing food is almost instinctive and I doubt if there's any human culture where this doesn't take place in one form or another.

The Canadian banquet was held in Stockholm's Grand Hotel, just a stone's throw from the palace. We could easily have walked there but that would hardly have suited the nature of the occasion so the big black limousines lined up at the palace door once again.

I'm sure nothing in Stockholm (or perhaps any-where else) can equal the sheer splendour of Karl XI's Gallery, but the banquet hall of the Grand Hotel comes close. It is a vaulted, gilded room lined with Italianate arches, lush draperies, and hundreds of mirrored panels. The ceiling resembles an inverted birthday cake, a confection of thousands of bas-relief flowers. One huge chandelier, that radiates more glit-ter than an acre of rhinestones, hangs from the centre of it.

It was once again a surprise to encounter this kind of opulence in a country that is usually regarded as the leader of the stringent principles of social democ-racy. Canadians have a tendency to equate politics of the Left with a certain drabness, as if embellishment were incompatible with social reform. Obviously the Swedes don't agree. And neither do I.

This evening I was seated beside the husband of the king's pretty, blonde sister, Princess Christina. Being married to a king's sister is not an altogether enviable situation. The husband still has to make his own way in the world somehow, but under much the same scrutiny that attends all royalty.

"Where is your home in Canada?" Tord Mag-nusson asked me.

"We manage to live in two places; one home in Ontario and another in Nova Scotia. Have you ever been to Canada?"

"Not exactly. I have been in the United States. I once lived there."

"They're not precisely the same," I insisted.

"Of course," he agreed, tactfully.

"Where did you live in the States?"

"In New York City. Christina and I spent a year there when we were students back in the 1960s. We were very happy there."

73

The engaging Mr. Magnusson talked about New York City at great length. Perhaps he had the idea that all Canadians must have an affinity with New York. Frankly the mere thought of the place fills me with dread. I visualize frightful poverty, decay in the streets, and triple locks on doors. Obviously there's more to it than that, but on my private list of the world's great cities New York ranks close to last place. For Tord and his royal wife, it had likely represented freedom — freedom from being royal. Although I found it enormously exciting to be in Stockholm dining with a king and chatting with his personable brother-in-law, for them this was just another routine event, perhaps no more noteworthy than the weekly trip to the supermarket is to me.

The dinner came to an end with a performance by the Galliard Ensemble, a chamber music quartet from Toronto. These four musicians travelled with us and played a short recital of four pieces at the conclusion of each reciprocal state dinner.

"They play very well. Very well indeed. Tell me, is this group popular in Canada?" Mr. Magnusson asked, when the applause subsided.

I found it hard to answer. Could one say that any chamber music group was popular in Canada? In truth, in 1981, the Swedish rock group ABBA was heard far more often on Canadian airwaves than was the Galliard Ensemble.

Back in our suite, I spent the usual hour packing clothes and preparing for the following day while Farley tried to stay awake long enough to make a few notes about everything that had been taking place in our lives. Since I didn't have time to do it, Farley had assumed the role of journal keeper.

"Umm. Meet anyone interesting tonight?" he enquired.

74

"Mr. Magnusson. Great guy," I said and went on to explain who he was and what we had briefly talked about.

"Uh huh. Anyone else?"

"No. Not really."

"Me either."

"So what are you writing about?"

"Oh, you know, what our destroyer was like, what the palace is like, the food, the cars. Actually, I'm kind of running out of commentary. It's amazing to be here . . . but nothing noteworthy seems to be happening."

"It is strange," I agreed. "All my life I've wanted to have an inside look at a real palace. And while it's all quite lovely to look at, I feel sort of . . . restricted."

"Right. Like a convent."

"Well, not exactly a convent. Nuns don't eat this well, I'm sure," I reflected.

"It's kind of narrow. I mean to say, if you worked here and didn't get outside much, it would be just as limiting as working in a coal mine or a department store."

"Oh, come on. All the VIPs who pass through this place? That's a lot different than a coal mine," I argued.

"True. But the staff doesn't get to know them. Even the king and queen only share a few meals with them and then poof! . . . they're gone, never to be seen again. I'm not saying that life is dismal in here, but it really isn't the least bit exciting," Farley concluded with a yawn as he closed his notebook. Then, as an afterthought, "Maybe I should ring the fire alarm . . ."

A state visit fills two solid days. Although the visiting head of state may remain in the host country for some

time after that, the continuation of the stay is designated as a private visit, more in the nature of a vacation. The terms are relative. As things turned out,
the rest of our time in Sweden was only one more
day and it was far from private. As well, there was
no escape from the rigours of a schedule.

On the first morning of our "private" visit we
were roused at 6:30 by our faithful major-domo bearing breakfast. (We never did find out where the rest
of the Accompanying Party got theirs, or even if they
did.) Late to bed and early to rise was evidently going
to be the norm. We had to be up even earlier this day
to be sure our suitcases were ready for collection at
7:30. All baggage had to be on board our plane, or
ship, well before we were, since for reasons of both
space and style, it could not accompany us in the
limousines.

The briefing-book stated that the "Farewell to
Their Majesties" would take place at 08:00 in the
Royal Guest Apartments. Once more, Farley and I
set off through the maze of corridors — and immediately got lost. Frantically we asked directions of
every palace servant we encountered until one of the
footmen, taking pity on us in our panic, volunteered
to guide us to the Apartments. He got us there on
time via a small private elevator, the existence of
which was well concealed behind an ornate eighteenth-century door.

Farley had a personal gift for the king and queen,
a copy of his book, *Never Cry Wolf*, in Swedish. Queen
Silvia, looking as queenly at eight o'clock in the
morning as she did at eight in the evening,
unwrapped the present on the spot. She smiled and
looked pleased with *Ropa Inte På Vargen*, although the
king appeared to be less enthusiastic. He is known

to be dyslexic and books are likely of less interest to him. Either that or he isn't fond of wolves.

The farewells lasted exactly eight planned minutes; then we had two minutes to descend the fairy-castle staircase for the last time.

It wasn't until we were on board a Scandinavian Airlines Fokker detailed to fly us south to Kalmar that Farley and I learned we had misread the briefing-book again. We had not been included in the royal farewells, Major Sangster told us. The only players in the final scene with the Swedish royal family should have been Ed, Lily, Jason, Esmond, and Léopold.

"Will we ever get it right?" I sighed, slumping into my aircraft seat.

"Isn't it nice that royal families are so gracious?" Farley said. "I mean, they could have booted us out of there. The bum's rush right down that palatial stairway."

Esmond Butler glanced admonishingly in our direction but he was diplomatic enough not to scold us. He had, after all, been trained to do his job at Buckingham Palace where politeness takes precedence over emotion. The palace has, for many years, incorporated representatives of the Commonwealth into the royal household on a rotating basis. Esmond, who had been working as a press attaché for Governor General Massey in the late 1950s, was chosen as the token Canadian. Two years later he returned to Canada to become secretary-chamberlain to Governor General Georges Vanier and since then his career had been devoted to smoothing the progress of each successive governor general.

On board the Fokker there was our own entourage as well as a platoon of Swedish bureaucrats, detectives and media people. The term "private" simply meant that the monarch was no longer our host.

Kalmar, a medium-sized city in southern Sweden, is at the centre of a popular holiday region. However, we were not going there for the scenery. We had come to tour two of Sweden's major industries, a Volvo automobile plant, which Ed had asked to see, and the Orrefors Glassworks, which had been requested by Lily.

Fog was wafting in from the Baltic as our flight approached the coast, and Kalmar airport was invisible. The plane gradually descended into the mist, but we were unable to see a thing. Down, down, down, and then suddenly the Fokker picked up speed and climbed steeply back up above the clouds. My heart started to pound. After years of being a passenger on every conceivable sort of plane, I still don't like flying, especially not when something appears to be going wrong.

"What now?" I asked myself, too alarmed to ask anyone else. Do we return to Stockholm and ask for our rooms back at the palace? Do we land somewhere else and take a bus to Kalmar? How are we going to maintain our precious schedule when the pilot can't find the runway? The plane circled, descended again and, on his second try, he found a gap in the low ceiling and slid us safely down. As we taxied towards the terminal, we Canadians gave him a hearty round of applause. The accompanying Swedes glanced at us in polite surprise. They clearly would not have done that sort of thing. Impulsive, emotional Canadians: what would we do next?

We were only fifteen minutes late as we strode down the now-familiar red carpet and shook another row of official hands. No national anthems this time, just the governor of Småland, the mayor of Kalmar and a clutch of municipal officials wearing smiles of relief that they hadn't had to scuttle the whole event because of the poor visibility. Within minutes we were off in a motorcade of, you guessed it, shiny new Volvos, on our way to the Volvo car factory.

After a ten-minute journey we arrived at a long, curving driveway that led through several acres of well-kept lawn. We stopped in front of a wide brick building, a modern structure that looked like one of the new universities in Canada, with lots of windows, lots of space, two storeys high, and surrounded by greenery. That this could be a factory seemed hard to credit. It bore no resemblance to its sister plants at home. But car factory it was, and the plant manager greeted us on the broad front steps and led us straight into the work area.

The first thing I noticed was the quiet. Not total silence, but an absence of the discordant clanging and banging we expect to hear in factories. There were no noisy conveyor belts. Partly assembled automobiles slid along at floor level in spooky silence, carried on electric trolleys controlled by unseen computers.

Men and a few women working in small groups glanced at us with little curiosity. The Kalmar plant is Volvo's showpiece and the workers are accustomed to visiting delegations. Thirty-two thousand cars are built in this large, pleasant building every year, yet there is no assembly line. The work force is divided into teams of about a dozen people, each assembling one car at a time in a group system that has been organized to feel like a small workshop. Within the groups the tasks are frequently rotated.

Someone who has been installing car radios one day may be attaching window frames the next. Everything possible has been done to alleviate the boredom that goes with repetitious work. Those who finish their assigned tasks ahead of schedule are free to go to their team's adjacent lunch-room to relax or read. Workers do not have to stand around pretending to be busy if they are not.

What delighted me most were the individual lunch-rooms furnished like modest living-rooms with pine tables and chairs and colourful drapes. Each had large windows looking out upon a park-like setting of forest and lawn and was designed for no more than twenty people. Employees didn't have to spend their meal time, or other free time, sitting in an echoing, concrete cafeteria surrounded by a sea of strangers.

The polygonal layout of the factory building was full of angles and projections that provided windows every few yards. This arrangement ensured that the workers didn't pass their days entirely under artificial light, far from a glimpse of the sky. I once spent four years working in an office without windows and I still have claustrophobic dreams about it. Even our bleak cafeteria had been windowless. Maybe that was why the conditions at the Kalmar Volvo plant made such an impression on me, every bit as vivid as my memories of the Royal Palace.

Canadian Volvos are assembled in Nova Scotia. Farley and I drive one and have owned a succession of four of them over the past twenty years. Like most car owners, we are partisan, convinced that our choice is perfection itself, so touring the Volvo factory was something of a pilgrimage for us.

''How do you like it here?'' Farley asked a man with a pneumatic drill in his hand.

"If one has to work in a factory, this is the best there is," he replied cheerfully in excellent English.

How I envy the Swedes their Volvo. The Saab is also a Swedish car but it is the highly successful Volvo that has put Sweden on the automotive map as surely as the Volkswagen did Germany. If Canada produced just one unique car of her own design it would do more for our national pride and international image than the Rocky Mountains, ten thousand red-coated Mounties and a billion maple leaves. It is demoralizing that we only manufacture other nations' cars and trucks. The Swedes have demonstrated that you don't have to be a big country to produce a first-class product.

After the Volvo tour we went to a restaurant in the centre of Kalmar where the governor was giving a luncheon in our honour.

Småland is one of the twenty-four *landskaps*, the historic regions that comprise the nation of Sweden. They are not the equivalant of Canadian provinces. The governor of each is appointed by the central government in Stockholm, and though there are governing councils they do not have their own parliaments. The only Canadian political structures somewhat similar might be the territorial governments of the Yukon and Northwest Territories.

Mr. Erik Westerlind, the governor, was a delight. A merry Swede is almost a contradiction in terms, but this he was, and he struck up an immediate rapport with Ed. Dining with a provincial governor turned out to be a picnic compared to the unbending court events of our first two days. There were only fifty of us at the table, and this luncheon felt almost homelike. We were a long way from the capital city, and the weight of royal protocol had lifted like the morning fog. Ed must have felt this too because after lunch he gave one of the best speeches I have ever heard from him.

When the governor general makes an official address in Canada, his or her speeches are usually drafted by the speech-writers of the household. When overseas, they are normally prepared by someone from the Department of External Affairs. This is the usual procedure for monarchs and presidents everywhere and probably explains why their speeches are generally so predictable, and so dull. But at a relatively informal luncheon like this, Ed could be his own man.

He began with some amusing reminiscences of what it had been like to be a young social reformer in the then Tory Blue province of Manitoba. He explained that Sweden had always been something of a spiritual home to him. When he became premier of Manitoba, Ed had looked to that society to see how they had solved some of the problems besetting those people in Canada who lacked an adequate share of life's necessities. Maybe his External Affairs mentors shuddered that afternoon, but his Swedish audience loved it.

The Swedes have such a commonsense approach to solving social problems. Most of their progressive policies are a legacy from the past half-century of coalition governments and their enduring belief in the importance of the social contract. My one regret about my only visit to Sweden was that I didn't have the chance to meet the legendary Olaf Palme. Palme was the prime minister for eleven years, and although the Social Democrats had been in power for all but six of the previous fifty years, they were out of office in 1981. After the election of 1982 Palme was returned to office to lead a coalition of the parties of

82

the Left. Tragically, he was assassinated in February 1986.

Canada still has a long way to go to provide the social services that are taken for granted in Sweden, where one-third of the annual budget is spent on the welfare of the people. In Canada the percentage is one-fifth. How long will it be before we have all-encompassing, subsidized day-care services for every family who needs them? And how long until our industrial workers can enjoy pleasant surroundings and enlightened work programs like those at the Kalmar Volvo plant?

After lunch we set out on a bus tour of the island of Öland. There's something jovial — folksy even — about conducted bus tours, even when they are composed of highly placed people. What a joy just to sit back and observe the passing landscape and let the tour director drone on with her hokey stories about Öland having once been the lair of pirates and brigands. How many places have I toured in the world that were supposed to have once been the preserve of pirates? Why, I wonder, is everyone so titillated by crime?

Öland (pronounced eúh-land) is an oblong island lying parallel to the south-east coast of Sweden. It is Sweden's smallest *landskap*. To reach it you must drive across the longest bridge in Europe, one whose causeways and spans stretch for six kilometres. I wondered why such an extravagant bridge had been built to connect this sparsely populated rural island to the mainland. Surely a car ferry would have met local needs. But the justification for the bridge is tourism. In summer this flat, limestone island teems with visitors, both Swedes and foreigners, who come to enjoy the sea and the Old World atmosphere of many pretty villages. It is Sweden's version of Prince Edward County in Ontario. But there were few visitors on that warm day in May and the uncrowded roads, tidy farms and old windmills of Öland looked much as they must have done for centuries.

Returning rather reluctantly to the mainland, we headed for the famous Orrefors glass factory.

If there is one thing that ensures a jubilant mood for any ceremonial affair, it has to be a brass band. And as we stepped from the bus in front of the factory, a band burst into a medley of marches and polkas. The bandsmen, all volunteers from the ranks of the workers at Orrefors Glassworks, looked especially festive in snappy uniforms of blue and gold. The music really lifted our spirits. There may be corporations in Canada that have volunteer bands with which to welcome visitors but I have never heard of them. The Orrefors band had been a company institution for eighty years.

Heralded with a trumpet flourish, we swept into the factory to watch the wondrous way that glass is made. I suspect that everyone must be fascinated by the ancient process of turning something as commonplace as sand into sparkling crystal. It takes about ten years to produce a first-class glass-blower or engraver, which puts them in the same category as doctors or ballerinas in terms of dedication. Despite the hard work and the years of study required, there is no shortage of willing apprentices at Orrefors. There was even one Canadian girl who was considerably surprised to find the governor general of Canada peering over her shoulder. She had come to Sweden to perfect her art because this, she told us, was the best place in the world to learn it.

Ironically, the glass factory was much hotter and noisier than the car factory had been. How different was the glass-blower's calling from that of the auto-mobile workers who alternated their tasks so that boredom wouldn't set in. Glass-blowing and design is a lifetime commitment, and ennui seems not to be among the occupational hazards.

Ed was offered the chance to "blow" something from a piece of molten glass that had just been with-drawn from a fiery furnace. Jason was the one who took up the challenge and managed to produce a bulbous vase that leaned slightly to one side when it cooled.

An art gallery adjoined the factory and here we looked at some of the masterpieces the Orrefors designers had produced. Graceful statues, prismatic vases, and multi-hued bowls were displayed on plinths. Sublime glass abstractions as tall as I am rested on polished wood tables. The contents of the room had that frosty, untouchable look of a Christmas window.

Happily, there was a discount glass shop beside the factory where crystal with slight imperfections was sold at bargain prices. We headed into it to see what we could find in the ten remaining minutes before our punctilious escorts moved us on again. It was impossible to make an enlightened choice in such a limited amount of time, but what proved even more confusing was trying to estimate the price in Swedish kronor. Although I'd been in Sweden for three days, I had not yet had an occasion to spend so much as an öre. Virtually none of us in the Accompanying Party had. Usually the value of the currency is the first thing one grasps on arrival in another country but that's not the case for a lady-in-waiting on a state visit.

Before we got back on our bus the Orrefors management presented Ed and Lily with a large crystal

85

bowl, and the rest of us with smaller ones. They were beautiful, but heavy. Fortunately we didn't have to carry them around with us, or try to squeeze them into our already-bulging suitcases. Captain John saw to that. His prime responsibility was looking after the four hundred pieces of baggage that accompanied us! It was an enormous task and fraught with difficulties. For one thing, we formed three distinct groups: the governor general and the Accompanying Party; the governor general's staff; and the Minister of External Affairs and his staff. Rarely were we all housed in the same building and quite often we travelled in separate vehicles. To add to the confusion, External Affairs minister Mark MacGuigan and members of his party kept departing from the tour and then rejoining it. At one point MacGuigan returned to Canada for three days and during another interlude he went to Belgium to attend a conference. Considering jet lag and exhaustion, I cannot imagine how he ever managed to do it all and keep his wits about him.

Keeping track of the destinations of the luggage of all these very mobile people was vitally important. Lost luggage on a state visit isn't just an inconvenience, it can be a national embarrassment, so the person in charge of keeping it all together is a key player in the whole trip's performance. The Canadian media got a lot of mileage out of an incident when former prime minister Joe Clark lost some of his luggage during a trip to Asia a few years ago. The implication that he had absent-mindedly mislaid it himself was pure nonsense: one of his assistants likely hadn't allowed enough time for the baggage to be transferred from one airline to another. It was just the kind of miscalculation that the governor general's staff goes to great lengths to avoid.

ADC David John had to know the whereabouts of absolutely everything: our personal luggage, the gifts we were giving and the gifts we received as we went along. Dave John, who came from British Columbia, was a career lieutenant in the Canadian Navy. A singularly good-looking man with silver hair, he was something of an anomaly as an aide-de-camp because of his age. He was thirty-nine the year he was assigned to the household of the governor general, and forty the year he joined our historic journey as the baggage officer. ADCs are usually between the ages of twenty-five and thirty when they are assigned to the prestigious but rigorous duties of Government House. There are always three of them, one each from the army, navy and air force, and they are also selected to represent the regional make-up of our country, English and French, east and west. In addition to a long list of stringent requirements for their arduous two-year stint, they must be single.

The bus took us back to Kalmar airport on a highway which passed alongside springtime-green fields of grain. It looked like a nice region in which to live. The Swedes have long had a policy of decentralizing industry to areas such as this, where jobs tend to be scarce. There are so many advantages to this policy. It brings jobs to people who might otherwise have to move away. Land is cheaper and housing is less expensive than they are in large cities. Even the air is cleaner. If the region also has the special appeal of scenery and the seashore, then it isn't difficult to lure management and skilled technicians to it. Successive Canadian governments have attempted to do the same thing but somehow it rarely works. Industries are born and often die prematurely in places such as Cape Breton Island or northern Manitoba. They become political footballs, with no one bearing the responsibility for their failure. The incentives the Swedes employ to coerce industry into moving to places like Småland are something Canadians ought to investigate. In truth, you can't visit Sweden — whether you're a backpacker or a courtier—without wondering how a mere eight million souls could find so many inventive and logical solutions to the dilemmas of twentieth-century life. Of course, the fact that there are only eight million of them may be part of the answer. Smaller aggregations seem to find their collective way with more democracy than larger ones.

Our visit was now almost over but our departure from Sweden was epic. Their excellencies, together with six of us from the Accompanying Party, were to journey to our next stop, Finland, aboard HMCS *Huron*, while everyone else would travel by air. Because of our tight schedule and the time required to sail from Sweden to Finland, the *Huron* had already put to sea. This meant that we would have to catch up to her by helicopter.

The *Huron*'s Sea King helicopter, which was waiting for us at the airport, could only carry four passengers in addition to its two-man crew and so would have to make two trips. Ed and Lily and Farley and I were the first to leave. In the tiny passenger cabin we sat facing each other with our collective knees almost touching. Nervously I buckled myself into a narrow canvas chair. The co-pilot handed each of us a pair of earplugs so that the noise wouldn't make us totally deaf. The pilot glanced back at us to make sure we were all ready to lift off. It was Harold Gear, the boy wonder. He looked as pleased as punch with his prestigious assignment. I smiled a constrained smile and tried to look calm.

Conversation is impossible in an airborne military

helicopter. The thudding of the rotor blades drowns out all but the most vigorous shouting. That was just as well because I was too frightened to make small talk anyway. Ed and Farley looked delighted by the whole experience as they inspected all the interior details of the menacing machine. Lily, who is a fearless traveller, was completely relaxed and quite content to have the chance to watch the pastoral coastline of Sweden slip by.

I was alone with my terror. Then I noticed that the fog blowing in from the Baltic was getting thicker. Soon the coast of Sweden disappeared completely. Even the surging dark water below us faded in and out of the mist. If I die now, I speculated self-pityingly, at least I'll be given an heroic funeral back home. As the chopper thundered onward in the murk, I wrote my own obituary in my head: *Lady-in-Waiting Dies in Service of Her Country. Medal Awarded Posthumously.* I resigned myself to the inevitable.

Helicopters don't land on the deck of a ship unless the pilot can see the target: that much I knew. How was Harold ever going to find the *Huron*, let alone manoeuvre this vibrating monster to a safe landing? We did have an alternate plan, of course. The Canadian military doesn't send a governor general or anyone else out over a foggy ocean without being sure it can bring them back to land if the weather closes in. But the logic of that was small comfort to me as we throbbed resolutely onward.

After what seemed like an eternity of flying blind, the bank of fog thinned into long wispy plumes and suddenly, just ahead of us, on a darkening ocean, we could see the *Huron*. She was heaving slowly in a heavy swell. The chopper leaned, circled, descended, and then hovered just above the painted circle of the landing-pad. From where we sat in the after-cabin we couldn't see the manoeuvres that were taking place below us so that our craft could land on the moving deck. I still cannot fathom how anyone does it, but Harold knew. Finally, we felt something solid underneath us and immediately a deck officer opened the door and helped us to climb out. Bent over double, we scuttled below the gigantic rotors to the lee side of the deck. There stood the commodore at attention, saluting the governor general. Within seconds we were being led down a companionway into the secure interior of the ship while our helicopter, with the dauntless Harold at the controls, took off to retrieve the rest of our party.

There could scarcely have been anyone happier than I was at that moment. As much as I hate to fly, I love to go to sea. With the ordeal behind me, the grey, unglamorous *Huron* seemed pure delight.

Accommodation in any military vessel is cramped. Farley and I had been assigned the doctor's cabin which the doctor had vacated for the night. The cabin was only about as big as the average Canadian bathroom but it held an upper and lower bunk, a sink, a mirror, a floor-to-ceiling unit of cupboards and a fold-out desk. Our luggage covered every inch of available floor space. We quickly weeded out the pieces we could do without and asked the steward to store them somewhere else.

On the deck above us our governor general fared considerably better. As the titular head of the Canadian Armed Forces, Ed was entitled to occupy the cabin space on a ship which is reserved for the commodore. This included a small saloon, a dining area, two miniature bedrooms, and a real bathroom containing that ultimate luxury on a no-frills vessel, a bathtub.

"Come up and take a bath any time you feel like it," Lily offered generously during the first real conversation we had shared in three days. We had always been surrounded by other people or separated by miles of corridors. Now, relaxed at last, we sat in the tiny saloon, sipped a pre-dinner drink, and exchanged stories and shared laughs about everything that had happened to us in Sweden. Lily kicked off her shoes. Farley took off his jacket. Ed lit a cigarette. A cheerful steward brought us cheese and crackers and some Canadian magazines. It almost felt like home.

For one evening we didn't have to weigh everything we said. We weren't on display, or at least we felt we weren't. Although having the governor general on board meant that the officers and crew were very much on their toes we, at least, felt that we could let our hair down. I began to understand why Queen Elizabeth is so fond of the royal yacht *Britannia* when she goes abroad. On a distant shore, your own ship is a welcome touch of home. Later that evening we were served a hearty meat-and-potatoes dinner, complete with bad Canadian coffee afterwards. I loved it.

After dinner, Commander Spalding invited us to tour the bridge and the operations room. I find it fascinating to be on the bridge of a ship. I believe that I'm in the presence of some great mystery amid the stern silence of the officers and the eerie blinks and blips of the navigational devices. I haven't a clue how any of it works, but that doesn't matter to me. I listened with feigned comprehension as the commander explained the machinations of the blinking lights and glowing cathode tubes. Our men were rapt. I have such a limited grasp of how any machine works that I could never qualify as an orthodox feminist. In my eccentric view of how the world functions, it is the men, thank goodness, who design, operate, and fix machines. Women do other things. While our husbands inspected all this amazing equipment, Lily and I cheerfully made small talk with the members of the crew. People are so much more interesting than dials, switches, and levers.

The waters between Sweden and Finland are hazardous. The shipping channel threads its way through rocky islands and reefs. It is also reputed to be one of the world's most beautiful maritime vistas. Prince Bertil, the widely travelled uncle of the king, spent a lot of time during one luncheon describing to Lily what a treat was in store for us when we sailed across the Baltic. But that night the fog was as thick as porridge and we saw absolutely nothing. So, with little to look at except those flickering consoles, we all decided to take advantage of the opportunity to go below and get some much-needed sleep.

Moments later, Commodore Riddell, looking very earnest, appeared at the door of the small saloon.

''Sir. We have just identified a Soviet vessel, apparently trailing us,'' he said, his tone of voice indicating a mixture of military urgency and boyish delight. After all, it wasn't every day he had the governor general on board while in the presence of a possible enemy.

Radar, and all the other electronic snoops had revealed that the ''signature'' of a vessel astern of us was that of a Soviet destroyer. Was it possible that she was tracking us, trying to unmask the secrets of the Canadian Navy? By then our ship was approaching the Gulf of Finland, international waters where anyone might legitimately be sailing.

We hurried back up to the darkened bridge. Curt

orders were given. We gathered speed. We would outrun our pursuer, by God. The Canadian Navy was going to show the Commander-in-Chief of the Armed Forces what the old *Huron* could do!

Half an hour later the first officer appeared with a message for Commander Spalding. Our electronic experts had now discovered exactly who was tailing us. It was a vessel of the Finnish Navy! Her commander had radioed a plaintive message to the *Huron* asking us to please slow down because his ship couldn't keep pace with us and it was his job to escort us into Finnish territorial waters.

Our naval intelligence had in fact got it right. The mystery ship *was* Russian-built. But the Finns buy their destroyers from the Russians, a fact of Finnish military economics that had been overlooked in the drama of the moment.

I climbed wearily into my bunk, pondering the insanity of military gamesmanship. All those dedicated, skilled, good people running this ship, whose purpose was . . . what?

I drifted into a fitful sleep, for naval ships are not quiet. There is activity in the echoing steel corridors all night long—the sound of heavy-booted footsteps and the intermittent clanging of signals and bells. The engines throb and thud. Nonetheless, we did manage to sleep until six o'clock when, by mistake, Farley and I got Bernie St. Laurent's wake-up call. Even then we went back to sleep until eight, when we were wakened once again by a distant roaring that we could feel as well as hear.

This time there was no going back to sleep. We had reached the offshore islands guarding the entrance to Helsinki and the ancient cannons of an outlying fortress were giving us a 21-gun salute. There was no way anyone could have slept through that.

Finland

Finland looks so much like Canada that it immediately becomes a landscape of memories. Approached from the sea, the rocks, the colour of the sky and the profile of the trees suggest to a Canadian that this must be the approach to the harbour of Halifax, or possibly to Thunder Bay. It isn't until you see the harmonious city of Helsinki with its mixed marriage of the architecture of nineteenth-century Russia and that of the recent Finnish renaissance that you know you are somewhere else.

The only one of us who was out on deck to catch the first glimpse of it was Ed. Even though no one on the distant shore of Kustaamiekka could possibly have seen him without powerful binoculars, he stood at attention, braving the chill breeze, to receive the ultimate greeting that one country can offer another —a 21-gun salute. I couldn't match his sense of duty that early in the day. Barely awake, I was still in my nightgown, peering out of a porthole, craning to see that bald little island from which the ancient cannon boomed its thunderous salutation.

The *Huron* sailed at a snail's pace for another hour as we glided into the spectacular harbour of Helsinki, escorted by a flotilla of the Finnish Navy, including that weary warship which had struggled so valiantly all night to keep pace with us. Those final moments as a ship approaches her mooring are, I think, one of life's most dramatic climaxes. A journey has been made; a destination has been reached. And in a ship, the conclusion of a voyage happens in such a slow sequence that you can savour it. I still remember the enchantment of my childhood voyages to Toronto Island on board the old ferry *Bluebell*. The crossing only took a few minutes but I loved every one of them. Arriving in Helsinki to the sound of cannons and the sight of fluttering flags brought back my childhood excitement.

The ceremonial arrival of a ship is infinitely more dramatic than one of an airplane. For one thing, you can decorate a ship and ours, decked out in all her ceremonial flags, was as spectacular as a blaze of fireworks. For another, a pier lends itself to a grand occasion more readily than some cordoned-off corner of an airstrip. Quite a crowd had gathered near the pier to see what all the fuss was about. A military band in flamboyant parade uniforms stood at attention, brass instruments gleaming in the sunshine. Behind them waited the inevitable line-up of black limousines.

Many of the world's capitals evolved as such because of their port facilities, so you find that piers are conveniently located near the downtown where the public can see what's going on. In security-conscious airports, the mandarins disembark in some faraway corner of the field to be seen only by newspeople, police officers, and a few invited guests.

As the gap between the *Huron* and the dock

slowly narrowed we had enough time to look down from the deck at all the Finnish dignitaries who were patiently waiting for us. We could easily identify the tall, bald man with the horned-rimmed glasses who stood at the head of the line, Urho Kekkonen, the 81-year-old President of Finland.

This was the first state visit a Canadian governor general had ever made to Finland and we could sense that the Finns were as excited about it as we were. At exactly eleven o'clock Ed, Lily, and Jason walked carefully down the gangplank and shook hands with the president. Bernie St. Laurent, standing tall this time under his statuesque hat, was immediately the centre of attention in his arresting uniform.

During the playing of the two national anthems, it occurred to me that being a military bandsman was not a bad way to live one's life. They get all the perks of the military and still have the chance to make music besides. Likely no one would ever take a shot at them either. Those bandsmen were our song-cousins that morning, enthusiastically tooting their trumpets and tubas. I wonder how long it took them to practise ''O Canada'' until it was perfect.

The schedule had allocated two minutes for the playing of the two anthems and at exactly 11:02 we proceeded down the gangplank and onto the red carpet where we shook hands with President Kekkonen, the man who, at that time, had been president of his country longer than any other European leader. There was the ritual inspection of the guard of honour which took place while we shook hands with a bunch of fair-haired VIPs. Then, with our accustomed split-second precision, we climbed into our designated cars and drove off.

A crowd of children waved pint-sized Canadian flags as we glided by. I waved back, full of bravado.

"This is a piece of cake," I thought to myself, free from the angst that had seized me when we arrived in Sweden. Our arrival had been letter-perfect and I had the feeling that all would go well for us in the land of the Finns.

I had been to Helsinki once before but the visit had been very brief. On a voyage Farley and I made from Canada to Leningrad in 1966, *Alexander Pushkin* had docked in Helsinki for a day. It had been a chill, overcast afternoon in October with the sound of crunching leaves underfoot. We passengers had only a few hours to wander around the city but I fell in love with the place—with its perfectly proportioned buildings, the subdued colours, the harmony between all that was man-made and natural. What impressed me most was the style with which the Finns did things. It wasn't just the architecture. All the smaller artifacts of city life — the telephone booths, garbage bins, bus stops, and traffic signs— looked as if they had been designed by a gold-medal winner from an art college. Even the people who passed us on the streets in their plain raincoats and flat-heeled shoes had the same well-planned look.

I had studied to be a designer at a time in Canada when the swingers yearned for cars with chrome-plated tail fins and the goal of just about everybody was a ranch-style house in the suburbs. In the late 1950s, most of the Canadian buildings that had survived from our slightly more graceful past were either being neglected, demolished, or covered with Angel Stone. To have landed in the country that produced Alvar Aalto and Marimekko filled me with the ecstasy of a pilgrim. It had been an immense frustration in 1966 not to have had time to see more of it. I could hardly believe my good fortune in having finally returned. Ed Schreyer may have looked towards Sweden for guidance in social programs but I, longing for enlightenment as I trudged through my student years on Toronto streets canopied with black utility cables, had looked towards Finland.

The four-minute drive to the president's palace was all too brief for me. I wanted to see the whole city right away. Mind you, as we wafted past a pair of ornate iron gates into the exquisite courtyard of the palace, it was some compensation. We found ourselves in front of a gem of a building that, unlike the enormous palace in Stockholm, had been built to human scale. It was three storeys high, classical in style and warmly welcoming. This tidy little palace had not been designed as the home of a king. It had, in fact, been built by the Russians as a home for their governor general back in the days when Finland was a duchy in the Russian Empire. Ed would not be the first of his kind to enter these hallowed halls. The colour of the outside of the building was distinctly Russian. It was the hue of distant goldenrod, the mellow yellow that you see on most of the old buildings in Leningrad. I love yellow. It has to be the perfect complement to the sombre skies that prevail for so much of the northern year.

We shook hands, for the second time that morning, with President Kekkonen as he welcomed us to his home and no further fanfare was needed to remind us we were honoured guests. After many smiles and few words, a servant quietly escorted us up one short flight of stairs to our rooms.

Inside the palace, the walls were painted in the light-hearted colour of daffodils. Farley and I were assigned one large, bright room with a wonderful view of the harbour. We were next door to the suite the Schreyers occupied and conveniently down the hall from Thelma and her indispensable iron. On a big table in the centre of our room was a flower arrangement that would have done credit to a Rosedale wedding, as well as lots of fruit, candy, cigarettes, and several bottles of assorted liquors. As if this wasn't riches enough, we discovered that the bathroom contained gifts of toothbrushes, toothpaste, shampoo, cologne, and shaving-cream. In case we had forgotten anything in our haste, the Finns had foreseen our needs.

We also found a gift from the president—a fluffy woollen blanket hand-woven in many shades of deep blue. It was soft and enveloping to touch and beautiful to look at. As I stood there cuddling it and wondering what I had done to deserve this, Jason came galloping down the hall.

"Guess what I got?" he asked proudly.

"Tell us."

"A bike! A Finnish *racing* bike! Is it ever neat!"

It was the perfect gift for a thirteen-year-old boy and Jason, I predict, will fondly remember Finland all his life.

The Finns had thoughtfully allocated sufficient time between our morning arrival and the family luncheon that we could get our bearings. I had nearly an hour to spare, time to have a chat with Lily, to change into another dress, and then to study the guest list. Reading the guest list before the beginning of an event is standard practice for heads of state and all who travel with them. It gives you some idea of whom you are going to meet. Britain's Prince Charles, for example, requests a short résumé about each person who will be seated within conversational distance of him at a dinner so that he will know whether he will be chatting with an athlete, a scientist, or a musician.

In our hectic initiation into the life of the court in

Sweden, I hadn't had time to read any of the guest lists. In Helsinki I did, but here I had to surmount the obstacle of the Finnish language. Finnish is not a bit like English or French. Swedish, on the other hand — for an English-speaking person — is not altogether alien. Swedish designations like *direktor*, *ambassador* and *ombudsman* speak for themselves. Finnish gave us no clues. And I could only wager a guess at the pronunciation of names like Ihamuotila, Maentakaenen, or Lähteinen. The Finns were doubtless having as much trouble with names like MacGuigan, Amyot and Mowat.

You can always get away with addressing the president of a country as "Mr. President" if you are uncertain how to pronounce his name. As I studied the seating plan for lunch I discovered that I was to be seated on the president's left while Lily would sit at his right. That put me on my mettle: I had expected to be placed a secure four or five seats away. What would I say to this august man if he asked me a question I couldn't answer? Could I speak intelligently about senate reform in Canada, or the imbalance of trade between Canada and Finland?

The president and I nodded cordially as we sat down to lunch in a small palace dining-room. Directly behind him sat Miss Pelkonen, his translator. She didn't eat. I hope someone had made her a sandwich beforehand. The president spoke English very well, but she was always close by in case there was some word or phrase he might have missed. It turned out we didn't need her services. When he finally turned to speak to me, the president wanted only to know what kind of wild berries grew in Canada. Relieved to be asked a question on a subject I knew, I cheerily listed strawberries, raspberries, blueberries, blackberries, cranberries, and that peculiar berry

101

that looks like a bloated yellow raspberry and which abounds in the subarctic bogs of both Canada and Finland, the bakeapple. It is known by the name ''cloudberry'' in the Nordic countries. I described the various terrains and seasons where all these berries could be found and thus the president and I continued our comfortable talk about the atavistic pleasure of finding one's own food.

President Kekkonen was known to hold dogmatic views about diet and longevity, views that seemed to have served him well. Not many people can still endure the rigours of public office when they are in their eighties. I was told that he ate a lot of brown bread, that he had been a marathon runner in his youth, a long-distance skier until he was in his seventies, and that he still went for ten-mile walks. A mystique had grown up around his indestructibility. I like to think that all those wild berries had indeed contributed to his enduring good health.

Presidents and monarchs, I would discover, rarely talk about their jobs on social occasions. The last thing they want to hear is one more opinion on how to solve the world's ills. Backstage, they're more likely to talk about their personal pastimes and pleasures. From that day I lost my fear of talking to people at the top. It's only those well down the totem pole who will try to humiliate you if you lack a clever answer.

The first event of our eventful afternoon was a wreath-laying ceremony at the Tomb of Marshal Mannerheim. Karl Gustav Mannerheim was the father of modern Finland, much like Sir John A. Macdonald was to Canada. Mannerheim was the man who united the country, the man who signed the constitution establishing Finland's independence in

1919. He led Finland out of the Russian empire and he also led the Finns into the disastrous Finno-Russian war of 1939.

Like most people, I had never given much thought to tombs and cenotaphs until I found myself on the periphery of the governor general's role, but I am now convinced that they do matter. People need visible reminders that their nations were not formed overnight nor sustained without sacrifice. The sacrifices of the Finns have been considerable.

Thousands of Finns moved to Canada during and just after the war. I remember meeting Finnish children at our elementary school, children trying to adjust to our way of life and our language. I had no idea then why they had come. Now I was beginning to understand.

If there are "developers" in Finland, someone has figured out a way to curb their worst instincts. Despite the destruction of the Second World War and the housing crisis that followed, no one tore the heart out of the exquisite city of Helsinki. Classical treasures from the nineteenth century still line the busy downtown streets.

Further uptown we visited the modern city hall, a building that dates from the post-war boom. We were ushered into a rotunda the size of a schoolyard that contained almost nothing but a broad bare stairway. In the stairwell, reaching from the ground to the third floor, stood one of the strangest pieces of sculpture I have ever seen. It was a tall column which consisted entirely of huge, plastic thumbs. Just thumbs. They overlapped and intertwined, weaving their way onward and upward, as tall as those gigantic totem poles in the Royal Ontario Museum. It is the thumb, most anthropologists believe, that has made man what he is, the ultimate tool-making, tool-using creature. I had never seen a tribute to the human thumb before and I have yet to hear a song sung in its praise. But in the Helsinki City Hall there was such a celebration to the thumb that it reached the ceiling.

We gathered in a large room on the third floor to celebrate not our thumbs but our state of accord. Mayor Raimo Ilaskivi, an amiable-looking man, spoke the obligatory words of welcome, those words we expect to hear but seldom remember. However, the welcome speech is part of the bonding process, an incantation of reassurance. It is notable only if it is missing.

While I don't recall what the mayor said to us, I distinctly remember the room in which we stood. Though it was as big as a tennis court, it was furnished with only one item: a carpet about forty feet square, woven in thick, looped wool in half a dozen shades of purple. This had to be the ultimate in the minimalist approach to decorating, yet the perfect solution to furnishing a large space in which brief gatherings are held, where no one sits down anyway. Just a carpet, an utterly gorgeous one. It provided people with a place to stand that was restful to the feet and it also dulled the cacophony of many simultaneous voices. I've been in innumerable reception rooms the world over and mostly they have been cluttered with uninspired chairs on which few people ever sit, while the floors where everyone stands were usually covered with something tawdry and synthetic. That purple carpet said so much about the originality of Finland. It was like a painting, an entertainment in itself. If the conversation grew dull you could lose yourself just staring into the dark, woolly depths.

The most unforgettable building we saw that day was a church — Temppeliaukio, the Church of the Temple Square. Completed only a dozen years earlier, it had been built by quarrying an amphitheatre out of living rock and then roofing it over. It was the antithesis of all the great twelfth-century cathedrals of Europe, which were constructed by piling quarried rock as high as was humanly possible.

At the door of the church we were greeted by the Lutheran pastor and his small daughter who presented Lily with a nosegay. Lily is always overjoyed to be greeted by either children or flowers, and she walked hand-in-hand with the little girl into the church.

Among us all, only Lily had grown up a Lutheran, yet we all felt at home there. The church was quiet, insulated from sounds that might remind us we were in the middle of a city. We sat down in the blonde oak pews and listened to more words of welcome, spoken through an interpreter because the pastor spoke only Finnish and Swedish, the two official languages of Finland. Then the organist played two fugues by J. S. Bach, and after that a tenor soloist sang an anthem.

Nothing could have been more welcome than the music. As long as it lasted none of us was obliged to say a thing. We didn't even have to react with a visible expression of interest. How tiring it was becoming to have to do so much smiling and talking. Silence was starting to assume the value of gold, with music coming a close second. If I am ever in the position of arranging a tour for some visiting potentate, I'll move heaven and earth to ensure that that person has time for musical interludes, preferably in uplifting surroundings.

And we were in an inspiring place. The building was circular, about as big as a skating rink, and most of it was underground. Despite its subterranean design it looked light and felt serene because it was encircled by 180 small windows just below its vaulted ceiling. The sun came streaming in and, against the background of chiselled rock walls, the simple brass liturgical symbols shone.

Inevitably I began to wonder why Canadians don't construct buildings like this — not churches necessarily, but any public buildings or even private homes. We are not short of bedrock. Apart from blasting it to smithereens in our quest for minerals or for the ingredients of concrete, we have not found much imaginative use for it.

In an information sheet, I was impressed to read that this church served a congregation of thirty thousand people in both Finnish and Swedish. Is there a parish or congregation in all of Canada with that many members? Or do the Finns have a different way of calculating the numbers of the faithful? Maybe they were counting every head in the surrounding, populous neighbourhood, whether those heads were ever bowed in prayer or not.

We made five more appearances that busy afternoon, including the parliament buildings and the national museum, but it was the church and the memory of those few musical moments that linger.

Back at the palace, our hosts had thoughtfully summoned a hairdresser for the convenience of Lily, Thelma, myself, and the women in the Finnish Accompanying Party. None of us ever had time to go out to a hairdresser even if we could have found one. We coped with our hair as best we could, using our own shampoo and portable hair-dryers. The plan was that I would have my hair done first since Lily still had one more event to attend. Thelma led me along a network of corridors that took us through the palace kitchen and then beyond it to a small salon with sinks and mirrors.

I sank gratefully into the big leather swivel chair as the hairdresser immediately began the shampoo. She was a tall, red-haired woman who spoke only a little English. Since I knew no Finnish, it seemed pointless to try and explain what I normally did with my hair. I just waved my hand skyward as if to say she had complete control. Besides, I could enjoy the surprise of seeing what she decided to do. There was also a cosmetician standing by, a younger woman who spoke more English than the hairdresser and who eyed me speculatively before she asked me the colour of my evening gown.

"Mauve."

She looked perplexed.

"Umm. Lilac?" I tried, wondering if the names for flowers in Finnish were remotely like ours. "Violet, but a very pale violet," I added. How tricky it is to explain a nuance of colour when you don't share a language. Finally I just pointed to a cake of mauve eyeshadow that was almost the colour of my dress.

"Ah," she said cheerfully, and then started to blend three or four shades of face powder in a tiny container.

"So, you see many countries on your tour?" the cosmetician inquired as she smoothed some kind of cream all over my face.

"Sweden," I answered. "Yours is our second country. And I like Finland very much," I added diplomatically.

"Sweden. Mmm, hmm," she nodded knowingly. "And did you see Silvia?" she smiled.

"The queen? Yes, several times."

She raised an eyebrow. "And she is very beautiful. Yes?"

"She is," I agreed, "and very charming."

The beauty salon staff, which included a third woman who appeared to do the cleaning-up, was now becoming very interested in what I was saying, inconsequential as it was. With the help of the cosmetician as translator, they asked about the queen's clothes, about her children, about the palace, about the king; fascinated to hear any scraps of information I could remember or cared to disclose. Queen Silvia is the queen of another country, a country that isn't all that popular among the Finns. I was surprised that they were so interested in her. Why do the citizens of republics regard royalty with such reverence? If pomp is missing from their own rituals, will the public invariably attach itself to foreign ones?

An hour later I emerged from the salon looking splendid. The hairdresser and the cosmetician had managed to make me look better than I could have possibly done myself. I should have written down their names. It would be worth a return trip to Helsinki just to find out how they did it. But I had to hurry away. I trotted down the hall and up the steps to the kitchen where the staff, less than an hour away from the start of the banquet, was frantic with activity. Then I saw Thelma and Lily rushing towards me, on their way to the salon.

"Wow! You look great!" Lily exclaimed, absorbing the transformation.

"I think I'll move to Helsinki," I said.

"I hope they can do as well by me!" Lily laughed.

"They will. And you'll feel so much better for just sitting back in that big chair."

"Oh, yes, my feet," Lily lamented.

"Your Excellency, we should hurry," urged Thelma, eying her watch.

Off they dashed at a near run, out through the kitchen and on down the stairs.

"Hey, look at you!" Farley exclaimed when I entered our room. He had been visiting the staff of his Finnish publishers, Karisto. Three of Farley's books had been translated and published in Finland during the previous decade, but until he got there he was unaware he had any sort of following in that country.

As we were assembling all our evening finery for the third time in four days, Farley told me about the surprises of his afternoon. Two attractive young ladies had met him at the palace gates where they greeted him with a kiss — right in front of the palace sentry. Then they summoned a taxi and drove him down to a pier on the waterfront where, among yachts and seagulls, a crew from Finnish television was waiting with a water taxi. Equipped with a cooler of white wine, the party sailed off to a nearby island where a young man conducted an interview with Farley for a local television show which is broadcast every day in *English*.

That interlude was followed by a number of press interviews held in a nearby bar. It was a happy discovery for both of us to find that Farley was well-known in Finland. When foreign rights to a book are sold, book reviews and sales figures rarely reach the author, who is lucky to even get a copy of the book in another language. And authors generally make a pittance from foreign publications. A payment of a few hundred dollars is about it; and agent's fees and local taxes take a bite from that. When one's book is sold and then translated into another language, its foreign publication is like dropping it into a distant ocean.

By now I was getting the dressing procedure down to a fine art. Following Thelma's system, I laid everything out in order — underwear, perfume, shoes, evening bag, dress, and jewellery. I allowed a few minutes to assist Farley who always had difficulties inserting his cufflinks and collar studs. But even he, the least foppish of men, was gradually learning to master his ceremonial garb.

We dined in the palace that evening in the Gothic Hall—a superlatively joyful room and the antithesis of everything that comes to mind when one hears the word "gothic." It was smaller than the overwhelming dining-hall of the Swedish palace, although smaller is a relative term. It was still big enough to seat one hundred people. The walls were painted the joyful colour of buttercups and the ceiling and mouldings were entwined with delicately sculpted leaves and flowers. And of course there were the real flowers. The room seemed to be full of them: tall bouquets that looked vaguely oriental with their asymmetrical arrangements of gladioli. I had not thought of the Finns as masters of the timeless art of flower-arranging but obviously they were.

At a Finnish state banquet it isn't necessary to find space for a retinue of royals. Consequently the seating plan was condensed and the Canadian lady-in-waiting was bumped up a notch. I found myself placed at the head table where, in a monarchy, a duke or princess would have been sitting. I nodded a "Good evening" to the gentleman on my right and then to the one on my left. Then I read the menu card

110

which told me we were about to eat *La Tortue Ninon; Sole en Gelée; Caneton à l'Orange; Pommes au Rhum;* accompanied by *Chablis Château Kirwan 1973* and *Veuve Clicquot Ponsardin Brût.* I supped my turtle soup, and I began to doubt that pork chops, pot roasts, and beef stroganoff—with the occasional bottle of *Lion d'Or*—would ever taste the same again.

It was with the lanky gentleman on my left that I talked the most. His place was at the very end of the table and so he was stranded with only me for a conversational partner. He had a wealth of salt-and-pepper-coloured hair, a craggy face, and a nice baritone voice with which he spoke flawless English.

"I've been to Canada," he told me.

"And where did you go?"

"Montreal. Toronto. And several places in northern Ontario. I was there in connection with the forest industry."

"And did you meet lots of Finnish-Canadians in northern Ontario?"

"Yes, I did. It was a surprise. Some of them have been there two generations, possibly three now. And they still have the language. A rather old-fashioned Finnish is what they speak. But, yes, certainly, I was able to speak to them."

My companion was not only knowledgeable about our forests, he seemed sincerely interested in us as a nation. It was a real pleasure to talk to him and I wouldn't have cared if the banquet had lasted all night. I glanced at the placecard bearing his name — Koivisto — but couldn't remember from our lists just where he fitted into the scheme of things. His position was printed on his placecard too but it was in Finnish and so was meaningless to me. He was sitting five seats to the left of the president. Did that mean he was a cabinet minister? A chief justice? The leader of the opposition (if there was such a position in the Finnish system)? As the dinner was drawing to a close, I decided to simply ask him what he did.

"I am the prime minister," he answered, matter-of-factly, as if I had asked him what time it was.

I was speechless with embarrassment. I tried to imagine anyone from another country dining with Mr. Trudeau and asking what his position was in the Canadian government. Oh, the shame! *The prime minister.* But something seemed askew here: why was he sitting on my left at the very end of the head table? In Canada, a prime minister would be in the middle and, furthermore, he wouldn't be sitting beside the lady-in-waiting. Other countries, other customs? No, other countries, other systems of government.

Finland has both a president and a prime minister, but in their protocol pecking order, the prime minister is Number Three, ranking after the president and the speaker of the house.

I quickly apologized to Mr. Koivisto, who was unperturbed. Prime ministers rarely feel slighted by lack of recognition. Doubtless they get quite enough of it in the course of any day.

Within the year, the venerable President Kekkonen retired. A few months after that, the electoral college elected a new president, none other than former Prime Minister Mauno Koivisto. If I should ever dine with him again I won't make a mistake about his position. He'll be sitting right at the centre of the banquet table!

The next morning we joined Ed and Lily for breakfast in the sunny sitting-room of their suite. We sat at a democratic round table, where everything from croissants to bacon and eggs was served. Captain St. Laurent, in his shirt sleeves, bobbed in and out a couple of time to discuss the day's events. Jason, in T-shirt and jeans, yawned and deliberated about what he wanted to eat. Lily wore her dressing-gown. It was a cosy scene.

We had even been supplied with copies of the morning paper, *Uusi Suomi*. Not even Ed could make head or tail of what it said; but we could recognize ourselves in the photographs. There was Ed, on the front page, flanked by a platoon of Finnish soldiers. Even Farley made the front page in a separate news item about his writing. On page two there was a long article about Lily. This was certainly the ideal way to encounter yourself in the press. If anything sniping or critical was mentioned, we couldn't read it.

Captain St. Laurent had also managed to make it onto the editorial page where he was the subject of a funny drawing that showed him trying to peer out from beneath his busby as he marched, blindfolded by fur, across a parade square. Bernie's hat—the like of which does not exist in the uniforms of the Finnish military—had been the hit of our arrival. Apparently a number of onlookers had thought *he* was the governor general, he looked so sensational.

However, on this, the less ceremonious second day of the visit, Bernie was dressed more comfortably in the anonymous dark green of the Canadian Armed Forces. Only the gold lanyard, which is worn at all times by a governor general's aide-de-camp, set him apart from his fellow officers.

The Men's Party departed at 9:15 to tour a nuclear power plant. The Ladies' Party wasn't scheduled to leave until 10:00 which gave me some badly needed extra time to unpack and dispatch whatever needed to be pressed. It was quite an adjustment for me to do a day's work dressed in my best. Usually I work in my own home wearing sporty, durable clothes that move comfortably from the typewriter to the stove, and elaborate hairstyles and make-up are indulgences saved for special occasions.

When it was time to leave, I suddenly found I couldn't open the door of our suite. What on earth was wrong? Farley had left through the same door half an hour earlier. I rattled it and shook it but it wouldn't budge. It was the only exit apart from the windows. What was I going to do?

It seemed undignified to yell for help. I knelt down and looked through the keyhole just as someone darted past it. I heard a gleeful giggle. Jason! With nothing on *his* morning itinerary and an active imagination, he had figured out a way to lock me in.

"Jason," I shouted, with a desperate attempt at authority, "your mother is waiting for me! We've got to be at the front door in three minutes."

No reply.

"Come on, Jason. Hurry up!" I coaxed, feeling like the victim of a boarding-school prank.

Only a muffled laugh.

Then I heard another voice. It was Thelma, sounding firm. I heard the door being unlocked as Jason innocently proclaimed that he thought Mrs. Mowat had already left.

"Just you wait!" I called back as I bolted along the hall and down the circular stairway.

The Ladies' Party, which, as always, included several men, was heading out to the countryside to see a restored eighteenth-century village. We drove beyond the city and then through a forest full of Canadian trees—birch, spruce, and pine. At least, to me they were Canadian. Doubtless the Finns didn't think so. The silvan vista could have been any one of thousands of places in the Canadian Shield. And the reconstructed village, when we eventually reached it, looked as if it had sprung straight out of a Cornelius Krieghoff painting.

Called Seurasaari, it smelled deliciously of pine needles. The sun filtered through an archway of evergreens. All other tourists had been put on hold for the morning so the place was ours alone. The director, Mr. Gårdberg, wore a pin-striped suit that looked out of place as he led us in and out of a dozen log buildings, all more than two hundred years old. We toured a church and a windmill and several solid houses and barns. With their tidy mitred corners, they were cosy but spartan and it was easy to see that rank-and-file Finns had lived much like Canadian settlers during the same era. Entire families camped in one room with only a sleeping-ledge to delineate the daytime space from the night-time quarters. There was precious little furniture: a crib for a baby, a spinning-wheel, occasionally a musical instrument.

During the Finnish winter, a season as long and as cold as our own, these simple houses had barely been heated. The director explained that in the morning someone built a fire on the dirt floor in the middle of the house. The warm smoke billowed around a bit before wafting up through a hole in the ceiling. It sounded to me like a sure-fire way to get everyone up and doing, though anyone who suffered from bronchitis would have been simply out of luck.

Most of the structures in Seurasaari had been brought there from Karelia, the easternmost province of Finland which, in 1947, had been ceded to the Soviet Union (or seized by the Soviet Union, depending on whether you are a Russian or a Finn). At some point the dispossessed Finns were given permission to dismantle the oldest buildings in Karelia and move them to western Finland. I was impressed that, in the midst of such hardship and upheaval, anyone would have been concerned about architectural preservation.

At length we were directed to the village square where we sat on rustic wooden benches and were entertained by a dozen folk singers and dancers in traditional costumes. Women wearing full skirts and loose-sleeved blouses, and men in dark trousers and colourful shirts danced a reel of the sort you'd expect to see at a party on Cape Breton Island.

It was a treat for Lily and me to sit idly in the sunshine watching other people performing. To let someone else be the centre of attention for a while is one of the best gifts a visiting celebrity can hope for.

"Let's just stay here all day," Lily whispered to me.

"They'll never miss us," I replied.

"We could have a sandwich sent in for lunch."

"Tell you what. Let's trade clothes with two of these dancers. Send a pair of them back in our place."

"I wonder if Ed would notice?"

"Or the police?"

Reluctantly we said our farewells to the staff of the village. Then, like a perpetual bridesmaid, I held Lily's bouquet while she signed the guest book. All too soon we were heading back into the city.

Prime Minister Koivisto was our host for lunch. By then the distinction between the president and prime minister was imprinted on my mind. The Government Banqueting Hall, at which events pertaining to the government (as distinct from the state) are held, wasn't far from the palace and so we were allowed to walk there. This was another unexpected pleasure and gave us a few precious minutes to see ordinary things in detail. The police in most countries are uneasy about these informal strolls, but the Finnish security police evidently didn't feel the risk to our safety was high. Even so, we were knee-deep in detectives as we strolled through the Helsinki market.

It was lunch hour for the downtown office workers and many of them were browsing among the stalls and barrows of food, flowers, and handicrafts. As we ambled along, they turned and craned to get a look at us. People always stare when one is surrounded by police.

"Hi, Canada!" called out a young man wearing jeans and dark glasses.

"Hi! Where are you from?" I called back.

"Massachusetts."

We stopped in front of a refreshment kiosk where the proprietor was selling something that looked like a perogy, a small pastry rolled up with meat inside. He handed each of us a sample. As I wolfed mine down I noticed that the canopy over his stall was decorated with photographs of a lot of famous people who had already passed this way: the king and queen of Sweden, the deposed king and queen of Greece, Henry Kissinger, and an assortment of European presidents. Evidently this walkabout through the Helsinki market was a ritual for visiting dignitaries, a light touch amid a round of official duties. A photographer was waiting to take a picture of the governor general of Canada eating one of these tasty little Finnish hot dogs, a picture to be added to the gallery of high-profile customers who have paused in front of this small Finnish business venture.

At the banquet hall we dined on turbot stuffed with spinach, followed by pheasant. The dessert was strawberry blancmange. It wasn't hard to take.

When it came time for coffee, the Ladies' Party was driven to a nearby restaurant called the Esplanadi Kappeli. A big room at the back had been cordoned off and here we were treated to a private fashion show.

Coffee and pastries were passed around and then, for the next half hour, a quartet of the most striking-looking women imaginable strutted and gyrated in front of us. Finns are a handsome race and these tall, blonde models were the crème de la crème. They were wearing fur and leather ensembles unlike any I had ever seen because the fur had been dyed in four unusual colours: wine, forest green, mauve, and grey-blue. Suède leather skirts and slacks had been dyed to match them. The colours bore no resemblance to the natural colours of wild animals. Imagine a woodland fox in a subdued shade of burgundy, or a muskrat the colour of a spruce tree. What a fantasy to brighten a long winter.

Even while I admired the clothing, however, I was acutely uncomfortable. I am a conservationist and I have mixed feelings about wearing any fur while new, lightweight coat materials can keep one warmer, and wild animals have been drastically reduced in number. I hoped that the furs we saw were not from trapped animals or animals on the endangered wildlife list, but as a guest of the state I didn't think that would be the appropriate moment to ask.

I felt distinctly more comfortable at the next event, a tour of the Finnish Design Centre. The best of everything produced in this inspired country is displayed at a central showroom. Here were dishes, textiles, silverware, clothing, and furniture. There were photographs of extraordinary buildings. Good design is a matter of national pride in Finland, the way only hockey seems to be in Canada. It would be as unthinkable to a Finn to erect an ugly building as it would be for us to cheer a Team Canada player who skated on his ankles.

In fact, there were so many beautiful objects in Helsinki that after a while I began a private game. As we were being chauffeured hither and yon, I tried to spot something ugly. But I didn't see one obtrusive, disproportionate thing. There were no scuffed soft-drink signs, no grimy auto-repair shops, no tangles of transformers and wires, no store windows plastered with signs shrieking about the bargains within, no battered aluminum doors. How have they managed this? Is there something in the Finnish soul that doesn't exist in the Canadian one? Do they legislate these things out of existence in Finland, or is it simply that no Finn would dream of putting a used-car lot in a place where everyone could see it?

"Most of us believe that the golden age of Finnish design is over now," remarked Mr. Ossi Sunell, the Finnish ambassador to Canada, while we inspected a display of photographs of Finnish housing projects. He had lived with all this architectural excitement his entire adult life and he wasn't as bowled over by it as I was.

"Our economy is stagnating at the moment," he said, a little sadly, "and, as well, our birth rate is very low. There is not the necessity to build many new buildings now."

"That may be true. But all this won't disappear," I replied with a sweeping gesture toward the roomful of Aalto furniture, Ittala wine-glasses, Arabia dishes, and Marimekko fabrics. "It will pass into history and become like . . . like England's Regency period . . . or the American Colonial. A classic."

"A satisfying thought," he smiled wistfully.

While we had been admiring this display of Finnish genius, His Excellency's party had looked at a totally different aspect of life in the capital city — a demonstration by the Helsinki fire department. They were taken to the top of a building from which they could observe firemen fighting a conflagration of burning debris on the eighth floor of an adjacent building that was under construction. While the fire-fighters were going through their paces with ladders and hoses, the fire department band was playing rousing marches up on the ninth floor of the same burning building! What a gesture of confidence, and what an irresistible spectacle: a band *and* a fire. When Farley asked if the band generally entertained at fires, the fire chief just smiled and replied, "Why not?"

It is a smart idea to have a brass band recruited from the ranks of city firemen, whether they play at fires or at children's picnics. A lot of the unoccupied time that firemen have while they wait for great and small catastrophes can happily be spent practising their music.

It was Canada's turn to entertain Finland that evening, and we held our banquet in the famous Finlandia Hall, a conference centre designed by the legendary architect, Alvar Aalto. This sublime edifice was built of white marble, glass, copper, and bronze. In the serene banquet hall, on a birch chair also designed by Aalto so that the furniture would be the perfect accompaniment to his masterpiece, I was seated between Chief Justice Olsson of the Supreme Court, and the Minister of Trade, Mr. Ulf Sundquist. This time I had made sure I knew exactly who they were beforehand.

Mr. Olsson, a white-haired man with black-rimmed glasses, was probably in his late fifties. He instructed me on the complex relationship which exists between the Swedish-speaking Finns and the Finnish-speaking Finns.

"My mother's first language was Finnish and my father's first language was Swedish, but both of them spoke both languages," Mr. Justice Olsson explained. "However, I had one grandmother who spoke only Swedish. Myself, I was educated in Finnish. But of course I always knew Swedish too."

Although there are two official languages, only eight per cent of the people of Finland speak Swedish as their mother tongue and most of these learn Finnish as well. They have to if they want to get a job in business or government. The chief justice told me that even though they are a small minority, the Swedo-Finns do not want to relinquish their language, nor the right to have their children educated in it. This isn't stubborn chauvinism as much as it is economic advantage. Swedish and its "cousin" languages, Norwegian and Danish, are spoken throughout the Nordic countries. Besides, anyone who knows Swedish will find it much easier to learn related languages like German or English.

The mild antagonism that still exists between the two linguistic groups is a legacy from the centuries when Sweden occupied Finland and dominated its trade, professions, and civil service. Naturally this special status was resented by those Finns who spoke only Finnish and saw the Swedes as interlopers. Although this state of affairs has not existed for over a century, the old resentment has not entirely evaporated.

"The bad feelings are disappearing now," said Mr. Olsson, who spoke English as easily as he did Finnish and Swedish, "but I can tell you that thirty years ago a Swedo-Finn like me would not have been appointed chief justice."

It all sounded too familiar. If I substituted Swedish for English, and Finnish for French, he could have been telling me about Quebec. The percentage of English-speaking Quebeckers is just about the same as the Swedish-speaking Finns. For a long time it was the English of Quebec who dominated the business life of the province, a fact not yet forgiven or forgotten by those whose mother tongue is French. And it would be surprising indeed to find an Anglo-Quebecker being appointed attorney general of Quebec in the 1980s, but who can say what will happen thirty years down the road?

After dinner everyone moved to the concert hall to listen to the Galliard Ensemble. This was a good move. In a stuffy room, replete with food and wine, the temptation to doze off during a concert is well-nigh irresistible, especially for those of us who had to listen to the same program over again. There was just one new selection at every performance. To honour each host country, the ensemble played one piece by a national composer. I fully expected that, since they had the rare opportunity of playing in the celebrated Finlandia Concert Hall, we would have heard a selection by Jean Sibelius, but we didn't. Perhaps our musicians believed that our Finnish guests might be tired of listening to their most renowned composer so they played a short piece by a Finnish composer I had never heard of.

This was the first time I had ever travelled anywhere accompanied by a chamber orchestra so it was something of a surprise to discover that flautist Robert Bick's opening remarks were exactly the same at every performance. I had innocently believed those ''off-the-cuff'' discourses which performers sometimes give about the composers and the compositions were precisely that — informal and unrehearsed. They're not. They're as carefully planned as one of the governor general's speeches.

Early-to-bed and early-to-rise was part of President Kekkonen's regimen, along with his faith in brown bread and long walks. He departed the moment the concert ended and, seizing the opportunity, so did Ed and Lily, with Farley and me right behind them. For us it was a luxury to be able to end the day by eleven o'clock.

The following morning we began our "private" visit to Finland. Ed Schreyer does not meander through a strange country; he devours it. He is endlessly curious and always investigating the ways and means other nations use to overcome their difficulties and increase their productivity. If you are a member of his entourage, trying to keep up with him is quite a challenge. Our first Saturday morning of "free" time was to be spent on board Finland's newest ice-breaker, *Urho*. Ice and ice-breakers are among Ed's boundless interests, a passion which Farley shares. To some extent, so do I. Finns, like Canadians, have had to figure out ways to combat that formidable obstacle to navigation, and in the process have become the builders of the world's best ice-breakers. In fact, the enterprising Finns sell ice-breakers to their next-door neighbour, the Soviet Union.

Urho (the name translates as "hero") seemed enormous. We had to ride an elevator to reach the bridge, seven or eight decks above the water line. From the spacious platform we had a panoramic view of the harbour and the city which, on a clear morning in spring, was especially lovely. A trestle table had been set up laden with drinks, coffee, and biscuits. We had all the ingredients for a celebration and I almost expected a shower of paper streamers as the powerful ship pulled slowly away from the pier on its way to an oil refinery at a place called Sköldvik.

Peter Bregg, a wiry, vigorous photographer whose assignment was to cover the governor general's tour for Canadian Press, was the only one of us who was permitted to carry a camera to every event. It would have been *infra dig* for the Accompanying Party to look like tourists. Peter worked long hours every night processing his films and sending them back to Canada through local wire services, and he generously gave us extra copies when he could. Still, I was frustrated that, in the midst of so much that was remarkable and beautiful, I could only take a hurried photo or two from some palace window. So on that morning of blue skies and one tall ship, I wasn't the only one who had brought along a camera.

Lily retreated to a sheltered corner of the foredeck where she could be alone for a while and soak up the sun. Ed conversed with the captain about his ship's capabilities. Farley studied the charts of the Finnish coast. I also find marine charts fascinating, with all the depths marked in fathoms, and the lighthouses and buoys neatly in position. I can get carried away imagining wonderful voyages just by looking at them. However, I wasn't going to waste this precious sunny morning doing anything that kept me indoors. I helped myself to a cup of coffee and walked out to the wing of the bridge. Gathering speed, *Urho* was steaming amongst a chain of islands, dramatic barren rocks that were home to thousands of seagulls.

"Hold it, Jay," I called out to Jason, as I snapped a picture of him leaning against the ship's rail, alongside Mike Thivièrge. Jason was probably wishing there were some kids his own age on board so they could go exploring together.

"This fresh air is something else," remarked Mike. "Puts me in mind of the Bay of Chaleur after the ice has gone out. That's what I miss, living in Ottawa."

We were idly watching a small launch with the

large white letters P.N. on its cabin. It was keeping pace with us a constant quarter-mile to starboard.

"Is that little boat going to follow us all the way?" I wondered out loud.

"Security," said Mike.

"Cops?" asked Jason.

"Yup."

"Nah. I don't believe it. That's the Polish Navy!" Jason guffawed.

After a while I went back to the bridge so that I could sit down for a minute and change the film in my camera. I climbed into the elevated chair usually reserved for the watch-keeping officer and had just got a new roll in place when suddenly there was a thunderous BANG, then a mighty jolt and a grinding, crunching roar. The whole ship shuddered as if a torpedo had struck her, and I was nearly flung out of the chair. Everyone grabbed some fixed object while the ship was briefly wracked by terrible tremors. Then she stopped dead.

Everything that was loose on the bridge had been thrown to the floor. Bells began ringing from every direction and we heard frenzied commands being shouted in Finnish.

"Where are Their Exs?" cried Colin Sangster anxiously as he ran to the bridge.

"Below! With the captain! In his cabin," called Mike Thivièrge who was already heading for the stairs. The two of them darted down the companionway. Whatever it was that had happened to us, the governor general's whereabouts and state of being were the primary considerations of the moment.

Farley suddenly reappeared.

"We've struck a rock!" he shouted, dashing excitedly from one side of the ship to the other.

He may have been relishing the excitement but,

being the practical soul that I am, I immediately located the nearest lifeboat and considered what chance anyone had of launching it from the great height of the upper deck. I checked out the nearest little island, calculating that I could swim the hundred yards or so to reach its slippery shore, but I wasn't so sure I could survive the frigid water of the Baltic or the impact of plunging from such a height. And what about everyone else? When we had joined this jovial voyage, no one had enquired which of us could swim. And we had certainly not bothered with a lifeboat drill on such a gala occasion.

Farley returned. "Just keep calm," he said reassuringly. "These fellows know what they're doing. They're working on damage control right now."

The most obvious damage was to the buffet that had been so nicely arranged for us. A pool of coffee, along with the contents of broken cups, bottles, and glasses, was spreading all over the immaculate floor.

Ed and Lily, who had just settled down for a chat with the captain when disaster struck, reappeared looking quite unruffled. The captain was nowhere to be seen since he and his fellow officers were frantically busy trying to determine exactly what had happened. They had to decide very quickly what was to be done. Abandon ship? Try to return to Helsinki? Or proceed to our destination?

It took only minutes to discover that the forward propeller shaft on the port side had been bent and was inoperative and that there was a gash of unknown size in the hull. Water was pouring into the ship's double bottom but all the watertight doors had been closed.

By then every member of the Canadian party had gathered on the bridge, watching with considerable apprehension as the captain gave orders to see if he could gently back the injured *Urho* away from the rock or reef which she had hit.

Slowly she worked up to full astern with all the power of her remaining three propellers. The huge vessel rumbled and shuddered ominously for a few minutes and then we realized we were free of the reef. After a few more minutes of anxious consultations, the ship's officers concluded that the pumps could keep the inflowing ocean under control. The captain decided to make for the dock at the oil refinery which would take less time than trying to return to Helsinki harbour. Once we had passed the last of the rocky islands, it was full speed ahead as we made a run for a haven that was still nine miles distant.

Though the light-hearted mood of the morning had vanished, it hadn't been replaced by terror. Everyone was calm; the police escort was close at hand and even if this flagship of the Finnish ice-breakers were to sink, we were confident we would all be picked up.

"I feel so badly for the captain," Ed told us. "He's served in the Finnish coast guard as an ice-master for thirty years and there isn't a thing he doesn't know about the operation of one of these vessels in these waters. This is a tragedy for him."

We all agreed. Although there was some anxiety among us as the damaged vessel gathered speed, we felt that the captain and his officers were handling the crisis with superb, calm efficiency.

The accident, we later learned, had nothing to do with the capability of the captain or his crew. We had been passing through a channel that the chart clearly showed was deep enough for *Urho*. But shifting ice during the winter had evidently tipped a huge boulder into the channel. It was an accident no one could have foreseen.

"Funny thing," said Don McKinnon who was leaning on the rail watching the far shore grow nearer with some relief. "I spent an entire career in the navy — years and years of my life on board ships — and this is the first time I've ever been in one that struck anything." Don, a white-haired bundle of energy in his early sixties, was the comptroller of Government House—the man who kept track of all our expenses, and hoped to balance the budget.

By the time we limped to the dock at the port of the Nesty Oy oil refinery where a battery of huge emergency pumps was waiting, the ship was about four feet below her Plimsoll line, the painted line on her side which indicates the depth at which she should have been floating. *Urho* was slowly sinking. The gash in her side turned out to be almost a third of her length. If she had not been fitted with a double hull and built for service in the ice, she would have gone down like a stone. That Saturday morning devoted to entertaining a party of Canadians turned out to be a very expensive proposition for Finland. The eventual cost of repairing *Urho* exceeded one million Canadian dollars.

Nevertheless, we were firmly convinced that the Finns build the strongest ships afloat.

"I knew she was a superb ice-breaker," Ed commented later. "But they really didn't have to show us she could be a rock-breaker too."

Visiting an oil refinery is not high on my list of priorities, but the expedition to Nesty Oy turned out to be more interesting than I imagined it would be. It was on our itinerary because of Ed's abiding interest in all sources of energy. Nesty Oy is the biggest industrial complex in Finland. Once we left our sinking ship, I looked around to see where the refinery was. Since I saw no evidence of it, I assumed that we had a fair drive ahead of us to reach it. Not so. I should have guessed that the inventive Finns had found a way to build an oil refinery so it wasn't a blot on the landscape. It turned out to be mostly underground, in chambers hollowed out of bedrock in much the same manner as the Church of the Temple Square is. Not only was the whole thing infinitely tidier than the kind we build back home, but putting it underground offered an additional military advantage in case of war. An underground storage facility is also less vulnerable to accidental fire or a spill than are refineries and storage tanks built as tall as cathedrals above the ground.

Finland has no oil of her own, so massive quantities of crude oil are shipped into this port to be refined. It was Farley who observed that the shore waters here were full of sea birds, including flocks of eider ducks. In Canada, most water birds have been eliminated in one way or another by pollution from similar regions of industrial activity. How can a nation of only four and one-half million people, who do not rank all that high on any of the scales measuring the wealth of nations, afford the kind of environmental protection which, in Canada, tends to be the last grudging consideration of government or industry? It is something our Minister of the Environment ought to find out.

The Nesty Corporation maintained a guest house on the refinery grounds. Our luncheon was served in a large log building on the shore of a lake surrounded by birch trees. It looked very much like one of those old-fashioned hotels that you can still find on the holiday lakes of Muskoka. Mr. Jaako Ihamuotila, the incredibly boyish-looking chairman of the Nesty Corporation, remarked that he was especially happy and very relieved to be able to welcome us that day. The mishap on board *Urho* gave us lots to talk about. Afterwards we sat outside on lichen-covered rocks that sloped down towards a Tom Thomson shore and could have sworn we were in northern Ontario.

Late that afternoon we left from Helsinki airport to fly north to Lapland. This was the occasion of our ceremonial farewell to the president. State visit farewells are arranged when they are convenient for both parties, and not necessarily when the visitors actually leave the country. As governor general, Ed spent a surprising amount of time travelling all over Canada just to formally say hello or goodbye to various members of the British royal family and other heads of state. Nineteenth-century protocol, twentieth-century jet travel, and the immense size of Canada can make official greetings a time-consuming duty.

Like Sweden and Norway, Finland shares with Canada an agrarian south which extends to an arctic north. Yet the south of Finland is so far north that only an hour and a half in a Finnair DC-9 took us across the Arctic Circle. As we approached our destination of Rovaniemi, we looked down upon a landscape of spruce forest, tiny lakes, muskeg and a river in flood. The green pastures were far behind us.

As we left the plane, we were surprised to find the weather very much warmer than at Helsinki. The airport workers were all in their shirt sleeves. Rovaniemi was one of the places for which Lily and I had armoured ourselves with warm coats and even snow boots. As it turned out, we were just one day too late to need them. Arctic summers, like arctic winters, arrive suddenly. Summer had come to Rovaniemi overnight.

The city is the capital of the Finnish province of

Lappi—which is what the Finns call the region that the rest of the world knows as Lapland. Governor Asko Oinas was on hand to greet us, along with the usual assembly of other local dignitaries.

"Summer has arrived for your visit."

"Two days ago we were in our winter clothes."

'How fortunate you arrived today."

We shook all the appropriate hands then walked through a modest little airport terminal to a waiting bus. This was indeed an exciting day to have arrived. The *Kemijoki*, or Kemi River, which flows through the city, had been frozen only a few days earlier and now was in full flood with torrents of water just inches from overflowing its banks. Ice cakes the size of houses were jammed against an iron bridge. Everywhere the land was saturated. As we came closer to the city we noticed that the local people were revelling in the sudden burst of warmth that had conveniently arrived on a Saturday. They were walking and bicycling along the road dressed in shorts and T-shirts, and many women were sunbathing in bikinis in their backyards.

Almost every building in Rovaniemi dates from 1945 or later. Forty years ago, the whole town was burned to the ground by the retreating German army. Rovaniemi is only a hundred miles from the Soviet Union's border, and the German intention had been to slow the Russian pursuit with a scorched-earth policy. The nine thousand people of Rovaniemi were forced to disperse as refugees — mainly to Sweden — in what must have been the grimmest winter in their history. Most of them eventually returned and now they have rebuilt the place, transforming a frontier town into a tidy little city of about thirty thousand people.

The Schreyers were immediately driven away to

a private lodge out in the forest to enjoy a much-needed evening to themselves. The rest of us were taken to The Polar Hotel, a long, two-storey building that looked not unlike the edifices we know in Canada by the incongruous name of motor-hotels.

The small rooms were beautifully furnished with pale, Finnish-style wooden chairs, tables, and beds. In anybody's arctic, builders do not indulge in the luxury of wasted space. During the long winter, every cubic foot of heated space costs dearly.

Our eleven pieces of luggage posed a serious storage problem. *Bring it all with you. You won't be carrying your own luggage.* I could hear Thelma's advice ringing in my ears. True—we didn't have to carry it, but we had to live with it. After much manoeuvring I managed to stack all the garment bags in the closet and everything else in the corners. In the corridor I could hear the merriment of the others in our party who were on their way to enjoy the world-famous Finnish institution of the sauna.

A knock on the door announced Major Sangster.

"Hi. Got a message from Their Ex's. They're inviting you to come out to Karhunpesa. Join them for dinner."

"Where?"

"Karhunpesa. The name of the log cabin where they're staying. 'Bear's den' is how it translates. About twenty miles from here."

"Sounds great."

"It is. But . . . we've run into a bit of a snag," Colin explained. "The governor has organized a little dinner for us tonight. We didn't know this was in the cards. Thought it would be a free evening. So, what we're hoping is that you two could, ah, preside. Be the Canadian hosts, as it were."

132

We looked at one another. What to do? The opportunity to spend the evening at a cabin in the woods was our kind of night out, for sure, but Colin ever so nicely twisted our arms. So we agreed, a little wearily, to act as a substitute for our vice-regal couple.

Because foreign celebrities are rare in remote places, everyone of any local importance expects to be invited to meet them. Few Canadians, and certainly no governor general, had ever visited Rovaniemi officially, so the "little dinner" turned out to be a full-scale banquet for about ninety people.

I sat beside a member of the district council. The council comprised forty-three members and just about all of them, and their spouses, were present. My dining companion, whose name I couldn't attempt to pronounce, was a high-school teacher in his thirties, with sandy hair, a round face and an upturned nose. He was a Sami, one of the indigenous arctic people of Europe whom the rest of the world refers to as Lapps. I was lucky to be able to meet him because he told me he was one of only five per cent of the adults of Lappi who *were* Lapps. An astonishing 95 per cent of the local population had moved to the region from other places in Finland since the end of the Second World War.

We drifted into a conversation about the concerns of being an educator in a northern town. The schools of Lappi tended to be larger than elsewhere in Finland, he told me. The population was relatively young and people in the north usually had bigger families than those in the south. Some Sami families, usually reindeer herders who lived a long way from the towns, had as many as ten or fifteen children who attended school intermittently and, in the opinion of the teacher, unenthusiastically. But in the modern world there are many ways to live the life of a Lapp. One may be a reindeer herder, or one may be a school teacher. However, you can be sure it is the herder in his embroidered costume who will have his picture taken when a foreign journalist comes around looking for a story.

I learned more from this informative man. I mentioned that I had once visited Siberia and that, to me, the terrain of northern Finland looked very similar. He nodded and agreed. Rovaniemi and the city of Murmansk, about two hundred miles away in the Soviet Union, are, in fact, "sister" cities.

"It is because our concerns are alike. At times members from our council visit Murmansk and talk to their council. Sometimes they come here to talk to us. That way we can make solutions together," he explained.

I had somehow imagined that the 700-mile-long border between Finland and the Soviet Union would have been impenetrable, something like the Berlin Wall, a no-man's land of barbed wire and military hardware. Not so. The Finns have managed to remain friends both with the capitalists in the West and the communists in the East. It had never crossed my mind that Finnish and Russian town councillors could exchange friendly visits to discuss such mundane mutual problems as plumbing in the permafrost or garbage disposal on the taiga.

During dessert it hit me that we were truly in the north. The windows in The Polar Hotel dining-room overlooked the surrounding evergreen forest and, as the evening wore on, it did not get dark. Even in May, a month ahead of the summer solstice, it was still twilight as midnight approached.

By midnight the party showed no sign of gearing down. We didn't adjourn for coffee until a quarter to twelve. As the long days of spring come to the polar regions, people do stay up later and later. And, since this was the first vernal weekend, the worthy councillors of Rovaniemi were in a buoyant mood. So were most of the Canadians. This was partly due to the less ceremonious temper of the far north and partly because of the absence of the governor general. Ed was never a forbidding presence but whenever he was present it meant that the household was on duty. Naturally, they didn't feel the same way about us. However, when the witching hour arrived we borrowed the vice-regal prerogative. We departed first. After a gracious good-night to the governor and his wife, we retreated to our room, leaving the rest of the revellers to party the night away if they felt like it. Most of them did.

A car and a driver had been provided to take Farley and me out to Karhunpesa early the next morning so that we could share in the final few hours of Ed and Lily's overnight vacation. We travelled on a gravel road through countryside that was indistinguishable from the Canadian Shield. Next to Iceland and Norway, Finland is the least crowded nation in Europe, and much of rural Lappi is devoid of human habitation. As we drove through it we saw the occasional field that had once been cleared but was now growing over with stunted trees. Some sturdy souls long ago had attempted farming in this poor soil and harsh climate, but they had quit.

Each of us had been given a book of facts and figures about this faraway corner of Finland. I read that an astonishing ten thousand people held jobs in that grey area known as "administration," while only half that number worked in the principal industry, which was lumbering. Only a few hundred still made a living herding reindeer. In the same little book, the Finns admitted a regional unemployment rate of 17 per cent. It was the same figure for the province of Newfoundland that year.

The road crossed a railway line and I was amazed to see such a thing this far north, but we discovered that it was possible to travel by rail from Helsinki as far as Kemijarvi, another fifty miles further east. I adore trains. I made a mental note that some day I would ride that train to Kemijarvi. That has always been my idea of the ultimate trip: to travel by rail to some uttermost part of the earth where I've never been. Of course there was one journey that was even more intriguing and it was the one we were on, way-farers in a Never-Never Land of palaces, princesses, and plainclothes police.

We arrived at a narrow lane leading down to a log house beside a lake. The house could have passed as a large summer cottage in Canada. We might have been just folks dropping in on the neighbours for coffee, except for the contingent of police. Their presence seemed wildly superfluous. Who, in that boundless wilderness, would pose any threat to the governor general of Canada? But security arrangements for heads of state are ironclad. There is a procedure and it must be followed. If the security service let down its guard, that might be the very moment some loony would come out of the woods.

There were half-a-dozen police on duty, and they had an enviable job of it that morning, loitering in a forest clearing in the ethereal northern spring, a silvan interlude when the sun is warming, the birds are returning, but the insects haven't yet arrived. There was still ice on the lake, but it was warm enough to sit outside without a coat.

There was one policewoman in the Finnish security detachment and she looked less like a cop than

I do. She was as slender as a dancer and her hair was dyed a vibrant magenta red. She wore gobs of eye make-up and was usually dressed in leather pants and spike-heeled boots. Some of the men in our party spent a fair bit of time speculating about where she kept her gun.

The log cottage was a larger, grander version of a cabin which my parents once owned near Fenelon Falls, Ontario. It had been built by Finnish immigrants. In the main room Ed and Lily were eating breakfast at a long wooden table. A waiter dressed in Sami national dress was serving hot rolls and cold meat. We walked in just as Jason charged through in his dressing-gown on his way to the sauna.

"At last!" exclaimed Lily, as if there had been some doubt we would ever get here. "Come and join us."

"You know, you missed a nice evening," Ed began.

"Ahem," said Farley. "We might have come sooner . . . but *somebody* had to take over. Duty, and all that . . . "

"I'll bet you were superb," Ed smiled, looking up from a large-scale map of Lappi spread out in front of him like the morning paper. He looked rested and relaxed. One good night's rest could instantly restore him. When he was tired, it showed. Lily, amazingly, never looked tired even when she was.

"I discovered something interesting here," Ed told us. "New idea—or, I guess it's an old one—for outdoor lighting. They take a length of log about two or three feet long, hollow it out, then bore holes through it like portholes in a ship. They fill the hollow with kerosene, light it and it burns for hours. Gives a surprising amount of light."

"It was actually warm enough to have dinner outdoors," Lily added. "So romantic."

Karhunpesa was the perfect spot for people, heads of state or not, to recharge their batteries. Oh, those thoughtful Finns! I could gladly have stayed for a week; but we only had two hours. Lily and I did take time to walk down to the shore of the tiny lake where we sat on a small wooden dock, pondering nothing more urgent than how long it was going to take for the ice on the lake to melt. It was already turning to slush. Maybe just one more warm day like this and it would be gone. It felt very Canadian, somehow, to be making that kind of calculation.

Because Thelma and Jean had remained at the hotel in town, we volunteered to help the family gather up their belongings. Their mountain of luggage had been reduced to a relative molehill for this short foray into the forest, but there was still a lot of it. Even in this humble place, every eventuality had to be foreseen. The head of state must not be left shivering for want of a warm coat, nor sweltering for lack of a lightweight one, nor soaking wet because somebody forgot his raincoat. It was all there, every garment a man, woman, and teenager might need for every possibility of northern Finland in the unpredictable season of arctic spring.

That day's program consisted of a meandering tour of Lapland — by helicopter. Since I am terrified of flying in helicopters and my services were not required that afternoon, the prospect of staying behind and just being alone for a little while was too appealing to resist.

At the airport, I stood and watched with apprehension as twenty-nine members of our entourage were swallowed up inside two gargantuan, vibrating, Finnish military machines built in the Soviet Union. They noisily lifted their dinosaur weight from

138

the ground and rapidly disappeared over the horizon.

Back at The Polar Hotel I spent my solitary afternoon busily scribbling notes about the tour. Then I washed my hair and, for about an hour, fell asleep. By the time I returned to the airport at four o'clock, I felt renewed. Soon I heard the distant thunder of the helicopters and in a few minutes they landed noisily.

"Hi! Where've you been? You should have come with us," exclaimed Peter Bregg. "We had lunch at some place in the back of beyond. Then we went to visit a famous painter who lives way off in the middle of nowhere."

"And he paints really weird pictures," Jason chortled.

"I'll tell you about them . . . later," Farley added quickly.

"You missed quite a show," added Inspector Mike Thivièrge, smirking a bit.

The painter referred to was Professor Reidar Särestöniemi. To be called a "professor" in Finland carries more significance than it does in Canada. It is an honour akin to receiving the Order of Canada, or being knighted by the queen if you're British. Särestöniemi, an energetic man in his fifties, lived and worked in a complex of log buildings in such a remote corner of Lapland that it could only be reached by a small boat on a nearby river, or else by helicopter. Short and sturdy, with a reddish beard, he looked not unlike Farley, a similarity that everyone noticed. A boisterous man, he had dressed in the bright trousers and embroidered shirt of the traditional Lapp costume to receive the Canadians.

"What sort of painting does he do?" I asked Farley.

"Well — big, bright things, kind of based on the landscape . . ."

"Like the Group of Seven?" I suggested. Words are always inadequate to describe the visual arts.

"Not that realistic. More like, oh, like Riopelle. At least the ones that were hung in the main gallery mostly were. Upstairs . . . well, up on the mezzanine some of us came across one of his other phases . . ."

"His blue period?" I joked.

"You could call it that," Farley grinned. "If they had been movies, you could definitely have described them as blue."

"Did Ed and Lily see them?"

"No, they were stuck downstairs, talking. But Jason did. He is certainly getting an education on his travels."

"Strange guy, Särestöniemi," Farley went on. "He lives there alone. No sign of a wife or anyone. Not even a companion. Just a local Lapp family who sort of look after the place."

"I wonder how he gets supplies — things like paint and canvases? And food."

"Haven't a clue. But one item he evidently doesn't get easily is booze. As we were leaving we asked him if there was anything he needed. Guess what he wanted? Two bottles of Canadian whisky."

"So did he get them?"

"Scotch. We didn't have any rye. Two forty-ouncers of scotch out of Bernie's hospitality box. Should brighten up his weekend."

"He'll have nice memories about visiting Canadians," I said, "as long as he can remember who his benefactors were."

One of the duties of a governor general's aide-de-camp is to take charge of a dozen bottles of liquor and wine contained in a special travelling case complete with lock. This case goes with the governor general but isn't intended for his or her personal consumption. At least, not all of it. It is to be used in the event that His or Her Excellency has to dispense unscheduled hospitality at times or in places where liquor is not available. The hinterland of Finland is such a place. In fact, all over Finland it is usually difficult and almost always inconvenient to buy liquor. The hours of sale are tightly controlled, the prices high, and the outlets few. The system is much like the alcohol-sales arrangements we had in most parts of Canada thirty years ago. The excesses of alcohol seem to be endemic to the world's northernmost regions for reasons not clearly understood, and most of their governments have, at one time or another, had to impose some form of limitation on the amount and the way it is distributed.

Less than ten minutes after the helicopters had brought the Canadians back to Rovaniemi, we were again aboard our Finnair DC-9 heading south to visit yet another Finnish city. The change of aircraft had been effected in a trice with none of the usual horrors of airports. There were no jostling crowds, no terse employees, no security checks, and no boarding passes. To travel in such privileged circumstances is to change the whole nature of the flying experience.

I am always surprised—naively perhaps—to discover towns and cities I never knew existed: complicated aggregations of unknown people studying, working, loving, dying, and leaving behind a legacy of street names, architectural oddities and other unnatural phenomena. Kouvola in eastern Finland is such a place. Even a geography buff like me had never spotted it on the map. Halfway between Helsinki and the border with the Soviet Union, Kouvola is about the size of Cornerbrook, Newfoundland, and, like Cornerbrook, owes its existence to the pulp and paper industry.

Unprepossessing as it at first appeared, Kouvola turned out to be extremely interesting. There, for a start, we encountered some of the happiest people we were to meet in Finland. Maybe this is where the most contented people live all over the world, in prosaic little cities and towns where the pressure isn't as gruelling as it is in the capitals, and the social dislocation isn't as unsettling as it tends to be on the periphery.

Half a dozen executives of the Kymi Paper Corporation and their wives greeted us at the airport with broad smiles, as if they were truly pleased to see us. On the journey into the city, Lily and I shared a car with the wife of the president of Kymi. By then I was becoming a connoisseur of those who had the job of squiring us around. From the outset, the elegant Mrs. Ritva Castrén got full marks. She was a pretty woman with straight, dark hair; worldly and witty; but best of all, she was a lady who knew when to keep quiet. There is a tendency to deluge ''high guests'' — as the Finns charmingly referred to us in their protocol dispatches — with too much information. Travellers can reach the saturation point rather quickly for absorbing statistics, and Mrs. Castrén understood this. She had just returned from accompanying her husband on a business trip to Australia, where she had been so inundated herself. She let us absorb our new surroundings at our own pace.

The Kymi Corporation guest house was a rambling old mansion in the middle of the city with accommodation for ten of us—the fortunate ones, as it turned out. The rest of the household and the External Affairs staff were booked into a nearby motel where they nearly expired from the same heat wave that had enveloped Lapland and that was now smothering all of eastern Finland. I noted that my wardrobe instructions for both Rovaniemi and Kouvola were "warm outdoor clothing."

"I must tell you that we had a governor general here once before," said Mr. Fredrik Castrén in his brief welcoming speech at dinner. "Unfortunately—for him—he was assassinated!"

The laughter was a bit strained, but he went on to explain that it had been the Russian governor general of what was, in 1906, the Duchy of Finland. Amid the growing nationalist sentiment at that time, his imperial presence among the Finns had been understandably unpopular. Only eleven years after his murder in Kouvola, Finland declared herself an independent nation.

No such fate awaited our governor general. Instead, he was showered with kind words, a superb dinner, and a beautiful bracelet was presented to Lily. These corporation men and women were a different breed from the career protocol people. The few speeches they delivered tended to include touches of humour and their gaiety made for one of the better evenings of the tour.

After dinner we adjourned to a drawing-room to drink coffee and *Lakka*, a Finnish liqueur made from cloudberries. In Canada cloudberries, or bakeapples, are only popular in Newfoundland, as a dessert, even though they grow in bogs all across the taiga of northern Canada. Someone should be turning this boundless resource into a beverage like the one we sipped that evening.

On Monday morning the men went to investigate an electric generating-plant that burned peat as fuel, followed by a visit to a logging operation. Our day began with a tour of a jewellery factory. The small enterprise manufactured jewellery solely from spectrolite, a semi-precious dark green stone mined in several parts of Finland. It is also found in Canada, mainly in Labrador, where it is called labradorite and is the provincial gemstone of the province of Newfoundland and Labrador. By pure coincidence I was wearing my earrings set with labradorite. The Finnish jewellery designer examined these with interest. The stones were indistinguishable from spectrolite but the setting lacked the style that the Finns gave theirs. The artisans in this modest factory had designed highly original silver settings that showed the iridescent stones to their best advantage. I am convinced a Finnish designer could craft a beautiful setting for a lump of coal.

We oohed and ahhed over all the brooches and rings in the showcase and then it was time to set off for the Kouvola Public Library. Public libraries tend to look much like one another the world over—which makes it difficult for a visitor to think of anything original to say to the librarian. But a children's choir was waiting to sing for us. We could applaud and congratulate them with real enthusiasm. They had competed internationally for Finland and won several awards. The songs, sung in Finnish, French, and English, provided that perfect touch of tranquillity to the morning's round.

Later, as we stood around watching a group of five-year-olds reading together with the help of earphones in which a recorded voice was pronouncing the words, Lily mentioned to the librarian that my husband was a Canadian author. The librarian nodded thoughtfully. She said something to one of her assistants who went away and fetched a copy of *Älä hukkaa hauku*, which is *Never Cry Wolf* in Finnish. Discovering Farley's book there that day was a revelation. What author ever knows what distant shores a book will reach?

Our morning ended with a tour of a large, bright, clothing factory. Artella Women's Wear manufactured no-frills ski jackets and pants, and washable summer dresses. There is a sizeable garment industry in Finland and their biggest customer is the Soviet Union. For reasons that I wager have nothing to do with politics, Finnish-made clothes are usually more flattering, comfortable, and durable than those produced by their eastern neighbours. Inspired design is second nature to the Finns. The Russians concentrate on other frivolities such as space science and the ballet.

Still, artistic proficiency is not the basis of the Finnish economy: it is trees. Trees are the most cherished resource in the nation and the Finns have a lot to teach Canadians about the use of forests. Later that day, as I listened to our men chatting about what they had seen, I was sorry that I couldn't have been part of their tour as well as ours.

Because the size of the land mass of Finland is relatively small the Finns don't share the Canadian illusion that the forests are limitless. It takes eighty years for a tree to mature in the south of Finland and one hundred and ten years in the north, so they regard trees as a finite resource that must be carefully husbanded. Finns really *think* about the kind of country their grandchildren will inherit. Whenever a mature tree is felled it is immediately replaced, not with just one seedling, but with three to ensure that the forests will never shrink. As a result, Finland has more trees now than it did at the turn of the last century. The clear-cut and cut-and-burn techniques that are standard procedure in Canada absolutely horrify Finnish foresters.

Ed and his entourage had been escorted through a pulp mill powered by wood chips and peat. Peat, with all its potential, has long been one of Ed's abiding obsessions. It is vegetable matter that has decomposed and carbonized and it ought to be of interest to many Canadian entrepreneurs because we have so much of it in our own country. We rarely use it for anything but garden fertilizer. It has long been an important source of fuel in parts of Europe. For centuries it has been used as a household fuel by those Scots and Irish who live on small farms, but theirs is a small-scale enterprise compared to the magnitude of the Finnish operation. The Finns harvest thousands of tons of peat for fuel every year, using a bewildering variety of sophisticated machinery.

Once the peat has been removed from a Finnish bog, the land is usually converted into farmland. If the soil isn't suitable for growing food, then trees are planted and the forest eventually takes over.

I reserve my last word on the genius of Finland for the matter of smells. I try to stay away from pulp-and-paper mills in Canada because of the frightful stench associated with them. You usually know twenty miles away when you are approaching a Canadian pulp mill, but in Kouvola I could not detect a trace of that all-too-familiar aroma of rotten eggs. Kouvola smelled more of the Tuomi trees—a kind of flowering crabapple — than it did of industry. The Finns had done it again; they had figured out a way to run a pulp mill that wouldn't make you gag.

As we flew back to Helsinki that evening, I felt optimistic about our future on this planet. Somebody was inventing and implementing ways to do things without completely destroying the environment, and they were prospering as well.

In Helsinki we found ourselves with a free evening for the first time in nine days. We had a room in the beautiful Hotel Kalastajatorppa, a magnificent complex that seemed to be built entirely of pale marble in a multitude of levels fitted into the side of a hill. Some travellers might have been tempted to explore a few more shops and parks, or try a new restaurant, but not us. It was amazing how much psychic strength was needed to face all those strangers day after day and still make sensible, congenial conversation. An evening of solitude was what we yearned for.

That night Farley and I ordered our supper from room service, a spare but delicious meal of cold salmon and mushrooms, and a bottle of Moselle. We indolently settled down in front of the television. We could only raise one channel and so we ate our meal while we watched, of all the unlikely things, a lesson in French.

Later, as Farley pushed the dinner trolley out into the hall, Captain Dave John came striding along. Tomorrow would bring another major baggage shuffle which meant he would be working late into the night and rising very early in the morning. Nobody worked harder than those ADCs. I'll never know how they found the stamina to do it and still behave so graciously.

"Bags ready by 7:30," Dave reminded us. "And, hey—you're not gonna believe this!"

"What?" Farley asked.

147

"That painter—what's his name—the guy living up in the wilds of Lapland."

"Särestöniemi?"

"The very one. We just got word: he's dead!"

"Dead? He can't be. What happened? The guy was so full of energy. Full of . . . oh-oh . . . Those two forty-ouncers!"

"Could be . . ."

"All we know for sure is that the family who look after the place just found him."

"We may be getting out of Finland in the nick of time," Farley said sagely. "Just think, we were guests aboard *Urho* when she ran aground. Now it looks as if we've done in another of their heroes. What's next?"

"Next is Norway, chums. And a whole new family of royals," said the captain as he took off down the hall. "See you in the cold grey dawn!"

Norway

One can usually gauge the status of a state visit by the rank of the official greeters who are on hand at the airport. That's the gospel according to Charles Ritchie, an author who has written a lot of witty, perceptive memoirs about his life as a Canadian ambassador. If that is the case, then we couldn't have asked for a better reception in Norway. The king himself was waiting for us. Even the weather smiled on us — at the last minute. It rains a lot in Norway and spindly rivers of cold water streaked across our aircraft windows as we began our descent into Oslo. But by the time our plane taxied through the puddles on the tarmac the clouds had moved east towards Sweden and the sky was bright.

By then we had scene one down to a fine art. The Schreyers stepped out to their accustomed spot at the top of the ramp. Then Captain St. Laurent immediately unfurled himself under his enormous hat. A Norwegian military band played "O Canada" and once again I became choked with emotion. I never feel as much love for Canada as I do when I am away from home. During those solemn moments when our anthem rang out over yet another foreign land, I was usually close to tears. The link between music and loyalty enveloped me and, for as long as it lasted, I forgave my native land most of its sins.

The green fragrance that follows a spring rain dissipated the usual airport smell of jet fuel. On the red carpet stood King Olav V wearing his gilded uniform as commander-in-chief of the Norwegian Navy. He was a robust 78-year-old with a patrician profile which looks very dignified on Norwegian coins. As I shook his hand, his aquamarine eyes bored into mine. He smiled warmly at each of us in turn while a battalion of television cameras zoomed in to capture the historic moment.

There has been no queen of Norway since the days of King Olav's mother. Olav's wife, Princess Martha, died three years before he ascended the throne in 1957. Olav V, the second king of modern Norway, has reigned alone. Crown Prince Harald, the king's tall son, was also there to meet us, together with his very pretty wife, Crown Princess Sonia.

Norway must be one of the last countries in the world where men are required to wear morning-suits at a state arrival ceremony. Not even the strait-laced Swedes had suggested anything more formal than the standard three-piece dark suit. The striped trousers and pale-grey swallow-tailed coats of morning are seldom seen in Canada now, although both Ed Schreyer, and Jules Léger before him, chose to wear morning-dress to open Parliament, in preference to a military uniform. It is still worn by the groom at ostentatious weddings and by undertakers at expensive funerals but despite its flattering lines, I suspect it won't be long before it becomes as quaint as a pair of spats.

150

As European capitals go, Oslo is a modest city, so we didn't expect our arrival there would be as overwhelming as it had been in Stockholm. Though it looks large on the map, Norway, like Finland, is actually a small nation of only four million people, roughly half that of neighbouring Sweden. Yet, when our sedate parade passed through the downtown streets all the lamp-posts were garlanded with hundreds of fluttering Canadian and Norwegian flags. The noon-hour crowds watched with evident interest as we passed by. But perhaps it would be a rare Norwegian who wouldn't pause to catch a glimpse of the king. And there was another aspect of our cavalcade guaranteed to draw a crowd. We rode in King Olav's personal collection of vintage cars including an ancient Packard, a middle-aged Cadillac with chromed tail fins, three or four elderly Mercedes-Benz and one fairly recent Rolls-Royce, all of them in mint condition. One would almost have to be a king to assemble such a parade.

One building in Oslo proclaims to the world that this isn't a run-of-the-mill provincial city — the royal palace. It dominates the commercial centre of the city from its majestic setting in a fifty-acre park, which, surprisingly, is open to the public.

"Hi, Farley!" someone shouted, as the gleaming old Packard which bore us inched through the crowd near the park's entrance.

Astonished, Farley gladly waved back. The greeter must have been a Canadian tourist but there was no time to find out. The cars rolled up to a portico and we had to step smartly into the palace, a few steps behind the king.

Our briefing-book told us we would enter the palace via the vestibule — a word I will always associate with the place you leave your galoshes — to be

151

greeted by Princess Astrid, Mrs. Ferner. Princess Astrid, the king's daughter, is married to a commoner so she is officially known by these two disparate names. She's not exactly one of your storybook princesses. A rather large woman who is the mother of five children, she wore glasses and, on that day, an elastic bandage on an injured ankle. It made her seem mortal and less threatening. And there was nothing fearsome about the palace lady-in-waiting, Mrs. Gøran Seip, who now had the task of escorting Farley and me to our quarters. She led us up a set of unprepossessing back stairs.

"This way is so much shorter," she said as we climbed the three flights. She was a bubbly, friendly woman of about forty with petite features, a trim figure and dark hair. She worked full-time for Crown Princess Sonia who, if the universe unfolds as it should, will be queen when fair-haired Prince Harald ascends the throne.

"Here we are," said Mrs. Seip, ushering us through a broad doorway, across an oriental rug the size of a junior baseball diamond and over to the tall windows on the far side of the room which opened onto a magnificent view of the royal gardens and the city beyond. In this drawing-room, the midday sunshine brightened a treasure trove of stately furniture and enough paintings to fill a small art gallery. Three gargantuan bouquets of spring flowers were placed strategically around the room. There was also a large, brocaded bedroom. This was the biggest and the most impressive suite in which we had been quartered so far. Mrs. Seip strode around purposefully, opening doors and explaining things to us, as if this overwhelming luxury was the most natural thing in the world.

"This is quite an old palace," she began apologetically, "so the bathroom is . . . well . . . "

"The bathroom is outdoors?" Farley suggested mischievously.

"No, no, no," she laughed. "It's just that it is rather old-fashioned."

It was indeed a venerable bathroom, much older than the Packard, and bigger than our living-room back at home. Two sinks, two toilets and the tub were all in separate compartments, and the tub looked big enough to swim in.

"If you need anything at all, there is a footman in the corridor at all times," Mrs. Seip said. "I'll come back and collect you five minutes before luncheon."

Since we had almost an hour to spare, I indulged myself by just staring out the window at the city of Oslo. It was enchanting: a green and leafy city in full spring plumage. Above the lilacs, I could see a lot of copper roofs on dignified Edwardian buildings. Some newer buildings had been added to the commercial downtown but their moderate height and style didn't intrude on the turn-of-the-century streetscape. I stayed at the great casement windows until my curiosity about our new surroundings impelled me to go exploring.

If you've seen one palace, you have definitely not seen them all. The Swedish royals had surrounded themselves with the ambience of the ancient regime of France; the democratic Finns had decorated their public buildings with furnishings they had recently designed themselves. The Norwegian royal family obviously had the English predilection for the eclectic mix.

Our drawing-room contained a massive Empire sofa framed in mahogany and upholstered in rose-coloured silk damask. There were two round Italianate tables of dark polished wood. The carpet doubtless came from somewhere in the Middle East, and the huge candelabra dominating the mantelpiece looked to be of Germanic heritage. It all looked like the home of an English earl. Of course Queen Maud, the mother of King Olav, had been born Princess Maud, the daughter of King Edward VII of Great Britain and his Danish-born wife, Queen Alexandra. The influence of Queen Maud remains much in evidence throughout the palace, and King Olav himself looked so much like his English grandfather that he could have played the role in a film, even without make-up, and have been utterly believable.

The paintings in our suite echoed other similarities between those two maritime powers. Most of them were realistic seascapes of schooners and clipper ships sailing on cold-looking oceans. However, the biggest painting was a life-size portrait of King Olav as a young man. With the sea in the background, he stands on a wharf wearing a yachtsman's blazer, cap and cream flannels, holding a lighted cigarette in his right hand. Styles do change. I doubt if there's a portrait painter anywhere in the world today who would paint a cigarette in the hand of a prince, nor a prince who would permit it.

The only room without paintings was the bathroom. Its decor consisted of a wealth of towel bars and hot water pipes. This changed my focus from the lofty realm of art to more mundane matters. I was concerned that we were both going to run out of clean underwear.

"This," I remarked to Farley as I viewed the two large sinks, "looks like the right moment and the right place to do some laundry."

"We could set up a commercial laundry in here

quite nicely but," he asked, "why should we? We can enlist that footman out in the hall. There must be a royal washing-machine down in the basement. I'll go and ask."

The young footman was instantly obliging. I hastily assembled a bundle of shirts, socks, panties, and bras which he dutifully carried away, although I did feel a certain reluctance at dispatching my grubby lingerie into the care of a uniformed servant.

Despite the flights of fancy that accompany the word "palace," the reality is that a palace in this century combines the functions of a high-class hotel and a modern office building. A royal family only occupies one corner of it. Apart from some grand rooms set aside for entertaining large numbers of people, for bestowing awards, or for housing royal artifacts, the rest of the building is given over to a staff of cooks, clerks, cleaners, and curators. And, inevitably, to someone who does the laundry.

That's one of my sharpest memories of the royal palace of Oslo, the certain knowledge that we were going to make it to the end of our tour with enough clean socks. I felt quite bucked by the time the energetic Mrs. Seip returned to lead us to the family luncheon.

We dined in a magnificent room called simply The King's Private Dining-room. If you're a king, you don't have to pussyfoot around giving elegant rooms names like Imperial Room or The Commodore's Table. You simply name the room after yourself or one of your ancestors.

All the senior members of the Norwegian royal family had assembled to lunch with their Canadian guests. This time, instead of a palace protocol official, I was assigned a seat beside a general. At least I assumed that's what he was since his uniform was draped with enough gold braid to trim a Christmas tree. I had learned that it was wise not to ask anyone's rank. Better to assume you were talking with a field marshal or a prime minister. People will always be flattered by your mistake if you err upwardly.

Three paintings as big as billboards dominated the room. Each one depicted, in great detail, a coronation at the precise moment that the crown was placed on the head of the new monarch while hundreds of still-life people looked on with rapt attention. Once upon a time painters made a living turning out boring pictures like these.

''I see three coronations here, but you have had only two coronations since your independence; isn't that correct?'' I enquired of the general. The subject seemed like a safe one with which to start a conversation.

The general, who had coarse fair hair and a round solemn face, looked perplexed. ''Don't ask me,'' he shrugged. ''I really don't know.''

I was hoping he would be impressed by my grasp of Norwegian history, but generals presumably have other things to think about. What he did know was the one subject dear to the heart of every general: war. And although that's not my favourite subject, it is what we talked about through most of lunch.

In Norway, the memory of the Second World War is never far below the surface. The country was invaded by the Nazis and occupied from 1940 to 1945. Those dark days are still not forgotten. That period was a particularly shattering episode for the Norwegians because in 1940 they had been a sovereign state for only thirty-five years.

In 1905, the same year Alberta and Saskatchewan became provinces, the Norwegians escaped from the political domination of Sweden without a shot being fired. They did so by holding a referendum and voting overwhelmingly to be an independent country. The Swedes sensibly respected their wishes and since 1907 the two countries have lived side by side in peace.

To be occupied at gunpoint by the military might of Nazi Germany just a generation later was a terrible blow to their pride. The Norwegians responded by producing one of the toughest Resistance movements of the Second World War.

The general — that really was his rank — became more zealous as he talked about the Resistance.

"The most difficult thing, perhaps, was to keep my role a secret. I was just a boy of fourteen when I joined. But secrecy was everything. The lives of many people depended on it, not just my own. Women. Children. We were all at war."

I don't like to consider the prospect of fourteen-year-old boys fighting in wars but I became engrossed by his tale. He described some ugly events I dimly recalled from the movies of my childhood but had blotted from my image of contemporary Norway. Canadians don't often think about Norwegians being tortured and murdered. As the years go on we are frequently reminded of those who suffered in concentration camps or who survived atomic bombs, but we have short memories for countless other tragedies of the Second World War. The Norwegians remember.

"I do not speak of it often," my companion told me, "but I had to watch from an attic window in a house near Akershus Castle while fifteen men from my Resistance cell were executed by the Gestapo. Two of them were my uncles."

Akershus Castle is one of the residences of the Norwegian royal family and after the family fled to

England to live in exile until 1945, the Germans turned the castle into a Gestapo headquarters. So it is at Akershus that Norway's most poignant war memorial stands. It was there, later that afternoon, that Ed laid the obligatory wreath to the war dead.

Across the courtyard from the memorial was a museum commemorating the Resistance. It contained a small, well-chosen collection that made one feel the grim impact of the occupation years. There were displays of clandestine radios. There were photographs of villages that had been levelled in German reprisals and pictures of grisly executions. There were several photographs of the late King Haakon, and of Olav when he was the crown prince. One showed Prince Olav seated behind a BBC microphone reading a Christmas message to the people of occupied Norway. Another pictured him holding a machine-gun as he led a group of Resistance fighters into the castle at the end of the war. Olav V has always been a very popular king and it's easy to understand why Norwegians dearly love him. He has shared the hard times with them and in their darkest hours inspired them to keep faith. Although that war is half a century behind us, I think it will take another generation before Germans feel entirely at ease when they visit Norway.

After seeing the museum I returned to the palace to find two hairdressers waiting at the door of our suite. A pair of smiling women, neither of whom spoke English, trotted in behind me and before I could even shake off my shoes, they swooped down on me like a pair of judo instructors. They herded me into the bathroom where they positioned a dainty chair in front of a sink. They sat me in it and had my hair washed in four minutes flat. After swaddling my head in a huge white towel, they steered me to another elegant chair in the bedroom in front of a full-length mirror.

While the younger of the two unloaded a bag full of brushes, clips and a portable hair-dryer, the other woman started to draw circles over my head with her finger. In the mirror I watched her finger going round and round. There was a quizzical look on her face. Why was she bestowing a halo on me? Then it dawned on me. She was asking, in sign language, whether or not I would be wearing my tiara that evening.

I must admit I was tempted to nod my head and let her believe I was some sort of duchess, while she styled my hair around a non-existent tiara. Amused, I shook my head. Somehow I would survive the occasion crownless.

Farley used this time to telephone his Norwegian publisher. Although several of his books have been translated and published in Norway, his work is not particularly well-known there. Even his publishers didn't recognize his name. When they finally twigged that he was the author of *Ulvene* and *Villrenens Folk* (*Never Cry Wolf* and *People of the Deer*), an assistant editor languidly suggested he might find time to drop by Farley's hotel and buy him a drink. Where was he staying?

"No. Not the Palace Hotel. The *palace* . . . where the king lives," I heard Farley say. "I'm sure you know where it is."

The editor did indeed know. But he had never expected to hear one of his foreign authors phoning him from it.

"He sure and hell changed his tune," Farley laughed. "Maybe they'll take a little more interest in my books now!"

The two hairdressers completed the job so quickly that I had time left over for that ultimate luxury, a long soak in the king-sized bathtub. Our bathroom had a very high ceiling and the wall between the tub room and a neighbouring room in another suite didn't quite reach all the way. From the other side of this partition I could hear taps being turned on and off and the sound of water swishing and gurgling. Someone was taking a bath in the next room. But who? Surely not the king?

Farley, who had wandered in to bring me a glass of white wine, couldn't resist trying to find out.

"Hallooooo there!" he yodelled, his voice echoing as if from a distant mountain.

"Hello yourself!" came the business-like reply. It was Esmond Butler. His suite and ours were back-to-back. I venture to say Esmond has bathed in more regal bathtubs than any other Canadian in our history, and doubtless could fill a book with some funny and not-so-funny recollections of his unique career. But I doubt he ever will. Discretion tops the list of the aptitudes required in those who hope to carve themselves a niche in the halls of protocol. Chamberlains to kings and governors general don't write candid memoirs about their former bosses; it's usually the housemaid who does that.

The acoustics of these two adjoining bath chambers rivalled those of Roy Thomson Hall, so Farley suggested that Esmond might join us in a song. But he wasn't to be tempted. In any case, we had to hurry and get ready to play our parts in the fifth state banquet which was soon to begin.

In the banqueting hall, every plate and wine-glass was etched with a crown. "*Hoffdame fru Claire Mowat*" read the small card embossed with the coat of arms of Norway that marked my place at the table.

160

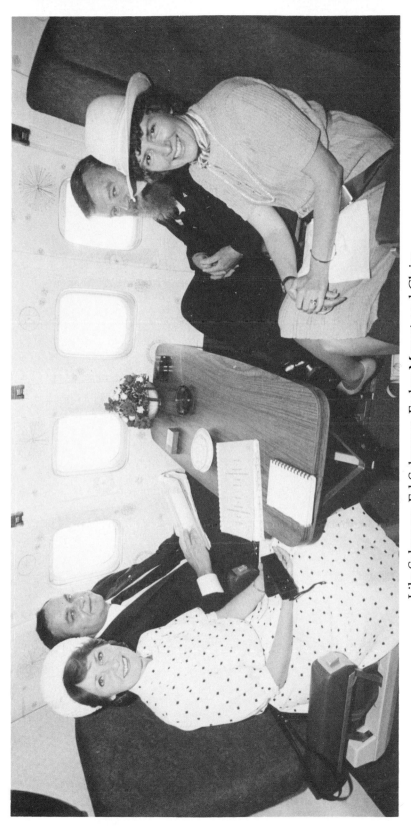

Lily Schreyer, Ed Schreyer, Farley Mowat and Claire Mowat on board the Canadian Armed Forces Boeing 707 en route to the state arrival ceremonies in Sweden.

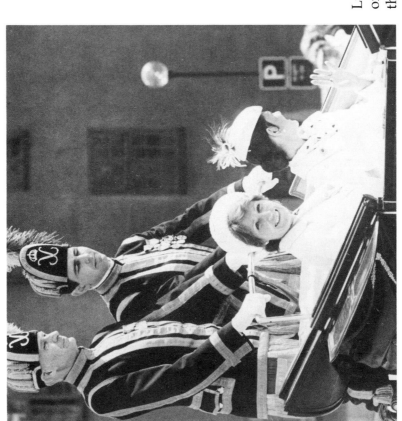

Lily Schreyer and HRH Queen Silvia of Sweden in the Royal landau during the state arrival in Stockholm.

Ed Schreyer and HRH King Carl XVI Gustav of Sweden, inspecting the Guard of Honour.

Receiving line prior to the state dinner in the Royal Palace of Stockholm. Left to right: HRH Queen Silvia, Lily Schreyer, Farley Mowat, HRH King Carl XVI Gustav and Esmond Butler.

Walking tour of Stockholm. HRH Queen Silvia, Lily Schreyer and Jason Schreyer. In the background: Claire Mowat and Colin Sangster.

Walking tour through Helsinki market. Ed Schreyer and Lily Schreyer. In the background: RCMP Inspector Mike Thivierge, Farley Mowat, Esmond Butler and Claire Mowat.

Watching Finnish folk dancing at Seurasaari Village near Helsinki. In the background: Claire Mowat and Lily Schreyer.

Observing a group of children in the public library, Kouvola, Finland. Lily Schreyer and Claire Mowat.

A procession during the arrival ceremony of the state visit to Norway. Ed Schreyer and HRH King Olav of Norway. In the background: Major-General Bjørn Egge, Commandant of Akershus Castle, Lily Schreyer, Crown Prince Harald and Claire Mowat.

Procession to the state dinner at the Royal Palace of Oslo.
In the foreground: Goran Seip, lady-in-waiting to Crown Princess Sonia;
Farley Mowat and Claire Mowat.

Waiting for the helicopter ferrying members of the party from Tune airport, Roskilde, Denmark. Lily Schreyer, Claire Mowat and Colin Sangster.

Receiving line prior to the state dinner in Copenhagen.
Lily Schreyer, HRH Prince Henrik, HRH Queen Margrethe,
Ed Schreyer, Claire Mowat and Farley Mowat.

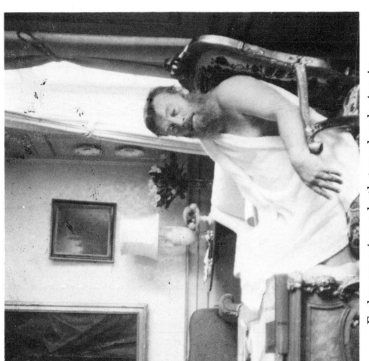

Farley wearing a bath towel, relaxing in the sitting-room of the King Christian Suite, Fredensborg Palace, Denmark.

Taking my own picture in the mirror of the bedroom in the King Christian Suite, Fredensborg Palace, Denmark.

In the Tivoli Gardens, Copenhagen. Lily Schreyer with Farley Mowat acting as lady-in-waiting.

State dinner in the Saga Hotel, Reykjavik, Iceland. Farley Mowat talking to President Vigdisi Finnbogadottir.

The farewell party after our final state dinner in Iceland. The Galliard Ensemble is playing. Farley Mowat is dancing.

"Court lady" it said. The walls and the ceiling were covered with handpainted flowers and the tall windows were draped with velvet. Above us, in the minstrels' gallery, a band began a medley of dinner music. The footmen marched in with the soup. Another international pep rally, with four kinds of wine, was underway.

I was seated five places to the left of the king, between a gentlemen who bore the office of a *Statsråd*, a minister in the Norwegian parliament, and our own ambassador to Norway, Arthur Campbell. It was a holiday to sit beside another Canadian because it was so much easier to find something to talk about. After we had made short work of the *saumon froid palais*, and as the music glided from Edvard Greig to Edward Elgar, Ambassador Campbell and I talked about the pros and cons of life in several regions and cities of Canada. He was soon going to retire and, after an absence of thirty years, he and his wife still hadn't decided which place they wanted to call home.

Coming home can be something of a letdown for a diplomat. Day-to-day life in Canada must look prosaic after a career in the world's capitals, peppered with state funerals, royal weddings and the occasional coronation. Many of our retired diplomats end up living in Ottawa where, despite the long winters, they are among a few colleagues who understand and appreciate what they have done with their lives.

My Norwegian dining partner was a tall man with a long, unsmiling face. After some predictable remarks about the weather, he enquired if I had another job besides being a lady-in-waiting.

"I'm a writer—of sorts. What I mean is that I am writing a book but it hasn't been published yet."

"And what is the subject of your book?"

"It's a memoir about a small community in Newfoundland. I used to live there. Newfoundland is our
easternmost province. Perhaps you've noticed it on
the map. It sticks out into the . . . ''

"The Atlantic Ocean. Yes, I know of this place. I
have read about it. There is a theory that Norsemen
settled there for a time in the tenth century. Do you
believe this yourself?''

"I do. They could have survived nicely in
Newfoundland.''

"Yet they did not stay long.''

"About four years. That's the conclusion of some
scholars,'' I said. "It's believed they left because of
conflicts with the local people—the *skraelings*, as they
call them.''

"So they sailed back to Greenland.''

"Where they lived successfully for about another
four centuries,'' I added.

"Yes, yes. Until the Eskimos killed them all,'' he
said gravely. "A Norwegian missionary, Hans
Egede, searched for them in the eighteenth century
and they had all vanished. Every one.''

It still remains a riddle of history as to just what
did happen to those blue-eyed Scandinavians who
preserved a European culture in Greenland for over
five hundred years. We know that during the fifteenth century they gradually lost touch with Iceland
and with Norway. Two hundred years later, the ruins
of their barns, homes, and churches could still be
seen, but by then the only people living in the green
valleys of south-western Greenland were short,
olive-skinned, hunter-gatherers, the Inuit.

"I don't think they were all killed,'' I said.

"Then where did they go?''

"Well, we do know that the climate changed and

it became much colder,'' I explained. ''So they would have abandoned agriculture and become hunter-gatherers. That's the only way they could have survived in an arctic climate. People can learn these skills when they must do so to survive,'' I said as I expanded my own theory.

''They would have learned,'' he affirmed. After all, the resourceful Norwegians could do anything. ''But that would not stop the Eskimos from killing them,'' he added.

I tactfully tried to persuade him otherwise. ''In my opinion, it was inevitable that the Norse would gradually marry into the Inuit community. That's how races have always melded. You must know,'' I said, a trifle flirtatiously, ''how women are attracted by success.''

He looked at me sideways with an expression of admonition. ''I do not agree,'' he shook his head.

''Why not?''

''Norwegians would not do that. We do not inter-marry with native races. We have a strong sense of our unity. It would not happen.''

''But it didn't happen in Norway. It happened in Greenland in the fifteenth century. Conditions were quite different.''

''No. It could not be. They were murdered. Such a tragedy,'' he lamented.

Good form keeps the lid on one's temper. If I had been anywhere else during this little discussion, I would have scolded the man for his racist views. Instead, I calmly began to tell him that in contemporary Greenland, mixed marriages between the Danes and the Inuit have always been commonplace. We were interrupted by the theatrical arrival of our final course, deep-fried Camembert cheese. It seemed wiser to drop the subject and just enjoy the treat. For all I knew he might not have had anything good to say about the Danes either.

Among the guests that night was Helge Ingstad, the explorer, and his archaeologist wife, Ann Stine Ingstad. These two had undertaken the first excavation of a Norse settlement near L'Anse aux Meadows in northern Newfoundland during the 1960s. The site is now a national park where visitors can sit inside a turf-walled reconstruction of a longhouse and imagine how a party of explorers lived there in the eleventh century. In 1963, several years before this marshy field was declared an historic site, Farley had gone there while he was working out his own theories about where the Norse had landed. He had found Helge Ingstad living in a rain-soaked tent. The two had shared some food and rum and pontificated long into the night about the earliest European discovery of North America. When they said goodbye in that windy place, neither of them could have dreamed that their next meeting would be in Oslo at a party hosted by the king.

After dinner the king circulated among his guests like the genial patriarch that he is. He laughed a lot and his forthright manner put everyone at ease. Perhaps, at his age, he didn't have to take himself and his kingship too seriously. The Norwegian royal family was proving to be a much more democratic lot than their counterparts in Sweden.

The only puzzle to me was why those turn-of-the-century Norwegians, after six hundred years without a king, had decided to install one at all. At a time when the French had long since turfed out their royal family and the Russians were soon to assassinate theirs, the Norwegians decided to revive theirs. They could not, six centuries later, track down descendants of their medieval kings, so instead they chose a Danish prince who was married to an English princess. That prince, whose name was really Carl but who took the ancient Norwegian name of Haakon, and his wife, Princess Maud, brought something a little magical to Norway's identity, some dimension which could not have come from the political process alone. Almost a century ago, Norwegian parliamentarians grasped the importance of ceremony in holding a human society together. They must also have realized that ceremony without a ceremonial chieftain lacks that final element to make the whole thing credible.

Kings used to have immense and terrible power. Today the seven remaining monarchs in Europe play roles that are more akin to tribal elders, admirable men and women who will still be there (and whose descendants will presumably carry on) beyond the changing fortunes of the politicians. For reasons of emotion, not logic, a lot of Canadians continue to cherish the British royal family many decades after it has ceased to have anything but ceremonial value in the way our country is governed.

The next morning we were treated to the most amazing breakfast. Thirty Canadians and Norwegians gathered around an enormous table laden with a smörgåsbord of cold meat, pickled fish, cheese of every sort, eggs, preserves, fruit, rolls, and butter. It was the sort of spread which, in Canada, would qualify as a full-scale buffet supper. Who would have guessed that Norwegians liked to eat so much at eight o'clock in the morning? Could this have been one of the reasons they wanted their independence from the Swedes, who begin the day with a mere croissant or two?

Our tenth day was starting well. There was even time to draw a breath and get some idea of where we were. The Norwegians, bless them, had scheduled our first event at the comfortable hour of ten-thirty, which gave us time to dally over a second cup of their delicious coffee. What's more, we were going to visit a place I really wanted to see, the Viking Ships Museum. And King Olav himself, that famous sailor, was going to be our personal guide.

Most people think they know what a Viking ship looks like. Children's picture-books, school history books, even packages of rye biscuits carry illustrations of long, narrow rowboats with dragon heads on their prows, usually filled with bearded men wearing funny helmets, hunkered down behind rows of shields. The movies have given us the same war-like image. But the reality is something else.

The three major vessels on display had been painstakingly excavated and reconstructed. The Oseberg ship came from an enormous grave mound; the Tune and the Gokstad ships were dug from the bottom of a silted-in harbour. All had been built in the tenth century.

You feel very small standing beside one of those reconstructed ships. Their size and their strength are awesome. Contrary to the popular notion they were not built for war at all, but are robust merchant ships. The Gokstad is 76 feet long. Both the Gokstad and the Tune were built to carry freight and passengers over stormy seas to faraway places such as Scotland and Iceland. Their carrying capacity was in the range of thirty tons.

How the Norse could have built these graceful

ships with only the tools available a thousand years ago seems a minor miracle. And what we were looking at was, for the most part, the original wood and ironwork. The cold clay of Norway had proved to be a good preservative. Equally remarkable is the fact that a nation as small as present-day Norway would have undertaken the extremely expensive project of resurrecting and restoring them. When Canada's most renowned ship, *Bluenose*, once the fastest fishing vessel under sail in the world, came to the end of her working life no one, neither private citizen nor public institution, tried to save her for her historic value. She was sold to a Caribbean country where she was eventually run aground on a reef and left to rot under the tropical sun.

The Gokstad and the Tune were cargo vessels but the Oseberg was ceremonial. Ironically, she had been built for the same sort of visit as our own, a special ship to be used in celebrations for visiting chieftains. The elaborate carvings with which she was decorated were primarily to make a grand impression. The need for ceremonial vehicles must be in our blood. We don't build ships like that today, but we do build bullet-proof limousines, Popemobiles and extravagant parade floats on which Santa Claus comes to town.

Every once in a while I had to remind myself we had a king in our midst. Olav ambled around like any other museum visitor investigating the displays. I dare say he knew the Viking ship story better than he knew the crown jewels. He was a man for all seasons, and being the king was only one part of his life. An accomplished sailor, he sailed in the 1928 Olympics for Norway and won the gold. He had also been a competitive skier and ski jumper. He had been a close friend of Roald Amundsen, the great Norwegian explorer who sailed through the ice of the Canadian Arctic before he became the first man to reach the South Pole.

When the king discovered that Farley was also a ship buff and just as fascinated by Arctic exploration as Olav himself, he steered my husband off to another room while the rest of us listened politely to an address given by the museum director.

"And what were you two talking about?" I asked Farley afterwards.

"Man talk," he winked. "Actually the king was telling me the inside dope on how Amundsen foxed Captain Robert Scott in the race for the South Pole. Apparently Amundsen didn't tell anyone where he was really going when he put to sea in 1911. Everyone at home thought he was off on a scientific exploration of just the coast of Antarctica. That's what the crew thought too. But Olav guessed otherwise. And he says he was the only one who wasn't surprised when Amundsen made straight for the Pole and beat poor Scott to it."

It was turning out to be a nautical morning. After we had looked at the Viking ships, the Men's Party went to another museum to see the nineteenth-century vessel *Fram*, the ship in which the intrepid Norwegian Fridtjof Nansen drifted in the ice across much of the Arctic Ocean while attempting to reach the North Pole. I wouldn't have objected to seeing it myself but we women had our own agenda. We were treated to a voyage on the royal barge *Stjernen*, the king's private launch, a 35-foot beauty that was all teak and mahogany, with an engine that purred like an ocelot. Except for the two-man crew, our entourage was all female and our hostess was the Crown princess.

168

It's no wonder that royal families love their boats. Slipping across the sheltered water of Oslo harbour on a balmy spring morning, it was easy to forget about being on display. We sipped cold white wine, ate dainty little sandwiches and no one could see us except the security police in their escort boat.

The crossing only took half an hour but offered us our first panoramic look at Oslo. It's a city without skyscrapers, a manageable-looking municipality that has the highest ratio of single-family houses of any European capital. With a little over one million residents, Oslo is roughly the size of Vancouver, a city that resembles it in some ways. The sea is always nearby; there are distant mountains; and most of the residential suburbs hug the shoreline.

The boat trip was the first chance Lily and I had to spend some informal time with Princess Sonia. She had not been born to royalty but came from a proletarian Norwegian family. Her love for Prince Harald, and his for her, was not sanctioned by the king for a very long time, or so the story goes. Each time I heard a version of Sonia-the-Commoner in love with Harald-the-Prince, the tale grew with the telling. Everyone loves a love story and, for Norwegians, this had been a real-life drama. The king believed that, for the good of the monarchy, Harald should marry a woman of royal lineage. The charms of several aristocratic young ladies, Scandinavian and British, were extolled but to no avail. Harald refused to marry anyone but Sonia. The king resisted. Harald persisted. The stalemate lasted for nine long years. Eventually Olav gave his blessing to their union and in 1968 they were finally married. In the end, the king took his daughter-in-law to his heart and they all lived happily ever after.

King Olav could scarcely have expected Crown

Prince Harald to agree to an arranged marriage. Harald spent four or five years of his childhood in the republican atmosphere of the United States where the royal children had sought refuge during the war. Later, after some military training in Norway, he studied at Oxford University, as his father had before him. Tall, handsome, and athletic like his father, the liberated prince must have been considered quite a catch during his bachelor days.

Legend also has it that the king arranged to send Sonia away to a fancy school in Switzerland where she could learn how to behave royally, but I doubt that anyone had much to teach Sonia about being a princess. For one thing, it isn't terribly difficult. Even I had been learning the trade secrets as I went along. But there is something more important than learning what to say in a receiving line or how to conduct oneself during a state funeral. A successful princess has to possess a certain indefinable blend of charm and polish, coupled with a lack of obvious artifice. I can't imagine a prince proposing marriage to any woman who didn't already have it. Sonia certainly did. She was friendly whenever we were with her and, like a true princess, her small talk was directed towards easy questions about *our* experiences, about Canada, about the other countries on our tour, about the weather. A princess does not babble on about her own concerns and her own opinions, however much I may have wanted to hear them.

Shipping is a major industry in Norway and the harbour was dotted with ships of all sizes heading for a tangle of exotic destinations. For a while we were absorbed in watching one elephantine freighter, about half a mile ahead of us, manoeuvring its way slowly towards the open sea.

"Where do you suppose that ship is going?" asked Lily dreamily.

"She is sailing for Svalbard," answered Princess Sonia. "She goes there regularly with supplies."

"That's Spitsbergen, isn't it?" I asked.

"Yes it is," she confirmed. "Far to the north. I have been there once with my husband."

"I've always wanted to go there," I said enviously.

Spitsbergen, which lies north of latitude 77 degrees, is a group of arctic islands near the very top of the globe. This territory of Norway is situated about seven hundred kilometres north of the northernmost tip of the Norwegian mainland. It is one of those ultimate destinations that romantics like me dream about seeing. The Crown princess was the first person I had ever met who had been there.

"It was most interesting," the princess continued. "In winter it is dark for six months and very cold. Not warm in summer either. There are no trees. About one thousand people live there. Most of them work in the coal mines. I was surprised when they spoke to me of being quite happy living in that isolated place. It would not be suitable for everyone."

"The Arctic has its appeal," I said. "For some people it's an addiction."

Happiness, as we would shortly be reminded, is a relative condition. Our next destination was a hospital for the permanently disabled, a special place for the worst of the worst—people who, because of accidents of birth or accidents of life, were almost immobile. None of them would ever stand and see a parade go by, and only a few could even wave a flag for a princess.

Sunaas Hospital was a low-rise building on the

side of a hill, above the infinitely interesting panorama of the port of Oslo. For anyone who had the
misfortune to be confined to a bed or wheelchair forever, it would be some small compensation to live
overlooking one of the world's busiest harbours.

The building was full of windows with views of
ocean and forest, and where they didn't overlook the
sea they faced little landscaped courtyards full of
shrubs and flowers. The hospital director led the
princess and Lily along the gleaming corridors while
we two ladies-in-waiting trailed behind.

We paused to observe a well-equipped physioth-
erapy room and then moved along to a sunny handicraft studio. There we watched while a lady
confined to a wheelchair, her arms held in place by
slings, painted tiny flowers on a glass vase. Some of
these patients lived in the hospital and others came
for rehabilitation for a few weeks or months. We saw
disabled people of all ages, from young children to
the very old. There were several young men who
were victims of automobile and motorcycle accidents
and now were struggling to learn how to sit up again.
We met an even less fortunate man who had been in
bed for eighteen years, kept alive by an artificial lung.

At the end of the tour we were introduced to two
angelic little girls, both nine years old and in wheelchairs. They presented Princess Sonia and Lily with
tiny reed baskets they had made themselves. They
were the lucky ones who had been chosen to meet a
real live princess and they could hardly contain their
excitement.

We joined the staff for coffee out on a broad terrace encircled with birch and pine trees.

"Our staff outnumbers our patients," the director, Mr. Øyvind Lunde, proudly told us as we min-
gled with a small army of therapists, nurses and

doctors. We even met Mrs. Sunaas, then in her eighties, the widow of the man who had founded this cheerful facility. Maybe cheerful isn't the right word. The quality was, I think, hope.

Luncheon was at Akershus Castle. This stone castle was capped with turrets and dotted with arrow slits from the days when all the king's men frequently had to take refuge here from their enemies. Inside, the castle looked like a setting for an Errol Flynn movie. The ceilings were low and supported by massive oak beams. The iron chandeliers had candles in them. The floors were made of dark bare wood, like a stage, and the rough stone walls were painted white. In the long dining-room the heavy chairs were of carved oak with red leather seats. We waited by our places listening to the approaching footsteps of the royal family and the prime minister as they proceeded to the head table.

For the second time on this journey I was seated beside the husband of a princess. Johan Martin Ferner, the other half of Princess Astrid, Mrs. Ferner, was a tall, no-nonsense chap who didn't appear to be suffering from an identity crisis just because his name was always listed after his wife's. He chatted mainly about their five children, and their busy household. It sounded much like the life of any well-to-do family anywhere, with a complex schedule of homework, riding lessons, music practice and summer vacations. Their biggest problem, he told me, was trying to find live-in domestic help. In classless Norway, even the king's daughter had trouble finding a reliable person who would work for them for more than a few months before moving on to some other job.

"You should try advertising in Canada," I suggested, thinking about those regions of our country

173

where unemployment was high and adulation for royalty even higher. ''You'd be sure to find someone.''

He nodded but said nothing.

It should have occurred to me that he and his wife wouldn't advertise — anywhere. Royalty doesn't. They hire their staff discreetly through agencies and through friends. They must go to great lengths to keep the world's weirdos away.

This time it was the government of Norway, and not the king, who was our host so after lunch we listened to a short speech by Norway's first woman prime minister, the brilliant, soft-spoken Gro Harlem Brundtland. Fru Brundtland had only been prime minister for a few months then, after being chosen as the leader of the Norwegian Labour Party. Dark-haired and attractive, she was just forty-two, and a woman destined to make a mark on the world far beyond her own country. There have been so few women prime ministers in world history that we still don't quite know what to expect from them. I can only say that Gro Brundtland did not remind me of Margaret Thatcher, Indira Gandhi or Golda Meir in any way. The mother of four children, she was also a medical doctor. Her gentle speaking voice belied the determined woman she must be to have moved so far so fast. Her party was defeated in an election later that same year, but in a subsequent election in 1986, she was again elected prime minister. Since that time she has inspired the world by forming a cabinet in which eight out of eighteen members are women. She has also headed the Brundtland Commission, a world-wide study on environment and development. As a role model for women in politics, as well as an example of the opportunities for leaders of small nations on the world stage, the prime minister of Norway shines like a diamond. We didn't know all this was about to happen, back in 1981. At that time, I was merely impressed to meet any woman who had accomplished as much as she obviously had in her forty-two years.

Later in the afternoon we were back aboard our sturdy old destroyer, *Huron*. She had steamed across the Baltic from Finland to be in Oslo in time to provide a floating base for our movable feast. This was our third reception on the ship's afterdeck and I was beginning to feel like part of the crew myself. The mood was always happy at these parties. For some reason it is always easier to entertain a crowd outdoors.

At first I chatted with a Norwegian businessman who exported fish-filleting equipment to Canada. His country and mine garner a lot of revenue from the export of fish. Canada, in fact, has the longest seacoast of any nation in the world and one of the world's largest fisheries. One would think that we might manufacture all our own fish-packing equipment, but we don't.

More interesting to me was the chance to talk with a group of women who had formed the Canadian War Brides' Association in Oslo thirty-five years earlier. These women had married Norwegian servicemen posted for military training to wartime Canada, most of them to Little Norway, an air training base in Toronto, and to a naval training base in Lunenburg, Nova Scotia.

I had a special interest in this group of young grandmothers. My own mother was an English war bride following the First World War, so I grew up on tales about the culture shock of moving from Britain to Toronto. Now I had to reverse my preconception that all war brides were women who came *to* Canada.

175

These brides had moved to Norway after the Second World War where, I venture to say, they had a more difficult adjustment to make than my mother ever did. Not only did they have to learn another language, they had to cope with the spartan conditions of post-war Norway and the obstacle of trying to blend into a tenacious culture that was even less accommodating to newcomers than Toronto.

"I was so thrilled to meet the governor general," gushed a trim lady with just a touch of grey in her brown hair and a trace of Toronto in her accent.

"All of us think His Excellency is pretty special," I agreed.

"He's so friendly. You can just go up and talk to him. Not like the others."

"Others?" I queried. How many governors general had she met?

"I mean . . . back when I was in high school . . . they were so — well — so British. Mr. Schreyer is so Canadian. Born right in Canada."

"Yes, of course. And he is actually the *fifth* Canadian-born governor general," I added enthusiastically.

"Oh," she said quietly.

I quickly switched the subject. I had embarrassed her. She hadn't lived in Canada since 1945. Our governors general were still Englishmen then. What seems like history to most of us was still the Canada of her distant recollections.

"So your group has stayed together all these years. How nice that you have kept in touch."

"We aren't as big a group as we used to be. In the beginning we got together for mutual support. We'd exchange tips on things like baby care and recipes. A lot of the food was strange to us then. Over the years we got used to the ways here. Mind you, some of the girls left. Went home. There were a few divorces. The rest of us got on with raising our families and living our lives here.''

''We mostly get together now for old times' sake. We've shared a lot,'' smiled another woman, who had been born in Hamilton, Ontario, and left when she was just nineteen.

That evening Jason, still two months away from his fourteenth birthday, decided he had endured enough state dinners. What he wanted most was to wander around downtown Oslo and see if he could find a pizza. A Norwegian pizza? Why not? Ed and Lily granted him his well-deserved night of liberty but on condition that Mr. Nadon went along too.

One of Jean Nadon's multitudinous functions was to be the family's *confidante*. A silver-haired dandy in his fifties, he was extremely fond of all the Schreyers and they of him. As maître d' at Rideau Hall he saw to their needs in the face of such obstacles as the temperamental nature of the sous-chef, the working hours of the kitchen staff, and the inevitable domestic ripples of a very large household. Most of his responsibilities were focussed on the planning of forthcoming menus with Her Excellency and such details as supervising the footmen when they polished the dining-room silver every day. But on the road he coped with whatever needs arose.

''I'm here so that their Excellencies won't feel surrounded by strangers when they need something — a cup of coffee, a dentist, a telephone extension — whatever,'' he told me. ''I'm a familiar face. It's my job to make them feel at home, to reduce the stress and strain. You'd be surprised at the number of people that some visiting heads of state bring to Ottawa to do just that. Queen Elizabeth travels with a personal staff of about twenty-five; the president of the United States with sixty, seventy or more."

As Jason and Mr. Nadon marched out to freedom beyond the palace gates in search of Norway's answer to fast food, the rest of us wrestled once again with our cummerbunds and curling irons. By the evening of banquet number six, I was into the reruns with my meagre array of only four evening gowns. Lily was travelling with twice that number which meant that she wouldn't appear in the same evening dress twice until we reached Iceland. This was not done out of vanity but rather so that the commemorative photographs would record a different gown at each event.

At the door of the Continental Hotel on a busy downtown street, a small crowd had gathered to watch the arrival of the king. As a prelude, they got to look at us first. We had to arrive ten minutes ahead of the royal family. When you have invited the king to join you for dinner, you make good and sure you get there before he does. A squadron of detectives and a harried-looking hotel manager ushered us from our limousines to a revolving door. Just as I reached it, I heard someone cheering and clapping. Who, in Oslo, would be cheering for us? I should have guessed. In the midst of the crowd, which was being herded to one side by a policeman, stood Jason and Mr. Nadon. As carefree as tourists, they grinned and waved.

"Yay, team!" I called back, before the revolving door sucked me in.

For a fleeting moment I longed to go with them, to share that pizza in some commonplace little café. We would soon be leaving Oslo and I had not even found so much as ten minutes to walk around and get a feel for the place. And I was starting to share Jason's impatience with banquets. It wasn't the food. I could cheerfully go on eating pheasant, caviar, white asparagus, and strawberries Chantilly for the rest of my life. What was becoming tiresome was the continual effort of making small talk with the many strangers who didn't share my turn of phrase or any fragment of my personal history.

In Canada I could usually find some common ground to make a connection with strangers. "So you're from Victoria . . . lovely city . . . my cousin lives there." "Prince Albert is your home? Well, I haven't been there but my husband grew up in Saskatoon and he has often talked about . . . " "New Denmark, New Brunswick! You know that's one place I've always wanted to see. You pass the sign leading to it on the Trans-Canada just south of Edmundston, isn't that right? . . . " "Oh, you're a McMaster grad. I wonder . . . were you there when George Grant was a professor of philosophy? I've always been a fan of his." All the givens that are part of the fabric of life back home were missing in the company of men and women who had probably never seen Canada, had only the faintest notion of what it was like and most likely weren't very curious about it. We often had to struggle for conversation once the subject of the weather had petered out.

Upstairs, in a private, guarded drawing-room, we fortunate few awaited the royal family. The plan was that, once they arrived, we would form a procession and our Canadian pipe major would lead us ceremoniously to the head table in the banquet hall. King Olav, Prince Harald, and Princess Sonia arrived exactly ten minutes after we did, right on schedule, but for some reason the start of the banquet was delayed. Instead of two or three minutes alone with them, the time dragged on to fifteen minutes. That might not seem like a long time if you stop to chat with an old friend you've encountered in your local post office but, standing face-to-face with the Norwegian royal family in full formal attire, it seemed like a very long time indeed.

Economy in conversation is a strategy that royal people learn early in life. Unless they're with one another, or with friends they know well, they don't indulge in idle chatter. Knowing that every word they utter may be remembered or recorded, they rarely take conversational leaps.

It wasn't until good king Olav sauntered over to take a closer look at Farley's medals that we finally found something to talk about. One subject that every monarch knows well is medals and decorations because they spend a lot of time at events where people are either wearing them or being presented with them. Of Farley's nine medals, six were from the Second World War and King Olav immediately recognized them. But the three Canadian civilian medals were new to him. He wanted to know why they had been awarded and Ed gladly explained the Order of Canada, the Canadian Centennial Medal, and the Queen's Silver Jubilee Medal.

"And you were awarded these for writing about the Arctic?" asked the king.

"Not exclusively the Arctic, Your Majesty. I have written about many other topics too. But the far north has been a recurring preoccupation with me."

"With me also," nodded the king.

"Strange to think, if the events of history had turned out differently, Canada and Norway would have been next-door neighbours," said Ed. "It was only in 1930 that Norway accepted Canada's claim to our high arctic islands.'' Ed has a remarkable memory for such data.

"Quite right. Quite right," added the king agreeably. "They should belong to Canada."

"That's what we think too," added Farley wryly.

It was mainly Norwegians, particularly Roald Amundsen, Otto Sverdrup, and Fridtjof Nansen, who explored and mapped many of the last uncharted regions on the face of the earth in the Arctic and the Antarctic. Many of our high arctic islands still bear Norwegian names: Axel Heiberg, Olaf Ringnes and Otto Sverdrup. The icy Queen Maud Gulf is named after King Olav's mother. Small wonder that King Olav, who was twenty-seven years old the year Norway relinquished its claim to what is now the north-easternmost edge of Canada, was so well-versed in the details of that golden age of Norwegian exploration. I'll wager, in his heart of hearts, that he wishes Norway had retained those inhospitable islands that his brave compatriots discovered.

The skirl of bagpipes ended the conversation just as it had begun to get lively. We trooped into the banquet hall while the other guests, waiting respectfully behind their chairs, watched us pass.

That evening I landed between two cabinet ministers and at first both of them appeared to be dour and uncommunicative. I held little hope for the rest of the evening and dined in silence for a while, gazing into the spectacular bouquet of flowers that had been placed right in front of me. Finally one of the ministers got around to speaking to me. Or rather *at* me, because once he got started, he delivered what amounted to a lecture about the 1972 referendum in which the people of Norway had voted to stay out of the European Economic Community.

It may sound boring but actually it fascinated me. The future of small nations and the tactics we will have to use to survive in a world of superpowers is a matter I take seriously. I paid attention, trying to fathom the reasons that had prompted the people of Norway to go it alone at a time when many Canadians wanted to sidle ever closer to the United States.

"You must understand that independence is recent for Norway, so we do not want to let it slip away from us again," he explained.

"Independence is recent for Canada too," I said.

"To join the EEC would make us an economic hostage," he declared. "Norway is a small nation. We must be in a position to make our own decisions."

"I share your concern. Canada is a small nation too."

"Small?" He looked skeptical.

"Twenty-five million people. That's small. On the map it looks as if we are a large country, but it's misleading. Even Canadians are deluded by our huge map. We have only ten per cent of the population of the United States. And ninety per cent of us live within two hundred kilometres of the border."

"Because you like to be close to the Americans?"

"Because that's where the good farm land is. And a better climate."

"Do you fear that the United States will absorb Canada?" asked the other cabinet minister who now joined the conversation.

"It does concern me," I said. "It won't be done with guns. They're doing it with television and with business deals. And we're letting it happen. Unfortunately it doesn't disturb enough of us that we've slid from the British Empire right into the American Empire."

There was a pause as each of these men considered the matter. The fragile nature of the Canadian will to exist had never crossed their minds. Then the second cabinet minister said, "Perhaps, then, Canada should join us. Join the Council of Nordic Nations," he smiled.

The first cabinet minister chuckled at the idea. "That might make it less easy for the Americans to swallow you."

"Thank you for the suggestion." I responded with a smile. "I will mention it to our prime minister if I happen to speak to him."

The rest of the banquet dragged on with many silences, and by the time the *melon royal* was finally served, I was beginning to feel depressed. It wasn't the surroundings. It was the sobering thought that we Canadians might be pretenders. Did we even have the right to be making state visits at all when so much of our economy, and our thinking, was controlled by another country? How could Canadians claim an honourable place among the world's truly independent nations in comparison to the Norwegians? Their four centuries of domination, first by Denmark and later by Sweden, as well as five years of military occupation by Germany, had hardened their resolve to survive. The very name of Vidkun Quisling, the man who headed the Norwegian Nazi party and who collaborated with the Germans, is now a synonym for treason. I was mired in gloomy thoughts by the time the Galliard Ensemble started to play their now-familiar recital. As the music of Mozart filled the room, I sat there speculating that Quebec would separate and then the rest of Canada would be destined to disappear — like Bessarabia, like Slovakia, like Scotland. And no one, least of all Canadians, would care.

There was enthusiastic applause at the end of the

recital. I was proud that we could at least produce first-class musicians even if we were less than proficient as economic nationalists.

Later, in the lavish Visiting Sovereigns Apartment back at the palace, Lily and I kicked off our golden slippers and curled up in a pair of French chairs. Our husbands gallantly poured us a nightcap and the four of us sat and chatted. We rarely had the chance to do this despite the fact that we were ostensibly travelling together. Under the watchful eyes of all the Swedish-Norwegian kings from the last century whose portraits lined the walls of the drawing-room, we seized the moment to reflect on the day's events.

"I really got lucky this time," Farley rejoiced. "I sat beside a lovely woman. She's a judge, as well as the wife of a cabinet minister. She had a great sense of humour. I had a wonderful evening."

"Same for me," added Ed. He had had Princess Sonia as his dining companion twice in the same day. "The princess is a very bright lady as well as being beautiful."

"Well, I didn't know what to do tonight," Lily said. "When a king nods off to sleep, is it polite to discreetly nudge him? Or do you pretend you didn't notice?"

"Poor King Olav. He has to sit through an awful lot of banquets," Farley said.

"He is seventy-eight years old, after all," I said. "And the dining-room was hot."

"I noticed that his own family just ignored the fact that he was dozing off. They must be used to it," Ed remarked.

"That was what I decided was the best thing to do. King Olav is so nice, I wouldn't want to hurt his feelings. I just wish those candlesticks had been better conversationalists.''

''Chin up, kids. Six down and four to go,'' said Farley in the tone of a coach in the locker-room ticking off the final games.

''At least there won't be another state banquet for a few days. Not where we're going,'' added Ed.

''Just where are we going?'' I asked. I was lost without my briefing-book. The events of the tour demanded such total attention that sometimes I couldn't remember exactly where I would be the following day.

''First we fly west. Then north,'' Ed began. He managed to keep the whole program in his head like a conductor with a symphony score. ''Stavanger, Bodø, Bardufoss, Tromsø, Andoy, in that order,'' he recited.

''Oh yes, I remember,'' Lily sighed. ''Raincoats and warm clothes. You know, I've got an idea. Wouldn't it be more fun if we went to Spain instead?''

''Now, Lily,'' Ed remonstrated. ''Some of the most spectacular scenery in the world is on the west coast of Norway. Mountains. Fiords. The midnight sun. Just wait,'' he added enthusiastically. ''Tomorrow you're going to see something truly extraordinary—the biggest oil drilling platform in the world.''

Lily and I exchanged looks of resignation. The wonders of fossil fuel technology didn't excite us.

''Lily, you go to Spain if you like,'' I laughed. ''I think I'll stay here and write a thesis about the paintings on the ceilings of the palace. Just think, I could do the whole project lying down.''

It seems to me that art historians write about the magnificent ceilings of Italy almost exclusively. Even

Norway, a minor player in the European economy, had once engaged some now-forgotten painters to spend years lying on scaffolds painting thousands of flowers, vines, and cherubs on the ceilings of the palace's grand dining-rooms and ballrooms.

Needless to say, Lily didn't go to Spain and I didn't stay in that palace one minute longer than the appointed hour the following morning when our group moved off. In Norway every one of us in the Accompanying Party had been invited to say farewell to the king. And the king even brought his dog with him to join in the goodbyes. I felt no hesitation in leaning down to shake the paw of this fortunate little black poodle — after I had shaken the hand of the king, of course.

I relished our last ride in one of the king's old Mercedes. All too soon we were at the airport pulling up beside our familiar Canadian Forces Cosmo, a plane that was starting to look kind of homespun (if you can call any aircraft that). There were the familiar faces of the crew welcoming us back with smiles, instant coffee, and a comforting assortment of out-of-date magazines. In no time we were off again into the wild blue yonder.

It wasn't blue for long. Oslo is located on the relatively sheltered east side of Norway. Our route lay south-west across the country towards the stormy North Sea. The chequerboard of farms disappeared into the mist as we neared the ocean. By the time we approached the airport of the city of Stavanger we were greeted, for the first time on our enchanted tour, by a steady, discouraging rain.

"A shame. The mountains are beautiful," said the mayor of Stavanger who, along with a bevy of district officials and Statoil executives, welcomed us to Norway's booming North Sea oil port. We were apparently surrounded by mountains, but we could only see the bottoms of them.

"We may have to cancel the helicopter flights. The ceiling is so low," the president of Statoil, the state-owned oil and gas monopoly, said apologetically.

"That won't break my heart," I thought but didn't say.

A motorcade of Volvos drove us over a hilly landscape. Norway is the physical antithesis of Finland and Sweden. Most of it is straight up and down. At Statoil's modern offices we were led upstairs to the boardroom, a large room commanding a spectacular view of the fiords which unfortunately were lost in the mist that day. We stared instead at a scale model of the world's largest drilling rig. The real thing was anchored in a foggy fiord a few miles away.

We were shown a documentary film about oil drilling operations in the North Sea, an occupation fraught with much the same perils of wind, storms, and ice as oil drilling off the east coast of Canada. Naturally the film did not emphasize the risks to life and limb involved in retrieving oil from the ocean's floor, even though a year earlier Norway had suffered the loss of an entire oil rig and over one hundred men of its crew. (Canada would suffer an almost identical loss in 1982 when eighty-four men went to their death on the drill rig *Ocean Ranger* off Newfoundland.) Generals do not dwell on the dangers faced by the enlisted men. Instead, the president of the company showered us with optimistic statistics about the oil boom which had come to Norway.

When that was over they served coffee and some delicious little biscuits.

"Thank goodness you've provided us with coffee," I said to the handsome executive with horn-rimmed glasses seated next to me at the broad boardroom table. That was the only subject I could think of to start a conversation since I didn't have anything original to say about the oil business. "I simply can't get used to drinking champagne in the morning. As a matter of fact, I'm not too fond of it in the evening either," I added.

"And you are not the only one," he smiled. "We had a visit from Queen Elizabeth a few weeks ago. Since we didn't know what to offer her to drink, we asked her secretary at Buckingham Palace what she would like. And do you know she doesn't care for champagne in the morning either?

"How reassuring," I said, "to know that Queen Elizabeth and I have at least that much in common."

"What place in Canada is your home?" he asked.

I gave him my standard answer that I have lived in four of our Canadian provinces, but Toronto was where I was born and went to school.

"Toronto! That's where I was. I studied for my engineering degree at the University of Toronto."

"How on earth did you happen to be there?"

"I worked my way to Canada on a Norwegian cargo ship in 1955. The ship left me at Bathurst in New Brunswick. I can still remember how surprised the immigration man was to see me. I don't think they had seen an immigrant in that place for a long time."

"Not since the return of the Acadians, I expect."

"I have such good memories of Bathurst. Everyone was so kind to me. A family took me to their home for the night. And the next day they drove me to the railway station for the train journey to Montreal. At Montreal I got a job on a Canadian ship right away. I saved my money and then after two years I was able to study at the University of Toronto.''

''I was an art student in Toronto at the same time,'' I told him.

''Such a small world,'' he laughed. ''We may have even been at the same parties.''

The weather had cleared just a little by the time our reception was over, so the Men's Party was able to take off in the world's biggest helicopter to see the world's biggest oil drilling rig, which was still under construction. The Ladies' Party, led by a gentleman from the local historical society, was taken on a walking tour of the ''old quarter'' of Stavanger.

What we saw was a neighbourhood that was not at all ancient. The houses were indeed about two centuries old, but they had all been moved from several nearby communities to a tidy, new subdivision when the old waterfront of Stavanger had been usurped for the construction of a port facility. The houses looked oddly plumb on their foundations in the planned streetscape. We trudged around in the rain, observing several dozen small, immaculate homes with cosy casement windows, low ceilings and Hansel-and-Gretel doorways.

It must have cost a vast amount to move them. Back home we usually find the funds to move the most venerable houses only if they are going to be used as tourist attractions. In Norway the old homes of ordinary folk had been saved from demolition so that people could continue to live in buildings they knew and probably loved.

The planners of the new era in Stavanger were primarily concerned about the future. Residential housing for the thousands of people moving into the area was not concentrated in the city itself but was dispersed among several neighbouring communities. It was the planners' intention that no single community would be swamped by newcomers, only to be left derelict when the oil boom ended. By law, Statoil had to devote a healthy chunk of its profits to developing secondary employment in the regions where it operated, as some protection against the unpredictable fortunes of the oil industry.

By noon we were back on board the Cosmo and heading north. As we munched our sandwich lunch, Farley told me about the gargantuan drilling rig.

''It was science fiction, like looking down at some fantasy city in outer space. We could only see it dimly through the mist and that made it look all the more alien. It was huge. And it was spooky. And what was even more ghostly was the glimpse we got of the up-ended legs of the rig that overturned last year.''

The thought of all those drowned men didn't improve my spirits on the flight to Bodø. The air was turbulent for the entire three hours and the seat-belt signal remained on while squalls and updraughts made the plane lurch and leap. Clouds obscured the famous view of fiords and mountains. I had always wanted to see this coast, but from the deck of a ship. Now I sank into my seat and daydreamed about snow-covered mountains and the picturesque fishing villages that were hidden somewhere beneath us. It still didn't help me to relax. Every time the plane jumped and jerked, so did my heart. I clutched the arm rest of my seat or else Farley's hand while he, as unconcerned as a baby, managed to fall asleep. Mark MacGuigan had retreated behind his black eye-shade. Lily's eyes were closed. Even Ed, who never dozes in the afternoon, had put down the book he was reading and appeared to be napping too. But I was just as alert as I hoped the captain was.

We landed at Bodø at five-thirty in the afternoon.

190

Fifty miles north of the Arctic Circle the late afternoon sunshine looked like high noon further south. The place was breathtakingly beautiful and the sight of it quickly made me forget the awful flight we had endured to get there. To the east of us we could see a range of jagged mountains with snow-covered peaks. To the west, a string of majestic islands loomed offshore in an ultramarine ocean. This, at last, was the Norway of the tourist brochures.

Bodø is primarily a fishing town and a railway terminal but it also has a large NATO base nearby and that was the reason we were visiting this community. The Norwegian military were our drivers for the motorcade from the civilian airport to our mid-town hotel. It was a relief to be on the ground again and the ten-minute drive gave me a chance to take in my new surroundings. As always, there was the unexpected — cattle were grazing in green pastures. There were even fields of winter wheat. No such agriculture is possible at the same latitude in Canada. Moose survive, not cows. Norway's good fortune is that most of the western coastline is washed by a branch of the Gulf Stream from Mexico. Without it, northern Norway would resemble Ellesmere Island and would be hospitable only to hunter-gatherers and not to farmers.

Like Rovaniemi in Finland, Bodø had been totally destroyed by Hitler's army forty years earlier. It was solidly rebuilt afterwards with efficient-looking public buildings and neat houses. The Polar Hotel was brand new, fourteen storeys high and by far the most imposing building in the town.

The entire twelfth floor of the hotel had been reserved for the twenty-six of us who were touring northern Norway. This was a chummy arrangement since, with no other hotel guests near us, we claimed

191

the corridors as our territory too. It also simplified the security arrangements and the detectives posted at the stairway and the elevator seemed less of an intrusion.

However, once in our room, I caved in. I sat on the edge of the bed, realizing that, for the first time on this demanding expedition, I simply couldn't go on with the show. It was the fourteenth day since we had left Canada. The turbulent flight — for a white-knuckle flyer like me — had been the last straw. My legs felt weak and my head was throbbing. And now we had an unexpected aggravation because an unscheduled reception was going to usurp the one free hour we had been anticipating. Lily and I were told we had just ten minutes to get ready to go up to the roof lounge to meet the wives of the big guns of Bodø. We bemoaned our fate together, wondering how we could avoid it. This extra reception seemed totally unnecessary to us since we would be meeting these same women, together with their husbands, later that evening at dinner.

Bernie St. Laurent hovered in the doorway worrying about how to deal with an incipient rebellion. It wasn't his fault that one more event had been tacked on to our crowded day but it was his responsibility to advise Ed or Lily when something was changed or added. He couldn't actually order Her Excellency to go to the gathering. He hoped to persuade her — but how? He looked, with mute appeal, at Farley.

"I'll make a deal," Farley suggested to Lily. "Claire is totally wiped out, but I'll volunteer to go along as lady-in-waiting. That way I can spring you in fifteen minutes."

"Fifteen? Guaranteed?" asked Lily skeptically.

"Promise. Just a token appearance."

192

Bernie looked infinitely relieved.

"Farley, my ever-ready lady-in-waiting," said Lily with a straight face. Her sense of humour always surfaced when the world looked dark. "Just call me an equal-opportunity employer." And off they went.

Ed meanwhile had been carried off by a possé of military helicopters to inspect the nearby NATO base where a Canadian Air Force unit was taking part in a training exercise. As I lay on my bed with my eyes closed, I could hear the ominous THUD-THUD-THUD-THUD-THUD as half a dozen of those ungainly machines chugged up, up, and away. And then I fell asleep.

By dinner time I had found the strength to face another roomful of strangers and another marathon of eating. An informal party was to be staged in our honour by Mr. Bjorn Bruland, the Norwegian Minister of Defence, at a hotel several miles out in the country. I didn't expect to find, in a place as remote as Bodø, a large restaurant that was even more remote, but the world is still full of surprises.

The Schreyers were borne off in a chauffeured car and the rest of us travelled in a chartered bus. It took about half an hour to reach our destination at Saltstraumen — Salt River — and a young Norwegian Air Force officer named Harald (a popular name in Norway) had been assigned to point out the interesting sights along the way. It was soon evident that being a tour guide was not exactly his forte.

"Over there is a fish-freezing plant," said Harald blandly.

We turned to look at it. It looked like fish plants everywhere.

"These are the homes of people who live here," he continued as we drove past a row of bungalows on the road that led out beyond the town.

193

He was silent for quite a while. Then he added apologetically, "Not much more to say about Bodø."

"Yay, Harald!" Peter Bregg called encouragingly from the back of the bus.

The rest of us applauded. Harald looked embarrassed. None of us wanted to hear a litany of facts and figures anyway. For the rest of the trip Harald said very little and we were free to look at the mountains and the harbours, which was the best memory we would carry home with us. In Norwegian harbours are some of the world's most modern fishing vessels, but one also sees the picturesque wooden ships that the inshore fishermen use-compact, double-ended boats that closely resemble their ancient Viking forebears.

There was no suburban sprawl once we had left the town behind. Only three per cent of the land in Norway is arable and its use is tightly regulated. Because so much of the country consists of mountains which, however beautiful they may be, do not sustain an economy, the government has iron-clad rules about the location of any building so that valuable farm land will not be nibbled away by subdivisions and shopping plazas.

By the wide Saltstraumen a hotel had been built, principally for sport salmon fishermen. It was a miniature version of one of those extravagantly lovely hotels that the CPR once erected in scenic locations all across Canada.

Pity anyone who didn't like fish. In the dining-room a circular buffet table offered us a choice of one hundred different kinds of fish dishes. There were octopus and squid, lobster and shrimp, salmon in abundance, and more variations on ways to serve herring than I could ever have imagined.

A dozen Norwegian military officers shared this

groaning smörgåsbord with us. I suspect that life on a NATO base in the north of Norway, once the novelty had worn off, might turn out to be pretty dreary. We, at least, provided some new faces in their midst.

As cordial as those majors, colonels, and generals were, I was finding it a limitation to visit a country and only meet people who were at the top. For most travellers it is just the opposite. Random contacts tend to be with hotel clerks, bus drivers, waiters, and shopkeepers. The following day I would be leaving this interesting country and I had yet to meet even one rank-and-file Norwegian, the descendants of the people who had inspired the plays of Henrik Ibsen and the paintings of Edvard Munch.

And I wanted to meet them. Before I left Canada I had been reading a Quebec novel called *Hamlet's Twin*, a story which is set partly in Quebec and partly in Norway. I was still trying to make sense out of author Hubert Aquin's love affair with Norway. To me Norway and Quebec are not very much alike, geographically or historically. But if they do share something besides long winters, who better to ask than the Norwegian Ambassador to Canada, Petter Graver, who was travelling with us. He had much experience with both places.

"I guess you know," I said to him, "that Norway is regarded as a role model for a lot of radical thinkers in Quebec."

"You refer to the 1905 referendum?"

"Premier René Lévesque quotes it as the best example of the way that one nation separated itself from the alleged clutches of another one."

"Yes, he has mentioned this in his speeches. And some scholars from Quebec have come to Norway over the past three or four years to study the events leading to our referendum, the wording and so on.

But I advise them that, historically speaking, it is not quite the same thing. You see we had *been* a nation once in the centuries before Denmark conquered us and then Sweden ruled us in turn. We had our own kings. We have a long, complex history.''

''Most Québécois will tell you the same thing.''

''Mmm. A nation, so they say. But not precisely a nation state.''

''Does a sovereign nation have to have a sovereign to qualify?'' I wondered out loud.

''Not at all. The world is full of sovereign states in which there is no monarchy and no aristocracy.''

''I wonder if they are at greater risk of disappearing?'' I mused.

Close to midnight we returned to our hotel in an airlift of military helicopters. Instead of thirty minutes in a bus, the trip lasted four or five minutes. The flight was blessedly short but I'll long remember it. The choppers lifted us just above the all-night fishermen in the chocolate-coloured river and flew in a noisy convoy only a dozen yards above dusky boulders and dim marshes. There was an eerie half-light that drained the land of its colour. Like the tones of an old sepia photograph, the landscape had turned to shades of grey and beige. The snow on the distant mountains was the colour of old lace and the ocean was as dark as charcoal.

Next morning we all shared an unceremonious breakfast in the hotel coffee shop. As usual, it was served buffet-style, a breakfast arrangement which struck me as being so sensible I'm surprised it hasn't been adopted by hotels everywhere. At a time of day when you may be grumpy, hungover, or in a hurry, you don't have to wait for coffee or anything else. We helped ourselves from a table laden with rolls, jam, fruit, and eggs and a big array of cold meat, fish, and cheese.

Afterwards Farley and I went back up to our room to collect our coats. And there was Jason in the hallway, wandering around with his dressing-gown over his trousers.

"Jay, better hurry," I urged.

"Thirteen minutes till we push off for the airport," Farley said, glancing at his watch.

"Yeah, but look! I haven't got a shirt," he said mournfully, pulling his dressing-gown open like a flasher. I guess it got packed last night . . . somehow . . . and now the luggage has all gone to the airport. I've got my jacket, but no shirt."

No shirt! This was no joke. There was going to be a farewell ceremony at the airstrip and we could scarcely spirit Jason through the line-up of officials and photographers wearing his jacket over . . . nothing. He didn't even have an undershirt.

Ed had already departed in a Canadian Forces DASH-7 aircraft for a private tour of a military base in the mountains near Bardufoss. Lily was still down in the coffee-shop.

"I'll try and find Mr. Nadon," I said, rushing back to the elevator. I felt sure Jean would have a solution, if I could only find him. Luckily he was standing in the hotel lobby when the elevator reached the ground floor.

"What? No shirt at all? But how on earth . . . Mon Dieu! Wait . . . I think I saw some shops downstairs," he said and dashed down a stairway that led to the lower level of the hotel.

It was great good luck for Jason that there was a men's wear shop in the hotel concourse that was open at 8:30 in the morning.

In the midst of the flags and flashbulbs at the

airport, Jason looked quite presentable in his new shirt — and a new tie that Jean had also bought for him.

In minutes we were off and heading still further north for Tromsø. When we had reached cruising altitude, Lily came down the aisle.

"Mr. Nadon, you saved the day! You deserve a medal."

"Ah, Madame," he replied with a deprecating gesture. "All in my day's work."

"You're too modest," Lily said. "You've saved the situation more than once."

"You know, Jean," I added, "you should write an article about all the near-disasters you must have avoided in your years at Rideau Hall. All those visiting kings and emperors . . . all those grand occasions . . ."

"Indeed, Madame," he replied gravely, "I could fill a book but unfortunately after it was published I would have to go and live in Argentina!"

Tromsø is one of the most northerly cities in the world and the natural setting is spectacular. Massive mountains crowd close to the sea. Gaily painted houses cling to the steeply sloping landscape. Tidy little fishing-boats bob about in the harbour and, on that cool, clear day, the sea was as blue as ink. At latitude 69.5 degrees north, Tromsø is one of those places that lie at the end of the highway and the end of the rainbow.

The only trouble with places renowned for their great beauty is that everyone beats a path to their doorsteps. From the moment we left our plane and boarded a small bus, we could see that Tromsø was a different quintal of fish from the straightforward little town of Bodø.

The first clue that one is in a tourist town is the

forest of signs that say "No Trespassing" and "Private" — in English. Other signs pointed the way to campgrounds. A large German cruise ship was moored down at the pier. And souvenir shops seemed to be everywhere.

Because the governor general was not with us, our visit to Tromsø was classed as unofficial. However, we did have the wife of the governor general in our midst so we could not slip into the city without some fanfare. The mayor met us at the airport and introduced us to four officials and a tour guide who were going to show us around.

Of all the aggravations that vex travellers everywhere, a boring tour guide ranks high on the list. As our chartered mini-bus proceeded through the narrow streets along the waterfront, we had to listen to the spiel of a very humourless woman. We would be stuck with her for the day. Her presence was a reminder to me that, when the ball was over, Cinderella Mowat would have to return to being an ordinary tourist, subject once again to the slings and arrows of outrageous folly.

With the bus's sound system turned up to full volume, our guide imperiously directed our attention to practically every old building in Tromsø. The driver periodically stopped the bus and we were forced to listen to contrived stories that must have been written by someone in the Norwegian Tourist Ministry to embellish local mythology. On we drove, our ears ringing with silly tales about trolls and gnomes. At one point, the guide, like a short-tempered school teacher, even chastized us for talking at the back of the bus. Tromsø grew less appealing by the minute. It was a relief when we finally pulled up outside the Peppermill Restaurant.

We had lunch on the second floor of this cosy little

auberge which probably wasn't as old as it appeared to be, but the half-timber decor and chequered table-cloths gave it a nice touch of kitsch.

One of the Norwegians assigned to accompany us in Tromsø was a soft-spoken man with thin sandy hair and a cherubic face. He joined us at our table for lunch, looking somewhat jaded. I wondered how often he had to accompany a group like ours.

"You're with the tourist department, are you?" Farley enquired.

"No. I am the chief of police."

The chief of police, no less. He looked a most unprepossessing cop. Still, his steady gaze suggested he would brook no nonsense.

"Is Tromsø originally your home?" I asked.

"I was born here, yes. And that makes me a minority. When I was a boy this was a small place. A quiet place. Now, it has changed very much," he volunteered.

"In what way?"

"We have forty-five thousand people here now. Most of them grew up in other places. Too many of them have nothing to do. It gives us problems," he sighed.

"Such as . . . ?"

"People come here but there is no job for them and not enough houses to live in. Many are drinking too much alcohol. And some are taking drugs. Selling drugs. Other crimes follow."

The police chief slowly shook his head as he lamented all that had happened to his home town in the span of his own lifetime. He was forty-three.

"There was always such a strong . . ." he groped for the right word, "force, yes, a strong force in our town, in all our towns, when I was a boy. Our parents . . . they were much respected. Now . . ."

200

"I think we would describe that as a sense of community," Farley suggested.

"Yes. Call it that. We do not have this now, not in Tromsø. Not in many places. There are too many strangers," he concluded.

Too many strangers. The world was too much with us, even in northern Norway.

As it turned out, the police chief was one of the two insightful men we met in Tromsø. His version of what this scenic paradise was really like was diametrically opposed to that of our garrulous tour guide. A solid community of reindeer herders and fishermen until a generation ago, Tromsø is now a regional administrative centre filled with bureaucrats, as well as being a mecca for tourists. The chief's story sounded painfully familiar. Traditional ways erode in the wash of newcomers moving in and local people moving away. Even those outsiders laden with all the good will in the world inevitably unsettle the delicate balance that used to keep communities from coming unstuck.

"I suppose tourism does bring in a lot of money," I conceded.

"Oh, yes. As much as fishing. But it also costs us much," he said. "Tourists," he lamented, "are the devil's way of spoiling things."

The devil, however, had apparently not tightened his grip on every aspect of existence in Tromsø. This small city possessed a new and remarkable cathedral. It loomed large on the inland horizon looking rather like an A-frame ski chalet, but on a monumentally larger scale. After lunch our bus tour resumed and we were taken to see it.

One has to admire the spirit of the Lutherans of Tromsø who found the will, and the money, to erect a cathedral in these secular times. Completed in the

201

1960s, this stark building was more welcoming once you stepped inside. The tall triangular wall which formed the reredos was ablaze with an abstract design in blue, red, and gold stained glass. In the unstinting light of this northern latitude, the window cast a warm glow over the pale wood of the pews and the brass liturgical symbols. The organist played a trumpet voluntary composed three hundred years earlier, and those few moments of baroque music brought the building to life.

Finally we visited a small museum at the edge of the city. It was full of artifacts of the ancient culture of the Lapps, or the Sami as they now prefer to be known. Nothing could have interested me more. Until that afternoon the Sami had eluded us—except for a fleeting contact with a few of them in Rovaniemi in Finland. An arctic people, the Sami are generally regarded as the aboriginal inhabitants of far-northern Europe. There are now only about sixty thousand of them thinly spread across the sub-arctic regions of Norway, Sweden, Finland, and the north-west corner of the Soviet Union. About thirty-five thousand live in Norway, the only one of the four countries in which they currently have their own regional parliament.

For the Sami, survival has been difficult. There are many parallels between their recent history and that of the native peoples of Canada, since all of them are being dispossessed of their ancestral ways. In prehistoric times the Sami lived as nomadic societies of hunter-gatherers. As early as four thousand years ago they had evolved into herders of reindeer, but today their old way of life is in abrupt decline.

The problem has little to do with the reindeer themselves or with the market for reindeer meat which is a growing gourmet industry throughout

Europe. The problem has to do with encroaching southerners. More and more of the tundra and alpine regions of Scandinavia, once considered worthless except to the Sami and their herds, is now being taken over for hydro-electric projects, reforestations, mineral exploration, and tourist facilities. With the loss of their ancestral lands, the Sami are losing their identity as a distinct society. Yet somehow they have retained their spirit and in recent years have begun to fight for the founding of a Sami nation which would stretch across the top of Norway, Sweden, Finland, and into the USSR. The odds are against them, but who can predict the future?

Understandably, the Tromsø museum collection had nothing to say about the problems of the contemporary Sami. There were displays of traditional Sami clothing embellished with intricate embroidery. There were photographs and artifacts illustrating the old reindeer herding culture. There was an exhibit of skis. The Sami invented skiing.

"It's almost as if the Sami are already dead and gone," Farley commented.

We trooped back into our bus, heading for the airport, but the tour guide wasn't with us. Her day's work evidently ended at the museum. Peace at last. It gave us a chance to initiate a conversation with a protocol officer from the Norwegian foreign office whose job it was to arrange the visits of foreign VIPs to this region of Norway. He was a pin-striped mandarin but his sensitivity belied his bureaucratic demeanour.

"These coastal communities," he said, "have been profoundly affected by two major events. One is the discovery of offshore oil. The other is the construction of roads in anticipation of an oil boom. You see, in this landscape of mountains and fiords, roads can only be built at a tremendous cost. That uses most of the money that might be available for such things as better houses for people, health care, a new school possibly. The bulk of the public money is spent on the road. Then the people spend much of their own money on cars. I can tell you the people here were more prosperous when they were served by coastal steamers. Once the road arrives, a community begins to disintegrate.''

''Shades of Newfoundland,'' I said.

''Shades of everywhere,'' Farley added.

''Have you the same problem in Canada?'' the protocol man asked.

''In many places, yes. And there's a tendency to fantasize about great wealth from offshore oil, which may never happen. That dream often clouds more fundamental needs. In eastern Canada the fishery is their enduring resource, but that often gets overlooked.''

''It is the same here,'' said the protocol officer. ''Fishing was our economic base for centuries. Only a few are making a living from it now. And all the oil in the world won't replace our old traditions, our community life, which grew around family endeavours such as fishing.''

''Dislocation,'' I sympathized, ''always makes people unhappy.''

''Yes, it does. However, I must tell you,'' he continued gravely, ''that I used to believe we had a disaster here on the north coast. That was a few years ago, before I was assigned to a post in Kuwait. What has happened there because of the discovery of oil is truly terrible. Those people had been living in the Middle Ages. Possibly it was the Dark Ages. Suddenly—there was television. Then roads. Then cars. Also many foreigners coming to live among them in a completely different way. Pooff," he lamented, and rolled his eyes to the sky. "Everything they understood and trusted exploded around them. Now they do not know who they are. And they are angry."

Half an hour after taking off from Tromsø we descended at Andøy in the remote Vesterålen islands. We stayed just long enough to retrieve our governor general, our Minister of External Affairs and three or four generals from Canada and Norway. Andøy looked uninviting, but most places do in the pouring rain. Its airstrip was the site of a military base, an isolated posting. There was nothing to be seen but a barracks-like terminal building, a concrete runway, and an infinity of rock that faded into the haze.

We were on the western extremity of Norway, a place considered strategically important if there is ever a military conflict between the Soviet Union and the United States. Under a commitment made to the North Atlantic Treaty Organization in 1967, Canada is obliged to send five thousand troops to Norway if that country is ever threatened by war. It is one of our two major military commitments in Europe, the other being to Germany. In readiness for the day we hope will never come, contingents of Canadian military personnel are stationed at several Norwegian NATO bases.

During the long flight back to Oslo everyone slept except the crew. Even I managed to assuage my terror and dozed off for a while (a sure sign of exhaustion) though the flight south was just as turbulent as the flight north had been. It was well that we got some rest between Andøy and Oslo because at the airport of the capital city our weary band encountered mild pandemonium. Our luggage had gone astray.

"Don't worry, love," Captain John, who was trying to cope with the impossible, told us. "We'll get it to you somehow before Monday." Monday was the beginning of our state visit to Denmark. "Just say a prayer that H.E. has one dark suit. Some bags went out with *Huron*, but some of them went ahead to Copenhagen. And right now I don't know which."

"And what about *Her* Ex? Or me, for that matter? What are we going to wear to meet the queen of Denmark?"

"Hey, come on. You gals look terrific no matter what you wear," was his less-than-reassuring answer.

"Thanks a lot."

"Happy landings," he called and returned to the hangar and his monumental chore.

Here at Oslo airport our group was dispersing. Some of the External Affairs staff were leaving the tour and returning to Canada, while the rest were flying directly to Copenhagen that night. The military officers who had joined us for the tour of Norway were returning to their bases. The governor general and those of us in the Accompanying Party were sailing in the *Huron* to the Danish city of Århus. No wonder there had been some mistakes in dispatching our bags and boxes.

It was turning out to be one of those days when things go wrong. The helicopter which was to have flown us out to the *Huron* had been grounded with mechanical problems. A second Sea King had been pressed into service and at lift-off she shook like a washing machine in its final cycle. As we thudded south along the Oslofiord, I glanced hopefully at the backs of the heads of the pilot and co-pilot, neither of whom looked to be more than twenty years old. Did they really know where they were going? Rain showers lashed our tiny windows and from time to time we saw flashes of lightning in the distance. Below us there was only water, dark, turbulent water with whitecaps trailing across it like tatting. I noted gloomily that the ocean was growing more stormy the further we got from shore. It crossed my mind that we might not be able to land on the deck of our beleaguered destroyer in that angry sea. The twenty-nine vibrating minutes of the flight felt like twenty-nine years. I wished I had never left home.

It was an enormous relief when we spotted the *Huron* down there, tossing in the ocean swell, but I was absolutely terrified by what followed. We descended, hovered, tilted, circled and then hovered again. For interminable minutes our helicopter hung in mid-air like an oriole's nest, swaying above the deck as the pilot waited for the precise second when the chopper could meet the heaving deck without a catastrophe. Finally we touched down, as gently as a snowflake, and the flight deck crew leapt into action to secure us. We climbed out and scuttled clumsily across the deck beneath the menacing blades. As ever, Commodore Riddell was there in his raincoat, standing at attention to salute the titular head of the Canadian Armed Forces. It's just as well that the media doesn't have the chance to photograph a head of state emerging from a helicopter in a storm. There is simply no gracious way to do it.

Huron plunged away into a south-easterly sea. Down, down, down . . . followed by a long, slow rise like a jerky elevator. Then she reached some invisible summit where she shuddered, paused . . . and then once again began the long descent into the trough.

Luckily I don't get seasick. Nor does Farley. I am so happy on board a ship that if only they had accepted women into the Canadian Coast Guard when I was younger, I might have had a career there. But Lily, our irrepressible prairie Lily, lay in her bunk with her usual spunk at a low ebb. Ed sat in the commodore's armchair manfully trying to read a magazine though it was obviously taking all his determination to stay there. The Brokenhead River of his Manitoba boyhood had never been like this.

Ed and Lily are the most enthusiastic pair of travellers one could find, always ready to investigate what's over the next hill; but the sea, as the saying goes, is not in their blood. To add to their misery that evening, the cook and his staff were knocking themselves out to produce the finest meal they could muster within the confines of the cramped little galley adjoining the commodore's cabin. The whole place was filled with the powerful aroma of food.

"Lily, they're serving dinner now," I told her hesitantly as I tiptoed into her cabin. She propped herself up on her elbows looking as pale as her namesake.

"Maybe you'd just like some soda crackers. Some tea. They can serve it in here," I suggested.

"I should be there," she responded feebly but dutifully. She got up and started looking for her shoes. "I'll be along in a minute," she said. "I just want to comb my hair."

Navy cuisine compensates for its lack of variety by sheer volume. Dinner consisted of five generous courses. Farley and I joined bleary-eyed Lily and stoic Ed around the commodore's table and the steward served the first course. It was cream of asparagus soup, served in wide bowls. As the ship lurched from side to side and plunged from bow to stern, the tide of thick green soup gravitated from one side of the bowl to the other.

"If only it wasn't green," Lily whispered.

I couldn't suppress a laugh.

"It's the old naval initiation rite," said Farley heartlessly. "The entire meal will be green. Just watch — the next course will be pasta pesto. Then a spinach salad. Spumoni ice cream for dessert, followed by Chinese green tea. It's the cook's way of testing us."

"Farley, shut up for Heaven's sake," I ordered as I observed Ed's mighty effort just to stay at the table.

The sound of the throbbing rotor blade on the deck directly above the dining-salon was a welcome interruption. It told us that the other four members of our party, Jason, Bernie St. Laurent, Esmond Butler, and Léopold Amyot—had safely arrived. By then the fog was almost as thick as the soup. There had been some doubt whether the second relay was even going to leave Oslo.

We were three-fifths of the way through what was turning out to be an exhausting state visit. Everyone went to bed early, too tired to think about the missing baggage; too weary even to hear the nocturnal rumbling, clanging, and creaking of our vessel as she thrust her way through a stormy sea towards Denmark.

Denmark

Århus is not the capital of Denmark. It is a medium-sized port city on the east coast of northern Denmark, and the reason *Huron* deposited us there on that peaceful Saturday, rather than at Copenhagen, was that we were in protocol limbo for the weekend.

State arrivals run on banker's hours, Monday to Friday during the business day. Even Friday isn't considered advantageous because by Friday afternoon media people are wrapping up their week's work and have been known to drift away, leaving stories unfiled. So there we were—in Denmark, but not officially *in* Denmark.

Nevertheless, disembarking from a warship decked out with a vice-regal flag and a tangle of ceremonial nautical signals was hardly an anonymous way to arrive. A crowd of curious people had gathered on the quay anyway. There was the ubiquitous line-up of long, black cars. Even without a brass band we must have looked noteworthy.

The city administrator was waiting on the quay,

a fair-haired woman with an aura of efficiency, who wasted no time in herding us into limousines bound for the city hall.

Denmark does not at all resemble the other Nordic countries. It is so much greener and flatter. The trees are bigger and in spring the flowers are more abundant. Travelling from Norway to Denmark in spring had overtones of a trip from northern Ontario to southern Ontario. Denmark even smelled different from its more northerly cousins. It smelled of grass.

By this time I had lost count of all the city halls we had visited. But Århus City Hall was unforgettable. It was an Art Deco treasure, a squarish building full of rounded corners, parallel lines, and recessed lights that at first put me in mind of some grand old movie theatre from the thirties. The City Hall, however, had more class. The architect had left out all the chrome and bakelite and substituted wood instead.

Not many public buildings were constructed in Canada during our impoverished 1930s, but a lot of movie emporia were. An entire generation of us think of Saturday matinées and the smell of popcorn whenever we see a certain kind of glass door with geometric steel bars and semi-circles slanting across it. Though the Bauhaus school of design — from which the trend originated — had its origins in Germany, the Danes adopted it and took it one stage further. For several decades the words "Danish" and "modern" were twin adjectives used to describe an instantly recognizable style.

The semi-circular council chamber was filled with curving rows of pale, practical, wooden chairs and desks normally occupied by the city fathers. We settled into the back row to listen to the inevitable, inconsequential words of welcome. What could the

212

mayor of Århus have to say in welcoming the governor general of Canada which we hadn't already heard a score of times?

A sip of champagne to toast enduring friendliness between Canada and Denmark (which has seldom been in doubt) and we were heading for the next event. The Men's Party sped away to visit the University of Århus which, unlikely as it seemed, contained a Department of Canadian Studies. The ladies got the best of it as usual with a tour of the Old City.

The Old City was a reconstruction, something like Seurasaari in Finland or Upper Canada Village in Ontario. Lily, Jason, and I strolled on cobbled streets, past ornately shuttered buildings with thatched roofs. We stopped to look in the window of a pharmacy full of ancient remedies, and paused in front of a bakery where the aroma of freshly baked bread replaced that of exhaust fumes. For a precious hour there were no cars, no schedule, and no speeches. Mind you, we were far from being alone. The director of this seventeenth-century village led the way, and a squad of very contemporary detectives trailed after us. But by then I had learned to blot them out of my immediate range of vision. Being treated like royalty was no longer awesome nor was it novel. It was work of a sort, mostly pleasant, but still work. And that day, in that comfortable provincial city, our task was easier because real royalty and the circus that surrounds them, weren't present.

"Hey! What the . . . " Jason suddenly yelped.

We turned to look at the normally unflappable Jason.

"Aw, lookit!" he cried indignantly. "Some bird . . . "

A passing gull had splattered a mess all down the sleeve of Jason's navy blue blazer. The director of the

Old City began to laugh, then checked himself to say, "In Denmark we believe that is a sign of good luck!"

"This means you will have an excellent visit in Denmark," his assistant echoed.

"Sure. O.K." Jason grinned manfully, wondering what to do about the mess.

I rummaged in my handbag and found one of those little packages with a moist paper towel in it. No lady-in-waiting should travel without one. I still don't know if being bombed by a bird is truly an indication of good fortune but I was impressed by the reassuring way our hosts had dealt with an awkward situation.

Among the books I had read before we began this tour was one which singled out the Danes as the "jolly" Scandinavians. I don't know how the author arrived at that sweeping generalization. There must, I feel sure, be some jolly Finns, Icelanders, Norwegians, and even a few Swedes. Nevertheless, we had only been in Denmark for about an hour when I remembered that book and made the observation that the men and women who were squiring us around did indeed smile, laugh, and even make jokes more often than their counterparts in the previous three countries.

Our next event was out in the countryside. We were driven beyond the edge of Århus, a city with about the same population as Ottawa. It covered only about half as much ground space yet still looked uncrowded. There was none of the suburban sprawl which is to be found on the perimeter of every Canadian town and city. How do the Europeans do it? How do they manage to pack so many people into those tidy towns which come to a finite end once the farmland begins? Denmark is the most densely populated of the Nordic countries with five million people in a land the size of mainland Nova Scotia. Yet it remains a nation of farms, a land where the madding crowd, in Jutland at least, must have long since emigrated to some other place.

It was here in the north-west of this country that the Jutes (one-third of that fabled triumvirate of Jutes, Angles, and Saxons, the ancestors of almost everyone who claims to be English) took their origins. As well as being blessed with lush farmland and the occasional stand of soaring beech trees, Jutland is also dotted with peat bogs. Because of the preserving qualities of tannic acid in the peat, some remarkable archaeological discoveries have been made in these bogs. Our destination was the Moesgaard Museum, which houses a unique if somewhat grisly collection of mummified corpses excavated from the bogs. In half-a-dozen display cases were the bodies of people who had lived a thousand years ago. They lay curled on their sides as if asleep, with peaceful, shrivelled faces that looked like those of dried-apple dolls. The skin on their arms resembled leather, their fingernails were still attached and so was their hair which the tannic acid had turned a dull auburn. They wore fragments of ragged, homespun clothing.

I was transfixed by these ghostly people who may well have been distantly related to me. The museum director explained that most appeared to have been murdered. One man had his throat slit. Archaeologists conclude that his assailant buried him in a bog about a thousand years ago, presumably hoping that his remains would not be found. And they weren't, until 1961. It is also believed that all the bodies were of ordinary people; this was not the usual display of kings, pharaohs, or saints whose remains had been preserved at great cost.

There is a macabre fascination in viewing the recognizable bodies of people who lived and died a long time ago. When I was a child, my favourite exhibit in the Royal Ontario Museum in Toronto was an Egyptian mummy. No matter what other interesting things my mother took my brother and me to see on rainy Saturday afternoons, I always wanted to look at that desiccated mummy.

We were all awed by this preservation of human history through the medium of peat, but none of us was quite as engrossed as Ed. His fascination with peat in all its manifest forms is limitless.

"Here's something even you haven't thought of, Ed," Farley suggested as the two of them stood side by side gazing at one of the ancient dead. "How about forming a corporation that will guarantee the preservation of a corpse for one thousand years! For a fee, we can bury a family's loved ones in the peat bogs of northern Manitoba. This could be an industry that would change the economic outlook of the whole mid-Canada corridor."

"That," said Ed sardonically, "is the kind of suggestion I'd expect from you. Imaginative, but highly impractical."

The mists of antiquity remained with us at lunch. Adjoining the museum was a restaurant suitably called The Viking, a replica of a tenth-century inn complete with a thatched roof. We were ushered into a rough-hewn log building where we sat on hard benches. In the middle of this windowless space was a smouldering fire. There was no chimney. The smoke—some of it—wafted up through a hole in the roof. The men and women who served the food were wearing sack-like homespun shirts which were just a trifle more dapper than the clothes on the bodies in the museum cases.

We were supplied with knives and spoons, but

not with forks, since they hadn't been invented by the tenth century. The lunch, or whatever it might have been called in the days when Danish pirates were feared all over northern Europe, consisted of salted fish, pickled fish, fish roe, and pork belly, all served as separate courses in wooden bowls. We ate unleavened bread. We were offered whey to drink and then mead. Instead of a salad, we dined on boiled angelica, a celery-like plant which also grows wild in Canada but which no one I know ever eats.

It was not a cuisine I would go out of my way to savour again, but the atmosphere in which we dined was delightful. In the midst of an expedition that was heavy on gold braid and red carpets, The Viking restaurant put us all in a good mood. There's nothing like sticky fingers to bring people together. The Danish protocol officers and archaeologists quickly became our buddies, even though we barely knew their names. I couldn't help but speculate that heads of state might feel a greater rapport with one another if the protocol staff organized picnics for them instead of state banquets.

The next event was in total contrast to what we had just seen. When the Nordic tour was being planned, Ed had requested to see a farm. He rarely travels anywhere without ferreting out fundamental facts about local agriculture. He grew up on a farm, but his interest goes far beyond the sentimental. He is well aware, as we all should be, that a nation that cannot feed its people will always be vulnerable.

Leaving Moesgaard, our cars purred along the smooth, paved highways of rural Denmark for half an hour. The landscape looked a lot like southern England. I was travelling with Lily and Jason. Lily and I were glad of the opportunity just to relax and watch all this greenery flit by, but Jason was getting bored. For a while he amused himself by calculating the height of the queen of Denmark.

Every Dane we met wanted to tell us something about Queen Margrethe II whom we were soon to meet. That she was charming and intelligent was axiomatic. Other reports centred around her astounding intellect, her energy, the fact that she smoked a lot, and her height.

"Very tall, oh yes. She must be at least 175 centimetres," one protocol officer told us.

I didn't know how tall that was, but Jason, who was familiar with both systems of measurement, figured it out.

"She's either five-eleven or six feet tall," he announced.

"And they tell me she wears high heels too," Lily added. "Goodness, she must be even taller than Ed."

We turned off the highway into a private tree-lined road. Our briefing-book told us that the name of the farm we were about to visit was Frijsenborg Castle and, in addition to viewing the farm, we would also be taking tea with the owners, Count and Countess Weddell. Their rank should have given me a clue as to what we were about to encounter but I was stunned by the reality.

The driveway into Frijsenborg meandered through acres of lawns bordered with hedges and geometrically arranged flowerbeds. At the door of a mansion of the sort of you see in magazines like *Connoisseur* and *Queen*, Count and Countess Weddell were waiting for us under a colonnaded, corniced portico. In front of them, poised to greet us, were two small children dressed in Little Bo-Peep clothes. They looked like Gainsborough's Blue Boy and Walt Disney's Snow White. A pretty young nanny in a dark dress and a starched white apron and cap looked as if she belonged on stage. Until that day, I would not have believed there were any families who dressed like this outside of illustrations in old-fashioned books for children.

"Hello there. How are you?" said Léopold, who was first off the mark to greet the appealing little girl and boy. They smiled, almost curtsied, and then shyly backed into their nanny's skirt.

"Your grandchildren are charming," said Léopold admiringly as he shook hands with the count.

"Our *children*," the count sternly corrected him. "They are twins, five years old."

Very rarely was Léopold caught off guard but this had been an easy error to make. The count, a handsome man with grey hair, must have been at least seventy years old, and the countess was probably in her middle forties.

The house and the children's clothes might have belonged to the nineteenth century but Countess Weddell was every inch a modern woman. From the outset it was clear that she was in charge of everything, including, I suspect, her husband. Slender, with dark hair neatly coiffed and wearing a navy-blue silk dress with matching pumps, she would not have looked out of place seated behind the president's desk of some big company. Running that estate was probably comparable to running a corporation.

The countess led us inside their vast house where we marched along a wide hallway with a chequerboard marble floor, past an elegant table inlaid with malachite, a desk ornamented with mother-of-pearl, beneath a gallery of paintings in gilded frames. I tried to peek into some of the adjoining rooms but no polite loitering was possible as we were hurried on through into the garden.

Lawns of manicured green stretched away into the middle distance, outlined with pathways of crushed white stone and beds of brilliant flowers. Sculpted shrubberies and evergreen trees dotted this totally planned landscape, at the centre of which stood a spectacular fountain with a quartet of bronze female statues robed in Grecian togas. The water trickled over their ample proportions and down into a round pool. This, I daydreamed, is the sort of garden I would have if I were very rich, along with a team of gardeners to look after it.

And this was only the garden. The "farm," which encompassed another four hundred acres, was sufficiently distant that its noises and smells didn't intrude into this pastoral idyll. However, the *raison d'être* for the farm was very much in the foreground: two enormous bulls held in tight rein by a couple of farm workers stood snorting below us at the foot of a flight of stone steps that divided the lower garden from the upper one.

The Weddells were in the business of breeding prize bulls and this pair of fidgeting behemoths had pedigrees as aristocratic as the Weddells themselves. Their production of sperm for artificial insemination was as valuable as rubies.

I am from the city but I have always enjoyed agricultural fairs. I marvel at the weight and force of farm animals. I love to see the colours of rare roosters and the plump contours of prize vegetables. Nevertheless I simply couldn't think of any appropriate comment to make to the count and countess about their prize bulls. In fact, it was impossible to find anything at all to say to these people whose assets probably exceeded the annual budget of the province of Prince Edward Island. *Nice place you've got here.* No: better to say nothing at all. Oddly, it had been easier to talk with kings; they were somehow less intimidating, perhaps because they seemed less personally possessed of their outrageous wealth. I avoided the front line and left the conversational ball entirely to Ed and Lily. (They, at least, had both grown up on farms although scarcely such farms as this.)

While we dallied, Peter Bregg took photographs of us dawdling in front of the glorious fountain, the statues, and the roses, until finally the countess steered us all back inside the mansion. At this point, the twins were escorted off-stage by their uniformed nanny. Somewhere amid the forty or fifty rooms of the castle the children would no doubt have a nice place to play, far from nosy strangers.

Our destination was an exquisite drawing-room, about fifty feet square, with a high, ornamented ceiling that rivalled those of the king of Norway. When a room has been so furnished that every last chair, table, carpet, doorknob, lamp, and ashtray is the finest money can buy, then the only place remaining on which to display one's wealth has to be the ceiling, and this one was covered with rosebuds and angels.

Two large round tables had been set for afternoon tea. They bore lace cloths, floral arrangements from the garden, and heirloom china platters loaded with scones and cakes. Nothing could have been more welcome than tea that afternoon because all the salted fish we had eaten at The Viking restaurant had left us with a terrible thirst. Two footmen wearing white ties and white gloves were kept busy pouring from the silver teapots while we gulped down the tea from dainty little cups.

Genuine aristocrats always know something about art because they inherit so much of it. There must have been fifty paintings hanging in that room alone, occupying every inch of the wall space that

221

hadn't been already claimed by the doors and windows. Our western civilization tends to embellish a room this way, in a display of wealth that we perceive as tasteful. Yet how cluttered that room would have looked to a Japanese eye accustomed to seeing a ceremonial room distinguished by only one carefully chosen object of beauty. How vulgar it would have appeared to an Islamic eye more familiar with lofty rooms with tiled walls and patterned carpets and no furniture at all.

Most of the paintings were portraits of worthy Weddell ancestors. A few depicted the Danish countryside painted in the drab tones of the early nineteenth century. The brightest picture showed the countryside covered in snow.

"Yes, that is Frijsenborg in the winter," explained the countess, noting my interest. "The wind from the sea blows the snow right across the plain. Jutland can be very cold."

My preconceived images of Denmark didn't include blizzards. To me Denmark was green pastures and blue cheese, along with Søren Kierkegaard and the stories of Hans Christian Andersen. Despite all the books, magazines, and films that flick past us, we never quite perceive the reality of an unknown land. There are millions of people in the world who, when they hear the word Canada, think only of snow, while I had never considered that the Danes would ever be snowbound. But then, I also hadn't imagined that Denmark included people like Count and Countess Weddell.

"We don't use this room at all in winter. It takes a week to get it warm. We have only ancient fireplaces in this part of the house," she explained, gesturing towards a walk-in chimney corner that looked like the sort of place in which the Little Match Girl might have hoped to sit.

"We have a shortage of portrait painters in Canada . . . regrettably," interjected Esmond Butler, who was also scanning the gallery. This was one of Esmond's concerns because every departing governor general must have his portrait painted before he leaves the office.

"Truly?" asked the countess. "It is the same in Europe. At one time there were so many. Now there are only a handful of good ones. We had Annigoni do ours," she added as casually as if she'd been giving us the name of her hairdresser. "But I can tell you it took far too long. He was here for six weeks."

"Ah yes. Annigoni," Esmond repeated. He was impressed.

Pietro Annigoni was the Italian painter whose reputation soared after he painted an innovative portrait of Queen Elizabeth in 1955. I suspect most people in the Commonwealth have seen a version of it at one time or another. In it the youthful queen stands crownless, wrapped in a dramatic dark cape with only one medal on it, gazing nobly and a little wistfully into the distance. It's a portrait much loved by the designers of biscuit tins and commemorative china plates.

"I've always admired Annigoni's work," I said, dropping a hint. I was dying to see what sort of job he had done with the count and countess. "Admired" was stretching the point, but I am at least interested in the magic realism of the man's work.

"Come and see them then," she suggested to Esmond and me.

Leaving the others to chat about bulls and gardens, we followed the countess to yet another sitting-

223

room. It was extravagant too but smaller and contained a television set and a big rumpled couch that looked as if people actually sat on it. There was a fireplace above which hung the two portraits of the count and countess. They were smaller than I had expected and both the Weddells had been painted to look as unblemished and purposeful as Queen Elizabeth. Portrait painting is a dying art. The price is high and few people care to spend so much time sitting still while the artist works. The photographer and the camera now occupy the niche that was once held by painters of distinguished faces.

"Six weeks," the countess said with some irritation, "and during that time he drank two bottles of red wine every single day."

When our convoy of Mercedes and Volvos rolled slowly down the private road and out towards the highway, I turned and looked back at the fantasy that was Frijsenborg Castle. The twins were standing under the portico waving a contrived farewell while nanny, in her Edwardian uniform, stood protectively behind them. We waved back as our car turned a corner, and then the scene was gone.

"That was unreal," I said to Lily.

"Did you have the feeling you were in a movie?" she asked.

"Yes," I laughed. "And it was an old British movie with an Agatha Christie plot starring Alastair Sim. I think it was the one where the butler was the culprit."

It was now late in the afternoon and we still had a long drive ahead of us. We were to traverse the mainland of Denmark from north-west to south-east, so we settled into the lush upholstery and tried to cat-nap. Lily can doze off easily when she travels and that day even Jason fell asleep. I tried but I couldn't.

For one thing, I didn't want to miss any of Denmark as it slipped by. And for another, I was hypnotized by the style in which we were travelling.

Usually our journeys in a fleet of limousines, flanked by police, were short. This one continued at high speed for almost ninety miles — ninety miles in which all traffic was stopped so we could swoosh past unhindered. I was in the second car. The lead car carried Ed and Farley and an aide-de-camp, and ahead of them was a pair of motorcycle policemen who rode with the kind of authority bikers dream about. It was a power trip of the sort we all long for when we're stuck in bumper-to-bumper traffic.

A second pair of motorcycle policemen sped ahead to make sure that each intersection was blocked by the local constabulary, and all oncoming traffic halted to let us hurry through. On and on we sped, past farms and villages, past rotund cattle and curious people who turned to stare as we swished by on our princely journey. It was an exhilarating trip.

Every corner of Denmark, except for the occasional marsh or woods, appears to have been put to use for some kind of agriculture. I am not an economist but there has to be a strong connection between the productivity of the land and any country's continued prosperity. Despite the industrial revolution, the technocratic age, and complex networks of aircraft and ships that can move food around the world, it is still axiomatic that poor soil means poverty and fertile soil brings affluence.

Besides being a wealthy country, Denmark also remains a rural country. Travelling across Jutland we saw many small villages and the outskirts of a couple of towns but we didn't pass through a single city. It was seven o'clock when we reached our destination on the south coast of the island province of Fyn. Falsled Kro (*kro* means inn), where we were to spend our only free evening in Denmark, consisted of a series of long, low, thatched-roof buildings surrounding a central courtyard. We were down the road from an ancient village in one direction, and the seashore in the other. This was the ideal place for us to drop anchor. What's more, the Falsled Kro restaurant, we were assured, was one of the finest in all of Europe.

I cared not a whit about that. On our travels we had not been lacking in extraordinary cuisine. What we were missing most was sleep, and nothing looked quite so appealing as the eiderdown on the bed in our slope-ceilinged room.

Jason couldn't shake a lingering cold. Ed was suffering from a sore throat and felt as if he were coming down with something. Lily had a headache, and the rest of us were hanging on by our fingernails. It was May 30. Being up front for thirteen days and nights, with almost no private time, was turning out to be much more wearing than I could have imagined — until I tried it.

Ed went to bed right after dinner, which was rare for him since his energies tend to soar in the evening. It was a sure sign that he was nearing the end of his tether. Farley managed to persuade him to cancel the first of the events that was scheduled for the next morning, a 9:00 a.m. visit to a museum of ship models. That way he could sleep for a full twelve hours. Convincing him that he should forego that one minor event was not easy. Justifying the cancellation to Esmond Butler was more difficult still.

"But you must realize the people who run that museum have been anticipating a visit from His Excellency for two or three months. They've undoubtedly gone to a lot of trouble — perhaps had

226

the building painted, cleaned, and polished everything. We simply can't cancel a visit by the governor
general,'' Esmond informed Farley.

''But Ed is . . . oops, His Ex is sick, dammit. One
little museum can't be of earth-shattering importance. At nine o'clock on a Sunday morning it's more
important he stay asleep,'' Farley insisted.

''We confirmed the visit with the director two
days ago,'' Esmond said firmly.

''And it could be the straw that breaks the camel's
back. It isn't worth it. Look, he has to meet the queen
on Monday. We don't want him arriving in an ambul-
ance,'' Farley persisted.

Esmond sighed. ''Well, I suppose I could go
instead. And Major Sangster. Make an appearance
on H.E.'s behalf. We can't possibly let the event take
place without someone showing up,'' he said,
accepting the inevitable.

After dinner, when we should have been in our
own beds, Lily, Farley, and I couldn't resist taking
one short stroll. The twilight had melded with the
fog and our surroundings had taken on a grey, myst-
ical mood. No matter how tired I was, I always
wanted to see our surroundings for myself. At the
bottom of the lawn, near the sea, someone from the
hotel staff had built a bonfire so that any guest who
wanted to savour the night could do so without shivering. Bernie St. Laurent, just back from a mile of
jogging, joined us. We sat silently by the fire enjoying
the sound of the waves, the flames, and the kind of
spooky evening that would have suited Hamlet.

Everything was so tranquil we felt we were miles
from anywhere, except for one thing—the dogs.

Danish security rivalled that of Sweden in its vig-
ilance. Along with the usual bunch of uniformed and
plainclothes police, a posse of four Alsatian dogs had

been assigned to guard the inn, and us, that night. While we were at the campfire, we could hear the dogs whining inside a police van parked nearby. Farley wandered over to chat with the officer in charge. The dogs were big and not the least bit friendly. Their handler told him that at midnight they would be released to patrol the grounds and that it wouldn't be safe for us to go near them. We took the warning seriously and made sure we were snug in our beds long before the witching hour.

We could hear the lulling sound of the sea as we drifted into sleep curled up snugly under the downy bedclothes. That, and the dogs' chorale. They howled and growled throughout the night, evidently imagining terrorists everywhere. I am very fond of dogs and the sound of distant barking doesn't usually disturb me. But I wondered about the other guests at Falsled Kro. Were they annoyed that they had to share their holiday with a party of people who were being guarded by killer dogs? Or would they be secretly thrilled? Maybe it was the highlight of their vacation, an anecdote they could tell their friends when they got home. *Yes, he must have been very important, that Governor of Canada. Police everywhere. Even dogs to guard him.* Guarding him from what we shall never know.

Sunday morning most of us slept until nine or ten o'clock, emerging to sit in the sunshine in the courtyard and nibble croissants. Sunday was the last day of May and, for the first time, it felt like summer. Both Ed and Jason were much better. Lily felt restored. And I sensed that I would find the strength to make it through to the end. One more queen to go. There was light at the end of the tunnel. Our night of rustic seclusion had done the trick. We all would have liked to have stayed at Falsled Kro for a week—even one more day would have been divine, but our schedule was utterly unrelenting.

Not far from the inn we came to the compact little city of Odense where Hans Christian Andersen once lived. He was neither rich nor famous during his lifetime. He was, in fact, an actor who hadn't enjoyed much success on the stage and so had turned to writing to eke out a living. The fairy tales he wrote in the last century are known to millions of people in dozens of languages. Even the titles are household words: "The Ugly Duckling", "The Little Match Girl", "The Red Shoes." The statue of the Little Mermaid, which is Denmark's most recognizable symbol, was inspired by one of his stories.

Andersen's house in Odense is now a museum, and that was our immediate destination. It was a small, plain dwelling, meagerly furnished with wooden tables and chairs but crammed with books and manuscripts. Andersen must have been a worse packrat than I am when it comes to keeping all the miscellaneous clippings and notes I think I am going to use as reference material—some day. Understandably, I am interested in seeing the homes of historic authors. I find it encouraging to look at the ordinary surroundings in which most writers have lived and to know where great thoughts and the writing of timeless prose took place.

In a small garden behind the house a reception had been arranged for the governor general by the Odense branch of the Danish Canadian Society. I had no idea such a society even existed. Most of its members were Danes who had lived in Canada for varying lengths of time.

Gatherings in gardens are a treat for people who travel in delegations. We had to spend so much time inside places: airplanes, ships, hotels, and even those fantastic palaces. Ambling around in the same garden where a frustrated actor once invented stories about mermaids and match-sellers made me feel closer to the man than looking at the relics in his house.

"Hello," I said to a young couple who had brought their small daughter. "Where are you from?"

"We live in Nyborg. It is near Odense. But we did live in Vancouver for two years. It was beautiful," said the man.

"We miss it sometimes," added his wife wistfully.

"We had happy times there. We used to ski often," he reminisced.

"But we came back here to be near our families."

"There's no place like home," I agreed.

"Yet we again think that we want to leave."

"Oh. And will you go back to Vancouver?"

"It's so far," she sighed. "We think that we may move to Norway instead. If we can find work. We want to live in some place where we can breathe."

"Everything around here is . . . " he shrugged as he groped for the best word—"It is owned."

"We once thought we might move to Finland," she added, "but their language is so difficult."

I understood what they were trying to tell me. For them the landscape of Denmark was without mysteries and it lacked challenges. There are no stretches of trackless wilderness. The few lakes are small and the rivers are what we would call creeks. Apart from the sea, the kind of untrammelled space Canadians take for granted is almost nonexistent in fastidiously cultivated Denmark. To some extent, it is within reach of people who live in Norway, Sweden, Finland, and Iceland. Citizens of any of the five Nordic countries are free to emigrate from one to the other with a minimum of red tape, but they are still faced with the obstacles of finding jobs and housing in whatever country they choose.

Later that day we flew from Odense to the city of Roskilde. There, twenty-five miles west of Copenhagen, we found ourselves once more being the visiting firemen in a city hall. Since it was a Sunday afternoon I dare say the mayor and councillors would have preferred to be doing something else but they had dutifully showed up so that we could all listen to another round of lacklustre speeches.

There was one benefit from those ritualistic words: they gave me a chance to just look around. This city hall had been built in the late nineteenth century and the semi-circular council chamber was a cosier space than its Bauhaus counterpart back in Århus. The windows had Italianate arches, and the wood and wallpaper were very dark. A row of brass desk lamps added a scholarly glow to the room where politicians gathered. There was an enormous tiled fireplace, even bigger than the one we had seen in Countess Weddell's parlour. I tried to imagine the Roskilde city council sitting by the glowing embers on some winter evening while they wrestled with their concerns about one-way streets, the high cost of garbage collection, or inadequate sewers. Could they ever argue furiously or even hold a grudge as long as the logs sputtered and their toes grew warm? It occurred to me that every council chamber ought to have one. Maybe the mood in the House of Commons would be kindlier if the Canadian government installed one there. People have to sit close together around a fire. We'll never know how much we have lost in terms of fellowship because of the tyranny of central heating.

The champagne reception that followed the speeches would have been forgettable except for one of the councillors. She was about thirty with long blonde hair and she wore a romantic straw hat and a flowery summer dress. While she and Ed were talking she casually mentioned that she was a Marxist, the only one on the council. But she was emphatic that she was a *Danish* Marxist, which was evidently a distinction that mattered.

In Canada it is an electoral impediment to espouse any form of communism. Yet, in what appeared to be a parochial Danish city, an avowed Marxist had been elected to the council and, equally startling, she felt perfectly free to identify her ideology to a visiting head of state.

Near Roskilde there is a museum housing a collection of historic ships. It was called, as you might guess, the Viking Museum. The oldest ships in the collection dated from the tenth century, that same era of derring-do that had produced the resurrected ships we had seen in Oslo, although these ships were much smaller.

The purpose of our visit was the launching of a Canadian-made birchbark canoe that had recently been donated to this museum. What better time to launch it than in the presence of the governor general of Canada? It was carried down to the shore of the Roskilde Fiord by a couple of museum workers and baptized with champagne by Ed.

Commodore Gordon Edwards of the Canadian Navy, who had been assigned to accompany us in Norway and Denmark, volunteered to take it on its maiden voyage. He was impeccably dressed in his summer whites, which looked a little bizarre in a canoe. A big man, he paddled with a strong stroke in a hundred-yard circle while the museum staff watched in admiration.

Nothing would do but Farley had to give it a try too since he has always loved canoes. He took off his jacket but he still looked comical paddling while dressed in a white shirt, dark tie, pin-striped pants, and city shoes. He looked even funnier when, after he had paddled a few hundred yards down the fiord, he couldn't get the canoe turned around again. A rising breeze was rapidly propelling them towards the sea. Using every shred of his strength and agility, Farley finally got the craft reversed and then had to paddle furiously against the current to get back to the landing-place in front of the museum. Everyone applauded.

"Thought we'd lost you," Ed said.

"Not to worry. I would have just paddled to Copenhagen and met you there tomorrow."

"But you had no chart," laughed the museum director.

"All I had to do was keep an eye peeled for the Little Mermaid."

By supper time we were ready to rejoin the *Huron*. She was waiting a few miles off the coast to carry us to Copenhagen for our state arrival the next day. This was to be our final helicopter airlift, a thought that put me into an optimistic frame of mind as I buckled myself once more into the canvas seat. I was almost beginning to enjoy living dangerously — on a sunny day. There wasn't a hint of cloud, wind, or fog. Even *I* felt certain that the pilot would find our ship as she rode peacefully at anchor on the murky waters of the Øresund, the strait separating Denmark and Sweden.

When the governor general travels in any Canadian Navy or Coast Guard vessel, the final evening on board is traditionally given over to a farewell celebration with the crew. On this occasion the gathering meant three consecutive parties, three more energetic events for us at the end of an already eventful day.

It began with an officers' reception on the flight deck, complete with a portable bar, canapés, and the ship's four-piece dance band. As the only two women on board, Lily and I should have been the belles of the ball. However, after our husbands had dutifully waltzed us around the deck a couple of times and then retreated to the bar with the commodore, none of the young officers asked either one of us to dance. I don't know if they were scared of us or simply felt we were too old for them.

The non-dance was followed by supper in the petty officers' ward room, a utilitarian space where the petty officers gathered in their off-duty hours for card games, films, and beer. A buffet of cold meat, salad, bread, and pie had been arranged on a trestle table. It was wholesome but plain, like a supper in a church hall.

I found a seat next to a young, sandy-haired man whose name tag proclaimed his Polish ancestry.

"Actually just my Dad was Polish. Mom was Scottish," he explained. "They were married in Scotland during the war. A few years afterwards they emigrated. I was only a baby at the time. I can't remember any place except Nanaimo where I grew up."

"So you don't speak Polish?"

"Not very much. But my older brother Stan does. In fact, he's in Poland now. He's studying to be a priest."

"In Poland? That's unusual."

"Seeing as he had the language, the church wanted him to complete his training there. Then when he comes back to Canada he can work with a Polish parish. Mom and Dad will be really glad when he's home. So will I. I was considered a security risk because of Stan."

"But why? Surely a priest . . . "

"Because of him going to Poland. Communist country," he said apologetically.

"But a seminary is hardly a hotbed of communist ideology."

"Oh, they got it straight eventually. Otherwise I wouldn't be up there in the operations room," he said with some pride, pointing his thumb skyward. His job was in the cerebrum of the ship, a room full of enormously complicated equipment and highly skilled men who made it all work. He talked about his job with the same verve and sense of purpose I had heard from Harold Gear, the helicopter pilot. Whatever limitations the Canadian navy may have in size or in public perception, it does not lack enthusiastic personnel.

After the pie, Ed, Lily, Farley, and I were ushered down to a still-lower deck for coffee in the seamen's mess. This low-ceilinged room was where the seamen spent their free time. It was crowded and smoky and we could feel the pulsing of the ship's engine.

The men stood in line to shake hands with us. Curiously, they seemed at ease with this formality, possibly more comfortable with it than if we had tried to circulate among them randomly.

Each seaman wore his last name on a plastic badge: a Landry and a LeBlanc from New Brunswick; a McDonald, a McNeil, and a Cormier from Cape Breton Island; another McDonald from Winnipeg; a

Parsons and an O'Brien from Newfoundland, and a Belanger from Quebec. One man bore the last name of Maracle, a family name shared by half the people on the Indian reserve near Deseronto, Ontario. Luckily I had once been there and Seaman Maracle was quite impressed that I knew where his home was, even before he could tell me.

The atmosphere in this mess had a happy, down-home flavour. If only it hadn't been the ninth event of a long day we would have lingered, maybe joined the guys in a game of darts. But the next morning would bring another round of full-scale pomp and pageantry, together with a new royal family. Sensibly, if reluctantly, we headed for our bunks.

On an idyllic summer morning HMCS *Huron* sailed proudly into Copenhagen harbour. Our stalwart head of state was out there on the bridge ready to receive the salute, but the rest of us were below decks in a state of consternation. Our distress was twofold. Not only had our missing luggage failed to arrive but Léopold had learned that the Danish protocol office was only going to give us a nineteen-gun salute — *two* cheers for the governor general of Canada, in effect. The view of their mandarins was that the governor general of Canada was not a true head of state but merely the representative of Queen Elizabeth of Great Britain and was therefore not entitled to full ceremonial honours. Our protocol staff was fit to be tied.

It might appear to be a trifling matter whether an ancient cannon on a Danish headland is fired twenty-one or nineteen times on a particular morning. Who would be counting anyway? But there was a principle at stake. What the Danes would be saying to all Canadians and to the rest of the world was that, in their opinion, the British government still had jurisdiction over us and we were not a fully sovereign state. Sweden, Finland, and Norway had given us full ceremonial recognition but the Danes doubted our authenticity.

Throughout the weekend there had been a lot of urgent phone calls between our staff at the Canadian Embassy in Copenhagen and the officers of the protocol division of the Danish foreign office, but the outcome of these deliberations was not known to those of us aboard the *Huron*. As soon as I heard, and felt, the first salvo from the saluting battery, I began counting: . . . 16 . . . 17 . . . 18 . . . 19. Suspense! Then, finally, 20 and then 21! Hooray! We had convinced Denmark that, some fifty years after the Statute of Westminster and one hundred and fourteen years after Confederation, we were no longer an appendage of England.

Lily and I felt like a pair of shipwrecked princesses that morning as we tried to achieve some semblance of style from our fragmented wardrobes. Fortunately we wear the same dress size. The garment bag containing both of my coats had gone astray but we figured that Lily's navy-blue jacket wouldn't look too incongruous over my purple dress. Lily borrowed one of my scarves and a pair of gloves and lamented the absence of her favourite shoes.

Only one piece of Ed's luggage had failed to show up, the bag containing all his clean shirts. No one else on board had any spare shirts that were large enough to fit him, so he would simply have to meet the queen of Denmark wearing yesterday's shirt.

However, the worst sartorial disasters fell on Farley and on Captain St. Laurent. The bag that held both Farley's dark blue suits was missing, leaving him with only his camel's hair jacket and brown slacks, totally unacceptable for a state occasion. There was nothing to be done but leave him out of the arrival and smuggle him ashore after the Accompanying Party had left the ship. Like someone in disgrace, he would have to sail to the quay in a proletarian motorboat with the remaining baggage. Far from being disheartened, he was quite looking forward to the prospect.

"Ship ahoy, love!" he crowed. "I'm going to town with the fleet!"

The only insurmountable problem was that Bernie St. Laurent's dress uniform had vanished. His red coat, bearskin hat, and ceremonial sword were nowhere on board. This was a catastrophe because Bernie, in his resplendent uniform, was a vital Canadian ingredient in the ceremony of presenting the two heads of state one to another. This was especially important in Denmark since they had been so grudging in acknowledging Canada's status in the first place. They may not have even realized that we have our own military and a whole host of traditions that go with it. This was the one place where we needed to make a spectacle of ourselves.

Esmond and Léopold were desperately rehearsing a new version of the ceremony, sans Bernie, as our ship was being secured to Buoy Number 2 in Copenhagen harbour, right on schedule at 11 a.m. We now had exactly twenty-two minutes until the queen of Denmark's barge would arrive to take us ashore. At this crucial juncture, a small grey motorboat rumbled alongside us and within seconds a dozen suitcases and garment bags were passed aboard.

Somewhere in some royal Danish closet, Captain John — our man on shore — had found the missing bags and hired a speedboat to deliver them to us. The day was saved! Bernie's uniform was found. Even Farley's uniform, his pin-striped suit, had returned to haunt him. He was the only one who was disappointed: he had been looking forward to arriving at the back door of the palace on top of a van-load of luggage. Ed disappeared to don a clean shirt while I rushed back to our cabin to help Farley unpack.

"Holy Mother . . . !"

I could hear Bernie cursing under his breath in the next cabin.

"You okay, Bernie?"

"Eccch! Look what happened!" he sputtered.

His crimson uniform jacket had fallen off the hanger inside the bag and had spent the weekend in a heap at the bottom. His relief had turned to dismay. How could he represent his regiment and his country wearing a rumpled coat?

"I'll bet the iron is still warm! Let me have that jacket!" I cried, grabbing it and bolting for the ladder to run to the steward's pantry on the next deck. By then I had become quite adept at climbing that ladder, even wearing high-heeled shoes.

The iron with which I had so recently pressed my silk dress was barely lukewarm. I plugged it back in and, with fourteen precious minutes to go, began assaulting the ridges on the serge jacket.

I was not making much headway when the chief steward, Petty Officer Halverson, appeared and took over the job. His strong arm pressed the jacket into presentable shape in jig time. By 11:22 a.m. Bernie had buttoned himself in, donned his fur hat and his sword and looked as if he were ready to take command of Denmark. When the royal barge arrived alongside *Huron* moments later, we all descended the boarding stairs as serenely as if nothing unsettling had happened at all.

239

The royal barge was a motor launch about forty feet long, a masterpiece of mahogany and brass. She looked like the ancestor of those venerable launches that well-to-do cottagers on the Muskoka Lakes used to own. Except for the crew. She was commanded by a silver-haired admiral of the fleet, whose uniform was so outrageous that Bernie's looked almost drab by comparison. The admiral, in a dark-blue jacket awash in medals, gold braid, and glittering epaulets, also wore a fussy, plumed hat. I would never have believed anyone still dressed that way anywhere in the world except in the Ice Capades. I tried not to stare at him. His three-man crew wore middy shirts of the sort little girls wore to school when I was a child.

We settled ourselves on leather seats in the cabin as the powerful engines gurgled into action. With all flags flying on both *Huron* and the royal barge, and with admiral, commodore, and captain saluting and bosun pipes shrilling, we headed towards the shore and Queen Margrethe. I felt a lump in my throat leaving the *Huron* for the last time.

Copenhagen harbour is quite lovely, I have since concluded from looking at photographs of it. Although the voyage from the ship to the shore lasted eighteen minutes, I don't remember seeing a thing. I was too distraught, concerned with regaining my composure after our frantic morning and with studying the briefing-book and the Order of the Cars. I was also trying to memorize the names of the prime minister of Denmark, the lord mayor of Copenhagen, and the Danish lady-in-waiting.

Esmond was giving Ed some final information about the inspection of the guard of honour — something to do with whether it was going to be done from the right to the left, or the left to the right. Such things are never left to chance: a head of state must not appear uncertain about which way he or she is heading.

The royal barge glided alongside a wharf festooned with bunting. A company of soldiers stood stiffly to attention, while close beside them a military band was poised for action. On a flag-draped platform before them stood the queen.

There is no mistaking the queen of Denmark. She *is* six feet tall and *does* wear high-heeled shoes, which brings her gaze up to the level of her handsome consort, Prince Henrik, who stands a towering six-feet-four. Queen Margrethe and Prince Henrik can be spotted in any crowd. They are taller even than the policemen who surround them.

The flags of both Canada and Denmark are red and white. Perhaps that was the reason the queen was dressed entirely in blue, royal blue, a colour that set her apart like a sapphire. It was the perfect complement to all those flags. The hem of her matching coat and dress just grazed her knees so her shapely legs were highly visible. But it was her unrestrained smile that held everyone's attention. As we shook hands with her she looked at each of us as if she was truly glad we had come. When she trotted off with our governor general to inspect the Royal Life Guards she managed to look as though she were enjoying the splendid moment too, even though she had likely lost count of the number of times she had done this before.

Farley and I had been assigned to ride with the wife of the court chamberlain, Mrs. Christensen, a rather stern-looking woman in her sixties. As we left the quayside, I turned to catch one more glimpse of what had been, if very briefly, a grand pageant. However, now that the military had moved off and the cars had departed, the quay looked abandoned. There had not been many spectators to share our glorious arrival.

"The Copenhagen newspapers are on strike, all ten of them," explained Mrs. Christensen, as if reading my thoughts. "What a shame more people could not have known of your arrival. Still, they will see it on television tonight."

We sped along a highway that skirted downtown Copenhagen and then on through a suburb where people carrying shopping bags and pushing strollers stopped at the sight of the queen's cavalcade. There was a 45-minute drive ahead of us to the queen's summer residence at Fredensborg, too long a time to spend in conversation about the weather. Fortunately we didn't have to. Mrs. Christensen had arranged to ride with us because she had somehow discovered that we had something in common. She had spent nineteen years living in Greenland when her husband served in the Greenland department of the Danish civil service. He had eventually become the governor. When he finally returned home he became chamberlain to Her Majesty the Queen.

Both Farley and I have long been aficionados of the people and culture of Greenland, that fascinating near-nation that is Canada's next-door neighbour. Once a Danish colony, then a province, it now has sovereignty association with Denmark. It didn't take long before we were engrossed in a discussion about the prospects for success of the recently established Home Rule government. Arctic buffs always find something to say to one another. Mrs. Christensen had even read one of Farley's books. What's more, she told us, so had the queen.

As the cars reached the private road leading in to Fredensborg Palace, the queen waved a graceful, gloved hand to a clutch of people waiting outside the ornate iron gates. Our parade drove on into a cobbled courtyard the size of a soccer field. A cavalry officer in a Wagnerian uniform shouted a command. The mounted guard of honour raised their shining swords in salute. Thirty dark horses stood patiently at attention.

"By Jove," said Farley. "This looks like home."

The palace surrounded the great courtyard on three sides yet, as palaces go, it was not a monumental building. This was, after all, merely the queen's summer home, although the Danish royal family is so fond of it they have all but abandoned their much grander palace in downtown Copenhagen. It was easy to see why they liked this one. We were miles out in the country and the view was as green as Ireland. Once all the queen's horses and all the queen's men had trotted off, we could hear birds singing everywhere. Fredensborg looked, if not exactly unpretentious, at least welcoming. Apart from a tall, central tower, most of the palace was only two-and-a-half storeys high. It had a white stucco exterior, an array of symmetrical square windows and a row of tiny dormers peeping from under a sloping copper roof. I envied any servant who slept up there and could wake up to this Normanesque splendour every morning.

The queen remained in the entrance hall with us, casually took off her gloves and chatted with Ed and Lily until a footman arrived to escort them to their suite. Just as Farley and I were about to set off for our quarters in the care of another footman, the queen turned, smiled warmly, and said something to us about not minding the prince's collection. Neither of us quite understood what she meant but we smiled back anyway.

We followed the servant up a wide staircase and then along an echoing hallway. We crossed a broad mezzanine which overlooked the Domed Hall — an atrium the size of a basketball court. Vast Renaissance paintings adorned the walls; a carpet-size tapestry of the royal family's coat of arms hung from the alabaster balustrade; marble cherubs were poised atop the doorways which, two storeys below us, opened upon a black-and-white, inlaid marble floor. On we went down another corridor until the footman opened the door of the King Christian Suite and ushered us in.

"Good God! What have we here?" Farley exclaimed.

"Wow!" I echoed.

We stood and stared. The antechamber of the suite, a room the size of a high-school classroom, was filled wall-to-wall with spears, masks and all sorts and sizes of carvings from Africa and Greenland. Here was a jungle of mahogany elephants, ebony gazelles, ivory bears and statues of men and women of remarkable proportions. Zebra skin rugs covered the floor, and scattered about were a few safari chairs, perhaps for the convenience of visitors who might be overwhelmed by their surroundings.

So this was Prince Henrik's collection. We wondered if he had become bored with kitschy little Danish mermaids and had decided to make a statement about himself.

This antechamber was only one of four enormous rooms in our suite. The other three were decorated and furnished in the fashion I had by then come to expect in palace interiors, predictable but pleasing Chippendale chairs, Oriental rugs, French Provincial tables, and a surfeit of portraits of past members of

244

the family. Royal families collect larger-than-life portraits of their ancestors the way ordinary families collect shoeboxes full of snapshots.

This suite—the ultimate in a journey full of ultimates—had two bedrooms, the larger of which contained a huge bed in which Winston Churchill had once slept. The sitting-room, whose brocaded walls were the colour of gold, contained a desk as big as a dining-room table at which, one can only guess, Churchill may have written postcards home, as doubtless a lot of kings and princes had done before him, and we would do after him. There was a generous supply of notepaper and envelopes embossed with the royal Danish coat of arms. Letters are mailed free of charge for guests who stay in palaces (as they are from Rideau Hall in Ottawa). The temptation to sit down and write to everyone I knew was curtailed only by the shortage of time.

Farley opened one of the casement windows in the sitting-room. Below us was an immense circular lawn with a solitary statue in the middle of it. There was only one living soul to be seen, and that was Peter Bregg, our photographer.

He spotted us and waved.

"Hey. Stay put for a minute," he called and proceeded to snap pictures of us.

"Don't you move either!" I called back, rapidly unearthing my own camera. "You look like a little lost prince down there!" He did indeed look as lonely as the statue, a foreshortened figure in a pin-striped suit against an infinity of green.

Peter always worked in a three-piece suit, which is not the traditional garb of news photographers. He claimed he was less likely to be shooed away by court chamberlains or detectives if he dressed the same way they did. Having grown up in the unremarkable city of Hull, Quebec, Peter had lived in several other countries and was a veteran of seventeen years as a Canadian Press photographer. He had covered such diverse historic events as the funeral of Haile Selassie and the inauguration of American President Jimmy Carter. He would soon be photographing the London wedding of Prince Charles and Lady Diana. Photographers are rarely photographed in any of the exotic surroundings in which they sometimes work so I took several snapshots of Peter. Then we had to hurry downstairs for the *en famille* luncheon.

By then I had decided that this ritual was the nicest part of a state visit. There were seldom more than thirty-five people in attendance so the heads of state and their entourages had a chance to become acquainted informally. These luncheons usually revealed a few personal tidbits about the monarch, or president, as the case might be; not gossip, but facets of their personal lives that transformed them from icons into real people.

"This is such an unusual room," I remarked to the gentleman on my left who was from the Danish Department of Protocol.

"Yes," he agreed. "The queen and the prince travelled to China last year." He nodded in the direction of a matched pair of antique Chinese cupboards dominating the end wall. "Those cupboards are new here. The queen has extraordinary taste and likes to bring home interesting souvenirs when she goes abroad."

The two rare cupboards were black lacquerware and inlaid with swirling ivory dragons. To continue the theme, three of the walls of the room had been covered in red wallpaper bearing embossed dragons.

But what made the room so striking was the fourth wall: it was painted bright yellow and hung with a collection of thirty-six antique plates that were as Danish as blue cheese. It seemed a wildly improbable combination of cultures and colours, and it worked beautifully.

"The queen has an excellent eye when it comes to colour," my companion continued. "All the royal residences have undergone much renovation in recent years. Her Majesty does her own decorating."

"She does it herself?" I asked in amazement, trying to picture this statuesque woman, who was sitting across the table from me, with a bucket of paint in one hand and a paintbrush in the other.

"She plans each room personally. Her style is unique."

"I'll say it is."

How I admired Queen Margrethe's gumption in taking on the challenge of decorating not one but two entire palaces. It would be an endless task. A building the size of Fredensborg would always have a room, or ten rooms, crying out for a touch of paint or some new curtains. Of course, there would be plenty of paid hands, and the sky would be the limit in her circumstances. Nothing would stand in the way of her creative ideas, except all those royal portraits. Come to think of it, maybe that was why they were in the guest rooms. That's where everybody's unwanted paintings end their days.

I warmed to this queen more and more. An imaginative decorator, an arctic traveller, a reader of Farley Mowat books. She even had a visible human frailty: she really did smoke a lot. The list of her accomplishments reads like the curriculum vitae of a Rhodes scholar. She holds university degrees in archaeology,

economics, and theology. She is an accomplished artist who has illustrated a dozen books for both children and adults. She has even designed a Danish
postage stamp. And in her spare time, if you can
imagine that she has any, she and Prince Henrik have
translated a Simone de Beauvoir novel into Danish.

The prince assumed the Danish form of his name
on his marriage to the queen. Born in France in 1934,
Count Henri de Laborde de Monpezat was working
with the French embassy in London in 1966 when he
met the then Danish crown princess. They have both
been heard to say it was love at first sight. They were
married the following year and within two more
years two sons were born to them. At long last Jason
Schreyer had someone to chum around with since
Prince Frederick was the same age as he was, and
Prince Joachim only a year younger.

Queen Margrethe was born in 1940 and baptized
Alexandrine Thorhildur Ingrid, the eldest of the
three daughters of the late King Frederick IX and
Queen Ingrid, now the queen mother. She was only
thirty-one years old in 1972 when she ascended to
the throne, the first woman in 560 years of Danish
history to become the monarch. (Queen Margrethe I
reigned from 1375 to 1412.) The Danes claim to have
the world's oldest continuous monarchy reaching
back one thousand years, almost a century earlier
than the British royal lineage.

After lunch, we gathered in a long, elegant room
for coffee. A dozen French doors opened onto an
ethereal garden and the panorama of a distant forest.
The queen and the prince moved casually among
their guests, as approachable as the Swedish royals
had been unapproachable. In the grand yet homey
palace at Fredensborg, one could almost forget who
the hostess was, but not quite. I experienced a

momentary flutter of butterflies in my stomach when the queen strode purposefully towards Farley and me. What was I going to say to this accomplished lady?

She had two things on her mind. She had lost her lighter and wondered if either of us could light her cigarette. Farley acted as Little Match Boy and we both lit up to keep the queen company. Then she straightaway opened a discussion on the subject of the ancient Greenlanders. The queen, or someone on her staff, had done her homework and she already knew that Farley had written extensively about the Norse voyages.

"How is it," she asked pointedly, "that the Greenland settlers could have built seaworthy ships when there is no ship timber in Greenland?"

"Your Majesty, historians don't agree about the answer to that," Farley began cautiously.

"Ah, but historians seldom agree about anything!" laughed the queen.

Farley took courage. "Personally, I've concluded that the Greenland Norse were sailing to Canada for wood, and a lot of other useful things, for hundreds of years. Of course, that's a minority opinion."

"I like minority opinions," said the queen frankly.

Queen Margrethe has visited Greenland eight times. Farley and I have been there three times ourselves. While we may not have had an awful lot to say to her about Denmark, nor the queen about Canada, we were able to meet one another half-way over our shared interest in Greenland. The conversation bounced along through two cigarettes and I realized that I was genuinely enjoying the queen's company, and not the least bit frightened.

Home Rule had been granted to the fifty-four

thousand citizens of Greenland in 1979, an arrangement that takes them one stage closer to becoming an independent country. While the radicals in this former colony would like to be rid of the Danish connection altogether, I couldn't help but speculate that they were going to lose something valuable if they severed their affiliation with their monarch. But of course it isn't their sensitive, well-informed queen who angers them. It's the bureaucrats in the Greenland Department of the Danish civil service, and the indignity of being controlled by people from afar.

When the queen moved on, I felt bold enough to talk with the prince consort. He was out on the terrace beyond the French doors talking with Ed. When I sidled over to them they were chatting, the way neighbours do, about the homey subject of pruning trees.

"It's an extravagance now," the prince was saying. "We leave them to grow naturally."

"Imagine that, Claire," Ed turned to me. "At one time they used to clip and prune that entire forest out there."

"Yes, you see, that way the trees were in perfect symmetry," the prince added.

He wasn't referring to shrubs and hedges. This garden, which looked like an enormous set design for *Swan Lake*, ended where a deciduous forest began. A hundred acres of hardwood trees flanked a central avenue which led the eye to tiny Lake Esrum about a kilometre away. At least it looked tiny by Canadian standards. Perhaps the Danes thought it was large. Back in the days when peasants worked for pennies, an army of them had once sawed and clipped the entire woods so that each tree was the same size and shape.

"I don't quite understand why they would have

wanted it that way," I remarked, "but I'm from Canada and I prefer the way trees look *au naturel*."

"Ah. The eternal question," observed the prince, "is why we always try to improve on nature."

Personable Prince Henrik, who in his private life prefers the name Henri with which he was born, is an intellectual, a man who was once destined for a major career in the diplomatic service of France. But falling in love with the Danish crown princess changed the course of his life. In the space of just over a year Count Henri de Laborde de Monpezat became a public figure, a husband, a Dane, a Lutheran, and a prince. He quickly learned Danish and his work has since revolved around his more public role as a goodwill ambassador on Denmark's behalf. He speaks many languages, including Vietnamese, the language of what used to be French Indo-China which was, surprisingly, where he grew up. His parents had business interests there. The philosophies of the Far East have been his life-long obsession, along with his collection of primitive art.

I was told that one of his ambitions was to spend a year in some remote corner of the world—in Africa or China perhaps—far from western civilization and close to nature. I doubt somehow that he will ever have the opportunity to do so, but the chance to gaze at and amble through that now-liberated forest any time he felt like it would be better than nothing.

Because Fredensborg palace was so far from Copenhagen, there had not been enough time that afternoon to schedule any events in the city. Consequently we had two glorious free hours. After lunch Farley stretched out on the big bed and started making notes about his impressions of Denmark. I tackled the never-ending chore of unpacking, sorting and packing clothes. Jason went swimming with the entire royal family in their pool, the only one of us invited to do so.

The palace concierge had told me that a hairdresser was available for Lily and for me. "The hairdresser will come to your suite shortly, Madame, but when the queen is ready for him please understand that he must leave."

Of course. I knew my place in the hierarchy, and patiently waited my turn.

The hairdresser arrived with the air of a man in a hurry. Young, lanky and fair-haired, he was dressed all in white, wore running shoes and spoke only Danish. In our bathroom he gave me a rapid-fire shampoo and then began working energetically with his portable hair-dryer.

The bathroom had been decorated in another of the queen's magnificent designs. A big, high-ceilinged room, it was covered with bold wallpaper in stripes of gold, wine, and royal blue. Along with the usual plumbing fixtures, the room contained a chaise-longue, an ancient wooden armoire on which garlands of tiny flowers had been hand-painted, and a couple of small chairs ornamented with the same folksy motifs.

The athletic hairdresser had managed to create one half of a coiffure when a footman arrived to tell him that the queen was ready for him. He literally stopped in mid-air, gathered his equipment, pointed to his watch to indicate that he would return in an hour, and took off.

My hair looked lopsided but I wasn't going to let the opportunity pass to take a walk in that Eden-like garden. The first obstacle was how to get there. Despite the relatively informal atmosphere, Farley and I still didn't feel that it was proper for us to simply wander the palace at will. Gingerly we descended the white marble stairway, then headed along a corridor which appeared to lead towards the back of the palace. We stopped to get our bearings in front of a window. In a small courtyard below us a peacock was strutting his stuff in front of his mousey mate. Just then a young lad of twelve or thirteen, dressed in jeans, came walking towards us.

"Excuse me," Farley asked him. "Can you tell me how we can get out of here?"

He grinned. "It isn't easy, sir. I've been trying for years."

It dawned on us that this was either Prince Frederick or Prince Joachim. Just a year apart in age, they were the same height. One was fair like his mother and one dark like his father, but they looked remarkably alike.

"This man will show you," he said courteously as a footman came hurrying around a corner.

"The garden? This way please," he said, and led us through a series of adjoining drawing-rooms. All of a sudden dogs started barking and running towards us. Not police dogs this time. These were the queen's pets, two boisterous little dachshunds and one elderly hound. The footman tried to shoo them away but we insisted that we would be happy to take them for a walk. He shrugged, with a look on his face that said, "take them if you want, they drive me nuts," and ushered us all out through a pair of French doors into the garden.

The dogs stayed with us for only a few minutes before returning to the palace and to what they must have believed was their larger responsibility, guarding the royal family. We did see them again several times as they meandered around their extraordinary home at whim. Despite the stateliness of it all, this palace was fundamentally the home of a family: a

253

man and a woman and their children, their pets, and their visiting friends. Sometimes it was hard to remember that.

I've no idea whether Queen Margrethe ever took time to wander in her remarkable garden where the fountains splashed, the hedges led you from one lovely corner to another and the grass was as dense as velvet. I daydreamed that, if I were the queen, I would spend every afternoon there.

Or would I? Lily once lamented that she and Ed and the children rarely spent any time in the gardens at Rideau Hall. She said there were always gardeners out there going about their work, or other staff members traversing the pathways on their way to some endeavour. Somebody always seemed to be erecting a marquee or taking it down. Apart from one corner where there was some deck furniture, the rest of the Rideau Hall formal gardens didn't feel like the kind of private space where a family might enjoy itself. Lily often escorted visitors past the showy flower beds, down the path to the miniature totem pole and over the gravestones of departed dogs of past governors general. Many times I had walked around there by myself, speculating that it wouldn't be a bad life at all to work as a gardener in such a place, a thought that again crossed my mind in the gardens of Fredensborg. Maybe gardeners are the ones who get the real satisfaction from these nurtured acres.

Cursing my luck that I hadn't been born with curly hair, I soon had to return to the palace for the other half of my hairdresser's appointment. I almost bumped into Ed as he came out through the French doors, chased by the same trio of dogs.

"Isn't this a great place to get some fresh air!" I exclaimed.

"Just what I'm after," he replied.

"Look, there goes Farley. He's on his way down to that lake. Hang on; I'll call him. Yoo hoooo!" I called softly. It didn't seem right to use full volume in a palace garden.

Farley heard me, turned, and waited for Ed. Soon the two of them were striding off in the direction of the miniature lake.

Of the six hundred acres of palace grounds, about four hundred are devoted to a working farm. One unpublicized luxury most royal persons enjoy is food that comes fresh from their own farms and market gardens. That used to be the birthright of nearly everyone in the agrarian world. Now only the affluent or the resourceful can taste free-range poultry, freshly laid eggs, farmer's cream, or tomatoes that haven't spent their ripening season in a tractor-trailer en route from Mexico.

To get out of the formal gardens, Ed and Farley discovered they had to climb a fence. Then they made their way through the forest down to the lake, which was the home of many swans and ducks. As they climbed back over the same fence on their return, they were confronted by two men wearing suits with conspicuous bulges under their left arms.

"Be careful. There's barbed wire, sir," one of them said politely.

It hadn't occurred to either of them that they had been under surveillance the whole time.

By the time my hair had finally been set and sprayed, it was too late to return to the garden, so I wandered down the hallway to examine my more immediate surroundings. I found Lily doing the same thing. With her elbows on the alabaster balustrade she was absorbed in watching the preparations for our evening banquet in the Domed Hall two floors below us. Because of the configuration of the atrium we now had the chance to observe how this well-orchestrated fête was put together. Half a dozen florists were carrying huge bouquets hither and yon, fussing over each arrangement to ensure every iris, tulip, and gladiolus was exactly where it should be. A pair of footmen was lugging a heavy wooden box full of silver cutlery and, under the eye of a house steward, five or six others were arranging the place settings. A crew from Danish state television was setting up cameras in strategic locations while three musicians were assembling their music stands. Every person down in the banquet hall looked very busy; the kitchen staff must have been working at fever pitch.

"Just think. They're going to all that trouble just for us," I said.

"Know what we should do?" Lily quipped. "Declare a holiday. Tell them they can just send a sandwich up to our rooms."

"One of those nice Danish open-faced sandwiches."

"After that they can all have a free evening. Go to the movies maybe."

"No way," I laughed. "I want my dinner."

"You're not getting fed up — pardon the pun — with all this?" She gestured to the scene below.

"Not yet. Not with the food, that's for sure. Anyway, I've decided that state dinners are therapy for me. I'm eradicating the memory of all those basements I endured in my childhood."

"Basements?"

"Right. Banquets were always held in basements. Dim church basements. Grey school basements. Why were all our celebrations held underground, back in East York?"

"Come to think of it, I guess they were in Grand-view too," Lily remembered.

"I shouldn't be critical. I suppose nobody had money for anything else in those days but I know I'll never get tired of eating in beautiful surroundings. Where I came from, splendour was presumed to be vaguely sinful. Gluttony was okay though — just as long as you indulged it in an unattractive place."

That evening I was especially curious to see the queen's hair which had been created during the interval between the right and left halves of my own coiffure. Her long hair was swept dramatically upwards to form a cushion for her diamond tiara. It looked quite wonderful, as did everything else about this singular woman. Even if she hadn't been born to be queen I believe she would have become something noteworthy anyway — the prime minister perhaps.

One of the queen's two younger sisters, dark-haired Princess Benedikte, attended the banquet too. Less renowned than Margrethe, she is just as tall and even prettier. She lives in West Germany with her German husband and their three children, and is the only one of the late King Frederick's three daughters who is not a queen. The youngest sister, Queen Anne-Marie, is married to the exiled King Constantine II of Greece and lives in Italy. Including their mother, Queen Mother Ingrid, there are currently three queens in the same family, which makes them unique among modern royalty.

"Good evening," nodded Mr. Ivar Norgaard, a short, balding man seated on my left. "I am the Minister of Finance."

"Oh, that's too bad," I smiled. "We won't have anything to talk about. I'm hopeless when it comes to money."

"Tell me then," he enquired graciously, "what it is that interests you."

I thought for a second. "Right now, I would say food. But as well as that I am interested in baroque music, contemporary art, all sorts of history, and eighteenth-century architecture. And," I added, for fear he would think me an unapproachable snob, "I also like canoeing."

"Ah. And me also. All but the canoe. I have not sailed in such a boat."

Mr. Norgaard had a nice dry wit that carried us through the evening. When I complimented him on his command of English, he said he had learned it in school in Denmark. He told me Denmark expected to be a fully bilingual country within this decade, in Danish and English. The Danes do not fear they will lose their identity by learning English. The number of Danish speakers in the world is small and the number of English speakers large. The educators of Denmark have concluded that every Danish child will benefit in adult life if he or she knows English. English, like it or not, is the first choice of a second language almost everywhere in the industrial world.

Only one question about the economy of Denmark had crossed my mind and Mr. Norgaard was the right man to ask. I wanted to know what percentage of the annual budget of Denmark was spent on the administration of Greenland.

He sighed and thought about it for a moment.

"Too much," he said.

"Then why," I continued tactfully, "has your country maintained the connection for over two centuries?"

He thought about that too. "Responsibility. We cannot abandon them. People must have the facilities of the modern world to survive as a self-governing nation. For example, Greenland does not yet have a university. Their professionals—civil servants, engineers, doctors, and the like — must all be trained abroad, usually in Denmark. When they can educate their own people, at all levels, then nationhood is possible.''

"Why not build a university in Greenland?''

"Universities are very expensive. It takes, I would say, a population of two hundred thousand to support one. Greenland has only fifty-four thousand people. Limited Home Rule is now possible but it will be some years before they can afford a university.''

Denmark in the 1980s has frequently ranked at the top of the prosperity polls conducted by the United Nations. On a scale measuring the availability of health care, education, housing, recreation, and the like, Denmark often takes first place, outranking the other Nordic countries, as well as West Germany, the United States, Canada, and Britain. Not even the Minister of Finance could explain to me, at least not in the time it took to eat dinner, how a mere five million citizens have managed to achieve this. The people of Greenland and the Faeroe Islands, Denmark's only two overseas territories, may be chomping at the bit to gain their independence but as former dependencies that are now maturing into self-governing entities, they could have fared much worse under other colonial overlords.

That night, as I prepared to join my already sleeping husband in the bed where Churchill had once tossed and turned, I couldn't find my nightgown. I consider it an invasion of privacy to have strangers unpack my clothes, however kindly the intention, so whenever I had the time I unpacked and hung things up myself. I thought I had left my nightgown on top of some folded blouses on the dresser but it wasn't there. I searched the armoire among Farley's suits and my dresses but there was no nightie. It wasn't under the pillow and it wasn't in the bathroom. In the end I went to bed without it, hoping I would be up and clothed before the footman arrived with our morning wake-up call.

I found it the next morning. It had been carefully laid out across the pillow of the bed in the *other* bedroom, the one place it hadn't occurred to me to look for it.

Palace luncheons and dinners followed predictable patterns, but the arrangements for breakfast were always different. In Sweden we had munched our croissants in solitude, while in Norway we had shared a big buffet with the entire palace household. At Fredensborg we began the day in company with Ed, Lily, and Jason in their sitting-room, a space so large and richly ornamented that it would have been classed as a ballroom in Canada. Here we were served soft-boiled eggs in porcelain egg cups, each one kept warm under a tiny, quilted egg cosy bearing the embroidered letter ''M'' atop a crown. It was the queen's monogram and she had designed it, although she hadn't embroidered it herself.

June 2, our sixteenth day, was especially complicated. There were several morning events; more in the late afternoon and a banquet in the evening. Since there wasn't going to be time to return to the palace to change for our reciprocal banquet, we had to pack our evening clothes in the morning so that a palace chauffeur could later deliver them to us at a downtown destination.

Two and a half hours in the middle of the day were free and clear. Lily and I couldn't believe our good luck. It was as if we had just learned that the teacher was sick and the rest of the school day had been cancelled.

"Would Her Excellency like a motor tour of Copenhagen during this interval?" the queen's lady-in-waiting asked me.

"Are you kidding?" responded Lily when I relayed the query. After more than two weeks on parade, the last thing she wanted was to spend any more hours in a limousine being driven past intriguing places she would have preferred to see at a pedestrian's pace.

"Thank you," I told Mrs. Anita Van Hauen, "but Her Excellency plans to take a short walking tour of the city."

"I see," she said flatly. "Then a member of the household will be her guide, if she so wishes."

"No thank you. Our travel officer, Major Sangster, has kindly offered to escort us."

What we were really planning was to play hookey.

Our final event of the morning was a visit to a home for the aged. Gedevasevang turned out to be an exemplary facility and I only hope that, by the time I'm ready for one, we will have homes like it in Canada. Built entirely on one floor, it was a bright building with lots of big windows overlooking lawns and shrubberies. The complex had been organized to accommodate every exigency of advancing age. We met people who lived in the residence and others who lived in their own homes but came in daily for meals, health services, and social reasons. Some were in good health while others in wheelchairs needed help. There were units for married couples and rooms for single people; a handicraft room, an exercise room, a physiotherapist, and a travelling library. Pets were allowed, and some cats, a couple of small dogs, and several caged birds were in residence. Arrangements were flexible: there was increased care for people who had been well when they moved in but became disabled later.

If one can judge a society by the way it treats its older citizens, then Denmark gets full marks. By the time we had said farewell to the smiling director and her staff and left the cheery halls of Gedevasevang I felt less depressed about the reality that all of us will grow old, unless we die first.

Then we asked the chauffeur to drive us to the centre of the city and leave us there. He deposited us at the junction of several busy, intersecting roads. On a raised quadrangle we found some public benches and sat down for a minute to get our bearings. Colin Sangster was now faced with the unenviable job of accompanying two women on a window-shopping spree, along with a pair of Danish detectives who had been trailing us all morning and trying to look invisible.

''Would you ladies like one of those hot-dog things?'' Colin asked, noticing that a street vendor was selling something that looked like a cross between a sausage roll and a hot dog. Lily and I both wanted one. We were always hungry.

Colin Sangster was proving to be a wonder, a man who could be either immensely patient or militarily efficient, depending on what the situation called for. On a June noon hour in Copenhagen, hot dogs on a park bench were just what we needed, that and a chance to sit in the sun doing nothing until the spirit moved us. Lily loves outdoor cafés and mediterranean climates. She bears up nobly as her husband, who has a passion for frozen oceans and peat bogs, tends to organize their travels in the general direction of the North Pole.

A plump, fair-haired woman of about sixty was sharing the concrete bench with us. Like us, she was just watching the passing parade of people and automobiles. Hearing us speak to one another in English, she turned and asked me if we were Americans.

"No, Canadians," I replied.

"I was in America for thirty years."

"It must feel like home then," I said.

"But I come from here, from Copenhagen. I went there to work for one year. I stayed. I got married. I had two children. I am on my own now. So I came back here to be near my sisters."

"And how are you finding it, after such a long absence?"

"Well, it's nice to see everything again. But . . . I don't know. I was spoiled living in Minneapolis all those years, I suppose. When I decided to come back to Denmark I thought I would stay for the rest of my life. But I'm not sure. It's very expensive here. You pay so much for what you get. The meals here, the restaurants — they cost far too much."

I didn't know what to say. At that point, I still hadn't seen what a krone looked like, let alone spent one. I just nodded sympathetically.

"And the hotels! Isn't it shocking what they charge? Where are you people staying?"

I didn't have the heart to tell her.

"With friends," I said.

"Well you're lucky."

"Yes," I said. "We are lucky. They have a beautiful home."

Colin had been studying a city map and he led the way to a mall-type street that had been permanently closed to motor traffic. We sauntered along past some tawdry shops, pausing now and then to look in the windows. We soon discovered that, though Colin's map had identified this as the shopping district, the merchandise was almost entirely pornographic. There were a lot of magazines with photographs of writhing naked people on the covers; there were shops selling T-shirts with explicit messages on them, and there were dozens of places where you could buy a massage, a tattoo, or watch a blue movie. It suddenly struck both Lily and me as very funny. What would the queen have said if she could see us now?

I admit to some embarrassment at being seen by the two detectives as I inspected a display of exotic contraceptives. True, they were supposed to remain silent about their work but they were human after all. I didn't want to be the butt of their jokes when they were sitting around later in some police lunchroom.

Say, Jens, you won't believe this but I was assigned to the wife of the Canadian governor general today and do you know what she and her lady-in-waiting wanted to look at? Well—

Colin began rapidly leafing through his guidebook in search of the *other* shopping district. I directed my attention to the pavement ahead of me and felt easier when we turned a corner and found ourselves surrounded by stores displaying Holme Gaard crystal and Georg Jensen jewellery. This was Stroget, Copenhagen's main shopping centre and Europe's longest pedestrian street. We weren't planning to buy any of the merchandise here either. We merely wanted to look at things in our own time. It was such an ordinary pleasure and it was surprising how we had missed this opportunity to browse in the world beyond the limousine. Eventually we sat down at a sidewalk café, ordered a Tuborg, and a sandwich and just watched the world go by instead of having the world watch us.

When our interlude of freedom was over, Lily and Colin Sangster were chauffeured away to join Ed at a reception at the Canadian embassy. I walked one short block to the Continental Hotel, where my evening clothes were waiting for me. I found my way to a large, cluttered reception room on the third floor in time to see three people from our protocol staff as they pored over the seating plan for the night's banquet. It was spread out on a large table like a blueprint.

"Hi, darlin', grab a coffee," offered chummy Captain Dave John, pointing to a percolator in the corner.

I helped myself and then sat down to watch our crew at work. In every capital city they set up a field office in one of the downtown hotels. Here the governor general's speeches were typed, messages from Canada were dealt with, all the accounting was done, changes to the schedule were added to our briefing-books, and the seating plans were arranged.

The seating plan is one of the trickiest jobs in protocol. Long before any guest arrives at a state banquet, his or her name has probably been shuffled on the plan several times. Generally speaking, everyone sits beside a person of the opposite sex. Every effort is made to put each person beside someone who speaks the same language or languages. Each country has its own precedence list which states where a monarch, president, prime minister, cabinet minister, archbishop, or military officer must be placed. The pecking order is inflexible. Career diplomats know what sort of relationship exists between their two countries based on where they sit.

It is the last-minute cancellations and, worse, the no-shows that throw the authors of a seating plan into a panic. If the king or the prime minister hasn't got any pals who are quickly available to fill in, the protocol staff themselves often have to jump in during the final hour to make sure the banquet room is full. Since no guest must ever be left to sit beside an empty chair, typists and speech writers have to be prepared to join the ranks of the lordly for a meal.

"We bring Canadian typewriters and even our own notepaper," Don McKinnon, the comptroller of Government House and of this whole operation, told me. "You might wonder why we bother. But paper and envelopes aren't the same size the world over. Then, on this trip, you'd have the Nordic typewriters with ø, æ and *å*s on the keyboard, and that would confuse a typist who works in English and French. We plan everything months ahead but we still end up with finicky details that have to be changed and decided after we arrive."

This was the same room in which our supply of liquor and wine was kept, under lock and key. When Canada is the host at a banquet overseas, the liquor is generally brought from home. This is done as an economy measure. The price of whisky and other spirits, it should comfort Canadians to know, is much higher in Europe.

I had half an hour to spare before rejoining Lily for a scheduled visit to the Tivoli Gardens. It was always a wise move to rest if there was a chance, since our day wouldn't be over until midnight at the earliest.

"Make yourself at home," said Dave John, tossing me the key to his room. "I'll be stuck here by the phone till six."

The captain's hotel room was also to serve as the

dressing-room where Farley and I would change into our evening clothes. It was small and rather dark, not a room that would hold anyone's attention for more than thirty seconds. I stretched out on the single bed and immediately fell asleep. I didn't wake until 5:30 when Farley arrived.

"What . . . ?" I cried, as he came through the door. "Oh, Lord, I missed it! I slept right through the Tivoli Gardens!"

"Relax. You didn't miss much," Farley reassured me.

"But I was supposed to be there! What did Lily say?"

"Don't worry. Lily was fine. I took over as lady-in-waiting. I even carried her bouquet."

"Thanks," I said, "but damn it, that's a famous place and I've always wanted to see it. Tell me what it was like."

"A lot of phoney baloney," he snorted. "Part circus, part Disneyland. Hot and noisy besides. Not my kind of place."

We took a shower and then changed into our evening clothes in Dave's cramped little room. Later Dave arrived to don his spiffy naval mess kit, a sexy uniform sporting a dark-blue bolero and a black cummerbund. It had the body-hugging contours of the clothes worn by male figure skaters.

Every palace limousine was occupied that evening because seven members of the Danish royal family were going to attend our banquet. Several extra cars had to be rounded up to transport the Canadians. A generous Danish banker had made his Rolls-Royce available and Farley, Dave and I were the ones assigned to ride in it from the Continental Hotel to the Langelinie Pavilion, a swankier hotel where the banquet would soon begin. The chauffeur, who wore a pale-grey uniform that matched the car, ushered us into the velvet depths of the back seat. A group of curious onlookers craned to see three ordinary mortals in full evening regalia depart in such splendid style.

In the banquet room of the Langelinie, our kilted pipe major led the procession to the head table. As he swaggered out of the room, a cabinet minister sitting on my right remarked, ''Such a colourful touch. Did you bring him from Scotland?''

''No indeed. We have our own pipers in Canada. Thousands of them. Most of them have never seen Scotland.''

I had been asked this question about our piper at every reciprocal banquet — in Stockholm, Helsinki, Oslo, and now Copenhagen. Few people in the rest of the world seem to realize that several million Canadians whose origins are classified as ''English'' are actually of Scottish ancestry and that the culture of the Scots has shaped many of our ceremonies. I don't have a drop of Celtic blood myself, but kilts and tartans, St. Andrew's Balls, Burns Dinners, and Scottish dancing are things I take for granted, along with pipers leading parades. I explained this to my Danish dining partner.

''How interesting. I didn't know that,'' he replied with sincerity, ''but I have only been in Canada once and that was rather a long time ago. My stay was very brief. I was actually travelling to the United States.''

''I know just where you were,'' I nodded. ''Gander. Gander, Newfoundland.''

''Why you're right! That's where I was,'' he exclaimed, as pleased as if I had been reading his teacup and got the facts correct.

Oh God. Oh Gander. What a curious image of our country Gander imposed on those countless thousands of European travellers who flew the Atlantic before the advent of the jet age.

The chief justice of the Supreme Court of Denmark, Mr. Hvidt, sat on my left and he was a charmer. He was sixty-nine years old, just one year away from retirement but as vivacious as a boy. We talked mainly about his summer cottage on the south coast of Zealand. He and his wife had spent their holidays there for many years and planned to live in their seaside home once he retired.

"We travel on the train for one hour. After that we take a bus a few kilometres. Then it is just a short distance to walk to our house."

"Couldn't you drive there?" I asked.

"I have never learned to drive a car," he chuckled. "I never wished to learn."

In fact, so he told me, he still rode to work every day on his bicycle. I liked his style. I couldn't imagine a chief justice of the Supreme Court of Canada riding to work on a bike every day. A non-driving Canadian chief justice would be provided with a car and chauffeur as a necessary adjunct to his dignity. But then in Denmark every second person regularly rides a bicycle.

"It sounds like a lovely place to be. Near the sea. A house with a garden. I'd love to see it."

"Then, please, you must come and visit."

"Thank you, but that must wait for another time. Tomorrow we leave for Iceland."

"I will be in Iceland soon myself. The chief justices of Denmark, Sweden, Norway, Finland, and Iceland meet once a year. This year it is Iceland's turn to be the host."

"And what are you going to discuss?"

"The law, of course," he smiled. "What else do five old chief justices have to talk about?"

"Are they the same laws in all five countries?"

"Not exactly. But similar enough so that we have a continuing dialogue among us."

This, our eighth state banquet, was the last one at which royalty would be playing a part. Queen Mother Ingrid sat directly across from me. A tall lady in her seventies, she spent most of the evening talking with Esmond Butler. Her jewellery fascinated me. I had never before seen so many jewels on one person. She wore a diamond tiara, diamond earrings, and several rings on each hand set with a rainbow of sapphires, rubies, and emeralds. She also wore a long necklace composed entirely of diamonds that graduated from the size of *petits-pois* to some as large as my thumbnail. They were so large that they looked —dare I say it—like fakes. Had anyone other than a queen been wearing that many jewels I would have been certain they were rhinestones.

When the banquet ended, no one was in a hurry to leave, least of all the convivial Queen Margrethe who seemed to be having a genuinely good time. During the coffee-and-liqueurs interlude I began to feel a little wistful that the grandeur was almost behind us. Whatever awaited us in Iceland would not be as dazzling as the events of the past weeks. It had been an exciting time as well as an educational one. I had learned how to speak to crowned heads without becoming tongue-tied, not exactly a skill that was going to advance my career but this small achievement mattered to me. What was more enlightening was my new respect for ceremony, for the various rituals that are an intrinsic part of all human encounters. A handshake, an introduction, a smile, or the offering of food are gestures we make to create a bond with strangers. These rituals aren't very different for heads of state except that they are performed on a grand stage where the drama of the encounter can be seen to be unfolding.

Farley appeared beside me. "Guess who I got stuck with?" he muttered.

"Who?"

"The director of the Tivoli Gardens."

"And did you tell him how much you enjoyed all that schlock and glitz?" I laughed.

"No, but it was a hell of a temptation. I told him that Jason loved it, which is true. Jason spent most of the day there with the two little princes."

"That Tivoli place," Bernie St. Laurent interjected, "is so American."

"This party," yawned Farley, who is an incurable morning person, "appears to be going to last all night. What I'd like right now is to go to bed."

Bernie glanced at his watch. "I'll let you in on a secret. I'm going back to the palace now. I have three hours' work ahead of me. Captain John will stay with Their Exs. You want to come too?"

"And just how are we going to do that?" I protested. "We can't traipse past the queen and just wave bye-bye-it's-been-fun."

"Trust me," whispered Bernie, with a conspiratorial grin.

We followed as he eased his way nonchalantly through the crowd towards a swinging door. We sidled through, marched along a short corridor and found ourselves in the hotel kitchen. The staff took no notice of us amid the commotion and clatter as they stacked mountains of dishes. Several flights of back stairs took us down to a fire exit leading to the hotel parking lot. Bernie's proper role in the military was that of a paratrooper. He could always find his way. Darting ahead, he soon found the great, grey Rolls that had delivered us and before the chauffeur had time to get out and greet us, we had all climbed in.

"To the Continental, yah?" the chauffeur asked.

"No. To Fredensborg," said Bernie, a bit surprised that the chauffeur didn't know. We were accustomed to drivers who had been drilled in every move.

"Where, please?" he asked again. He was either having trouble understanding or he didn't believe us.

"The palace," Farley repeated.

"Where the queen lives," I added grandly.

"To the best hotel in Denmark," Bernie turned and winked at me.

Despite Bernie's gold braid, Farley's medals, and my sweeping evening gown, the chauffeur seemed reluctant to drive us there. Half an hour later, as we approached the gilded gates of Fredensborg Palace, he stopped the car.

"The palace . . . " he pointed. "Now . . . is it back to the Continental?"

"Just drive right in," Bernie ordered in his best voice of command.

It's a rare moment when you can instruct the chauffeur of a Rolls-Royce, especially a skeptical one, to drop you off at the queen's front step. At that moment the palace concierge rushed out to open the door for us and greeted us like old friends, which must have quelled the doubts of the banker's chauffeur.

The Rolls streamed away into the night while Farley and I lingered in the silent courtyard, postponing the moment when we would have to say good-night

to wonderland. Then a detective suddenly appeared
and the concierge began hurriedly to pull on his
white gloves. The queen was coming! The detective
had been told, via his insert earphone, that her car
was less than a kilometre away. We realized we
would turn into pumpkins if we didn't get out of
there fast.

We dashed into the palace and raced up the marble stairs. I had to clutch my long skirt in front of me
like a bundle of laundry so I wouldn't trip on it. We
zoomed along the corridor and into our suite, breathless and relieved that our hospitable queen would
never know we had defied the rules and left the party
before she did.

The next morning we piled our luggage into its usual
hillock to be carted away by a team of footmen, then
joined Ed and Lily for breakfast. When this tour
began, it had often seemed to me that we would
never make it as far as Iceland, yet here we were just
a few hours away from our final stop.

"I hope the coffee is this good in Iceland," Lily
remarked as we sipped our first cup of the day.

"And the weather," I added. I already knew
about Iceland's fickle climate.

I scooped another spoonful of gooseberry jam on
my croissant. The jam was made from berries grown
on the grounds of the palace. If this was to be my
final breakfast in a palace, I would be as self-indul-
gent as I wanted.

"Lily, are there scales in your bathroom here?"

"Yes."

"Were you brave enough to step on them?"

"No. Did you?"

"Yes, and you know what? I'm two or three
pounds *lighter* than when I left home."

"Seriously?"

"It must be true," echoed Bernie, who was check-ing off things on a sheaf of papers. "I've lost about five pounds. And Captain John says he's lost seven."

Every one of us had lost weight, despite a daily calorie intake that would have sustained a polar bear. And the only one who had taken any exercise at all was Bernie who occasionally jogged around some palace garden. Our immense expenditure of psychic energy was evidently absorbing all those cream sauces, desserts, and liqueurs as fast as we could put them away.

There was a sudden stir outside the suite. We could hear voices and footsteps. The door stood open and just beyond it we were appalled to see the queen. She was dressed to perfection in a matching coat and dress and a broad-brimmed hat — the sort of clothes a queen wears for an official farewell. She was accom-panied by several people from her household but — heavens above — she was ten minutes early!

Ed, who had been immersed in reading dis-patches from the Department of External Affairs, hurriedly got to his feet and looked apprehensively at his watch. He was still in his shirt sleeves. Bernie, also in his shirt sleeves, rushed to don his tunic. Had something gone wrong with our timing? The Queen must never be kept waiting!

We grabbed assorted jackets, hats, and gloves and followed her and her party down the stairs to the main doorway. But there had been no cause for alarm and we had indeed been running right on schedule. The queen had decided to arrive a little early to have a few informal minutes with her departing guests. She well knew that nothing ever gets said at an airport depar-ture. Those farewells are strictly for the cameras.

I decided to throw caution to the wind and speak to the queen before she spoke to me.

"Your Majesty, we have enjoyed staying in the King Christian Suite and I want to tell you how much I admire your flair in decorating these rooms."

"Ahh," she gave a little laugh. "I hope you didn't object to sleeping beside the prince's collection."

Object? I wouldn't have objected to anything in that palace.

"It was our pleasure," I told her truthfully. "I admired the entire suite including that beautiful bathroom."

"So you liked the Roosky bathroom," she beamed. She was clearly proud of it. Perhaps none of her previous guests had the nerve to compliment her on it. "It is one of my favourites."

As our cavalcade headed for the airport the name she had given the bathroom suddenly clicked. *Roosky*. Of course, the Russian bathroom. It explained the decor of embroidery and hand-painted flowers, the traditional crafts and patterns of Old Russia. It was not, as Farley mirthfully suggested, that the queen was a closet communist. The Danish Royal Family, I seemed to recall, had intermarried with the Romanovs somewhere along the line. Queen Margrethe no doubt had some distant cousins who were Russians.

Until this century, marriageable European princesses were traded around the way hockey players are today. It must have been awful for them. Now this has changed: royal people are more likely to marry someone from their own country, and not necessarily from the aristocracy. In the late twentieth century, when monarchs are retained for symbolic reasons of ceremony and continuity, an heir to a throne may likely marry someone with whom he or she has fallen in love.

Queen Margrethe was the only monarch who personally came to see us off at the airport. At Vaerlose air base the breeze was brisk. Our mutual red-and-white flags quivered over the heads of the Danish guard of honour. Despite my best efforts with my hatpin, I could feel my black straw hat starting to lift. I had to keep one hand on it or it would have blown away. But then, so did the queen with hers. Peter Bregg caught us on film, both clutching our hats with our left hands as we said goodbye.

The plane took off and began to climb. Within minutes cloud cover obscured the lush landscape of Denmark. I wondered if I would ever see it again. And if I did, would I feel the same way about it in more ordinary circumstances? I think most of us on board felt some sense of loss because, for a long time, there wasn't much chatter among our usually sociable team. But maybe it was just late nights taking their toll.

I settled down with a booklet of dull facts about the economy of Iceland. There wasn't another glimpse of land until we passed over the northern tip of Scotland about an hour later. After that the weather changed. The north Atlantic Ocean became brilliantly blue and, long before we reached it, we were able to see the mountains and glaciers of Iceland. When the high, dramatic cliffs of the island's south coast became visible, everyone on board crowded over to the right side of the plane to catch a look. There it was, the westernmost nation in Europe.

The excitement of one more new country spurred us on. We may have been exhausted but we were not jaded. What's more, in a land that is notorious for its stormy weather, it appeared that the sun was going to shine on our parade. We could now smugly believe that we were charmed. All five of our state arrivals had occurred in sunshine. Quickly — find the hat-pins, the lipsticks, the gloves, and the briefing-book. Léopold, where are you? How do we pronounce Finnbogadottir, the name of the president? Get ready. Look out, Iceland! The Canadians are coming!

Iceland

One of the world's largest islands and one of the world's smallest nations, Iceland lies midway between the Old World and the New. It was the last European country to be settled, when Celtic people arrived sometime during the eighth century followed by the Norse in the late ninth century. It is a land of amazing contradictions, not the least of which is the fact that, almost alone among the world's nations, it possesses no armed forces and does not intend to. We were not, therefore, treated to a display of military aerobatics the moment we entered Icelandic air space. At Keflavik airport we were greeted by an unarmed, stolid guard of honour of the Icelandic police. Yet, ironically, in order to enter this, the least militaristic of the western nations, we had to land at an air base operated by the most aggressive one. Keflavik international airport is located within a United States Air Force base that has been in Iceland since the middle of the Second World War. The menacing presence of parked American bombers and fighter aircraft surrounded but did not entirely over-shadow our peaceful mission.

Waiting inside the plane, we listened to the Reyk-javik police band play their hearty rendition of "O Canada." Then we heard the national hymn of Ice-land and I concluded that Canada had won hands down, musically speaking, against all the Nordics. The people of Iceland may be moved to tears when-ever they hear their lugubrious anthem but, in com-parison to its lumbering rhythm, ours sounded downright exciting.

The ritual red carpet looked brighter than ever as we emerged into a day of undiluted arctic sunshine. There wasn't so much as a breath of wind although this was a land famous for it. In the crystalline atmos-phere we could clearly see the snowy cap of a vol-canic mountain a hundred kilometres away. Where was that legendary weather I had warned Lily about? We had transported a load of raincoats and boots across Northern Europe and scarcely even unpacked them. That serene morning we didn't even need our hatpins.

Statistical oddities are the norm in Iceland and the fact that they had the prettiest head of state in all the world in 1981 was just one more pleasant surprise. President Vigdisi Finnbogadottir was a slender blonde with innocent blue eyes and a pert little nose, the kind of face that puts you in mind of Anne of Green Gables. She was forty-nine the year we met her but no one would have taken her for more than thirty-five. Dressed in a dark suit and small white hat, her bearing was tidy and efficient, more like a lawyer than the actress she had once been.

Our arrival was no ordinary event. Because Can-ada was the first country outside the Nordic group ever to pay a state visit to Iceland, I suspect that all of their cabinet ministers and the entire staff from the protocol department were there to greet us. Iceland has only 240,000 people — about half the population of Newfoundland — and it looked as if everyone of any importance had turned out to welcome us. Like many pocket-sized countries, Iceland has often been overlooked in the international diplomatic circus. Neither Great Britain nor the United States, both of whom have had long-standing trade and military agreements with this country, had yet honoured Iceland with a state visit. Our motorcade was long and every car was full.

The paved highway which links Keflavik with Reykjavik, the capital city is not the most scenic route in the country. It crosses a flat, coastal plain strewn with great and small cinder-coloured boulders, the remnants of an ancient lava flow. Travellers who arrive by air get their first real look at Iceland over those lumpy fields. A painter would need gobs of Payne's grey and burnt sienna to capture the pallid tones of this Martian landscape. Yet, scattered among the rocks and lava, we did see a few lonely sheep foraging for random tufts of green grass. The desolate appearance was deceptive.

I was to travel in a car with Esmond Butler and a protocol man from President Finnbogadottir's office. Once we had driven past the chain-link fence surrounding the base, and beyond the American soldiers who grimly guarded their outpost of empire, the three of us got into the inevitable conversation about the weather. Understandably, Icelanders are preoccupied with the subject. "If you don't like our weather, wait five minutes and it will change," they'll tell you knowingly. However, on the June day when Canada came to call, the weather was as intoxicating as gin and it remained so. The sun shone virtually until midnight.

"Tell me . . . " Esmond leaned forward to catch the ear of the protocol man, "how far along would your gardens be at this season?"

There was a pause. The protocol man, who had thin hair and rimless glasses, looked perplexed.

"For instance," Esmond elaborated, "would your roses be out yet?"

"We have roses sometimes. Now, perhaps," he replied vaguely.

"What about vegetables then?" Esmond persisted. He was a keen gardener. "Do you grow peas here? Would they be ready yet?"

Another pause. Then the officer turned around and looked apologetically at Esmond.

"I don't know," he admitted, as if he had been asked for some obscure statistic about his country's gross national product. "I am not interested in gardens. Me, I like mountains and glaciers." He pointed in the direction of Snaefelsjokul, a mountain that looked as if it were floating on the distant horizon, its wisp of volcanic smoke melding with the clouds.

That, I thought, was a sensible preference. All of Iceland lies north of latitude 63 degrees and despite the Gulf Stream, gardening must be a difficult proposition at best. We soon dropped the subject of flowers and vegetable gardens and, for the remainder of the journey, diplomatically talked about volcanoes instead. Active volcanoes with their unpredictable tempers erupt with alarming frequency, so they loom large in the thoughts of every Icelander.

That particular morning I would have liked to have been in the same car as our insatiably curious governor general. For so many years he had wanted to visit this unusual country and I could imagine how pleased he must have been. Because of his initiative Iceland had been made the last stop of our tour. The Department of External Affairs would have been content if we had ended our trip right after Denmark. However, partly because he believed it was only fair that all members of the Nordic group be treated equally by Canada, and partly because of his curiosity about this anomalous place, Ed had convinced the department that Iceland must be included too.

Almost anyone who grows up in Manitoba has met someone of Icelandic descent. The towns of Gimli, Arnes, Hekla — and even a tiny village in the Interlake region named Reykjavik — were all settled by Icelanders during the late nineteenth century. By the year 1900, one-third of the population of Iceland, defeated by volcanic eruptions and crop failures, had migrated to western Canada, most of them to Manitoba.

In 1973, while Ed was the premier of Manitoba, there had been an eruption in the Westmanni Islands near Iceland's south coast. The disastrous effects of the volcano left five thousand people homeless. The province of Manitoba had donated sixteen pre-fabricated houses to help with the resettlement of the unfortunate Westmanni islanders. The houses had been manufactured, ironically, in a factory in the vicinity of Gimli where third-generation Icelandic Canadians had helped to build them. And because there was an abandoned but still usable military airstrip at Gimli, Ed had asked that the Canadian military fly these partly assembled houses to the homeless Icelanders. It was not surprising that the premier, who later became the governor general, had received a heartfelt invitation from the government of Iceland to come for a visit.

Of the five countries on this tour, Iceland was the only one that Farley and I knew reasonably well. We, too, had always been interested in the country. Its early history had been the cornerstone for Farley's book *Westviking*. He had read volumes about its past and its present. We had also spent three weeks there three years earlier. We were not disappointed and promised ourselves that we would return, though never dreaming we would do so in such style.

Our first destination was a luncheon at Bessastadir, the official residence of the president. Located just outside Reykjavik, it is a square, frame mansion situated on the side of a hill overlooking the ocean. Built originally as the summer home of the Danish governor of Iceland when Iceland was a colony, it is now an historic treasure. It is the sort of house that could pass unnoticed in one of the wealthier neighbourhoods of Copenhagen or Halifax, but in Iceland, where all construction is very expensive and where the cityscape is dominated by utilitarian corrugated-iron roofs, Bessastadir stands out like a jewel.

An unpretentious servant took our coats and nonchalantly directed us towards a large reception room. I felt as if I were arriving at the home of some affluent Canadian friend. There was even a guest book on a hall table. The house was exquisitely proportioned in the Danish manner and furnished in the French. From the generous windows we could see both the ocean and the mountains and, on a nearby hill, there was a flock of grazing sheep. A sunroom on the leeward side of the house looked out over a rock garden full of tiny spring flowers, alpine blooms that would surely brighten the president's day whenever the rain obscured the more dramatic view.

President Vigdisi Finnbogadottir is the single parent of an adopted daughter. I don't know if she has ever been married; her last name gave no clue. In Iceland a woman's surname consists of her father's first name and the suffix "dottir." Married or not, she keeps this name for life. Similarly, a son takes his father's first name and the suffix "son." This is their ancient system of nomenclature and not a recent feminist manoeuvre. For a woman, it is her father then, and not her husband, whose name provides the basis of her lifelong identity, a system which is not necessarily as equitable as it initially appears.

In the dining-room my placecard read "Claire Mowat Adstodarkona landstjorafruar." Heaven only knows what that meant, particularly in this country that has no court tradition. Icelandic is a very complicated language which has changed little over the past thousand years. It is ancestral to modern Norwegian and bears more or less the same relationship to it that Anglo-Saxon does to modern English. Because it has remained constant, it is possible for Icelanders to read for themselves the ancient Norse sagas, a legacy of their own literature that has survived the past millennium. Many of them do. In our disembodied culture you would have to be something of a scholar to feel at home reading Chaucer or *Beowulf*, by comparison.

We lunched on *lax*, smoked salmon, the ultimate epicurean delicacy of all the Nordic countries in spring. I never got sick of it. But then no matter what they put in front of me, I devoured it. Right up to the last hour of the tour I was as hungry as if I'd spent my days digging ditches.

None of us was staying overnight at Bessastadir; there wasn't enough room. Everyone, from the governor general down, had been booked into a brand new hotel in the city. It's odd how your recollection of a city can change greatly from one visit to another.

On my first journey to Iceland, it rained every day and my overall impression of Reykjavik was that it was drab — tidy and clean, but without much visual charm. I remembered streets without trees and small houses painted in sombre colours against a background of everlasting grey skies. This time, in sunshine, the whole place looked unexpectedly mediterranean. The terracotta-coloured roofs and pastel walls against the clear blue sky bespoke a city in Portugal or Greece. Only the absence of tall trees reminded me of the northern latitude. Reykjavik is the world's northernmost capital, a medium-sized city of mostly single-family homes, plain schoolyards, small, pleasant parks, and a surprising number of statues. It harbours almost half of the country's population and gives the appearance, at least, of being the epicentre of a classless society. If there are any Icelandic billionaires (many are paper millionaires, but only because of the devaluation of the Icelandic kroner) you see no trace of them. There is no evidence of great wealth nor of shameful poverty.

Since few buildings in Reykjavik exceed two storeys, the eight-storey Saga Hotel loomed over one corner of the city, as visible as a pyramid. In relative terms it probably cost just about as much to build. Without forests for lumber, clay for bricks, or even local cement or building stone, the construction costs of a really large building in Iceland must rival the national debt.

What this country may lack in building materials, however, is balanced by a bonanza of natural energy. There is an abundance of heat for everyone. Most of it comes in the form of hot water that is piped from the innumerable hot springs underlying much of Iceland, directly into bathrooms, radiators, and swimming-pools. There are also mighty waterfalls that are harnessed for electrical energy. Like Canada, Iceland is capable of producing more renewable energy than it needs. In Reykjavik, whose name translates as "smoky harbour," the only air pollution comes from the wispy smoke of a distant and slumbering volcano.

The hotel manager escorted us up to our rooms. Then the Men's Party departed to visit the University of Iceland where a Manuscript Institute houses a famous collection of ancient maps of the new world. That left me free for an hour. I was contemplating going for a walk when the phone rang.

The call was from Njördur Njardvik — novelist, poet, and professor of literature — whom Farley and I had met at a writers' conference in Bulgaria in 1977. We had become fast friends and he had urged us to come and visit his homeland, which we did the following year. Now he was eager to see us again.

Everyone visiting another country should be blessed with a friend like Njördur. He and his charming wife Bera, a teacher of English, enthusiastically introduced us to Iceland, to its intriguing local food, spectacular geography, and cordial people. Their two little daughters, Urdur and Hilde, who were only seven and eight years old at the time, did their best to teach me Icelandic. Children make ideal language coaches because they will repeat words over and over and over until you get them right. I learned a lot of nouns but the grammatical intricacies of old Norse were beyond me.

Njördur arrived at our hotel room shortly after Farley returned.

"So, we meet again!" he exclaimed, giving us both a crushing hug. "But," he added dryly, as he observed our luxurious quarters, our mounds of luggage and all the detectives out in the hall, "under different circumstances this time."

On our previous visit, we had travelled with only one suitcase each and had been grateful for the opportunity to camp out in Njordur's mother's flat on Snorrabraut Street while she, poor lady, was in the hospital. Hotel accommodation in Iceland costs two or three times as much as in Canada.

Njördur is a tall bear of a man with sombre grey eyes, a square face, and thick grey-brown hair. He settled his long legs in the only chair in our room that wasn't cluttered with clothes, gave me a penetrating look, then turned to Farley.

"When you wrote that you were coming back to Iceland you told me that Claire was now a lady-in-waiting."

"That's the job description," I explained. "Basically, it means that I assist the wife of the governor general when she attends official functions. You know — talk to people, remember names, carry the official photograph—"

He started to laugh. "I thought he was saying that you were expecting a baby!"

"No, no, no!" I giggled. "Not waiting *for*. Waiting *on*."

"So. Tell me this. Why do you have a governor general?" he asked.

"Why?"

"Why don't you have a president?"

I sighed. It wasn't going to be easy to explain the intricacies of the Canadian system of government to Njördur. He was a left-wing intellectual and a rebel and, like most Icelanders, was suspicious of anything that smacked of colonialism.

"Umm, let's see. We call our head of state the governor general because — well, because of tradition. That has been the name since the days when we were governed from England."

"So you keep this title to remind you of the authority of the queen of England?" he asked sardonically.

"No. Not the queen. The Crown," Farley tried to explain.

Njördur raised a cynical eyebrow. He failed to make the distinction, and of course he couldn't share the emotion we feel about our own traditions. That's the ingredient which always sounds awkward and illogical when you try to explain your political system to an outsider.

"And who wears this crown?"

"Well, in Canada, no one does really," I replied.

"The crown is a symbol, if you like, of our particular brand of democracy, based on the British one. The crown is the state. But the queen has no power in Canada. None," Farley added.

"Then why don't you change the title of this person who governs without a crown? If this person is actually a president, he should be called president."

"Perish the day!" said Farley. "That sounds too damned American for me!"

"Yes, but in Iceland we have a president and a prime minister. Both are elected. With the American president the political power and the ceremonial role are combined. And that can be dangerous. Dictatorship becomes a real possibility, especially when the president commands the military too."

"Exactly," Farley agreed. "The prime function of the governor general is to defend the constitution of Canada. Same function as the queen—in Britain."

"But people in other nations will believe the queen rules Canada if you continue calling this person a governor general," Njördur insisted.

"I know," Farley conceded, "but our ceremonial head of state has a lot to do with the traditions and roots of many of us. The British royal family, good, bad, or indifferent, represents continuity. We have to assume that's a reassuring element in this unstable world."

"I understand what you're saying to us, Njördur," I added. "And we still have trouble convincing the world that we're a sovereign state. The Danes, just a few days ago, doubted it."

"Those Danes!" Njördur snorted with disdain, then added triumphantly. "Ah, but we got rid of them."

If there was one thing I had learned from my first trip to Iceland it was that you don't compare anything Danish to anything Icelandic in a way that favours Denmark. Former colonials, as Canadians ought to know, don't like to hear praise for people who were once their mentors and overseers.

"And you got rid of them peacefully," I lauded.

"We did. In the referendum of 1944, we voted 97 per cent in favour of becoming our own country."

"That's evolution, not revolution. The better way" was Farley's comment.

"It is. So you will keep this governor general but change the name, yes? What shall it be then? What about 'Chairman'?" he suggested.

"That," Farley laughed, "sounds altogether too Chinese!"

"Maybe Governor in Chief," I suggested. "That was what his predecessors were originally known as, a couple of centuries ago."

"Meanwhile, you must meet Our Man, by whatever name. You're going to like Ed," Farley said. "Among his many sterling virtues is his great interest in Iceland."

Farley phoned Ed and arranged a meeting later in the afternoon. Meanwhile Njördur went home to retrieve his wife as well as a copy of the book he had recently written about the history of Iceland. When they returned to the hotel around six o'clock, Farley and I had just finished getting dressed for the banquet. I opened our door to greet them. Bera and Njördur stared at us in astonishment.

"I don't believe this," said Njördur in mock horror. "And you a social democrat!" He began to laugh at the sight of Farley in his evening dress. "You look like the last Great Auk!"

"Nothing wrong with being a Great Auk," Farley said defensively.

"Except that they are extinct, of course!" Njördur laughed even more heartily.

"These are our costumes," I explained. "Think of us as an opera company on tour. Only we don't sing."

"We just eat," Farley added.

"Claire, this is a beautiful dress and you look very nice," said Bera with a reproachful glance at her husband.

Most Icelanders live their lives in comfy wool sweaters, tweeds, corduroys, jeans, and sensible shoes. Bera may have had occasion to wear more frivolous clothes from time to time, but Njördur wouldn't have been caught dead in white tie and tails. Of course, until this epic journey, neither would Farley.

"And what did you get all those medals for?"

Njördur enquired, noticing the miniatures on Farley's chest. "Not for killing people, I hope." Njördur was a dedicated pacifist who even objected to the Boy Scouts because of their paramilitary origins.

"They came as a result of my being in the right place at the right time," he winked.

We rode the elevator to the top floor. Detectives observed us without expression as we headed for the penthouse suite, the deluxe top-floor quarters which hotels the world over set aside for visiting tycoons. I knocked. Captain Dave John, decked out in his dress uniform with enough gold braid to rival a drum majorette, opened the door.

"Hi, guys," he greeted us. His offhand manner hardly matched his authoritative uniform. Njördur and Bera, citizens of a country without a military tradition, didn't quite know how to react to him. Although the ADCs used first names among those of us who played the supporting roles in our road show, they never ever spoke to Ed or Lily that way.

"Sir. The Mowats and their friends are here," Dave announced tersely, standing at attention.

Ed was delighted to meet a couple of Icelanders from outside the strictures of government and protocol. This had been the missing ingredient throughout the tour, the opportunity to talk for more than a fleeting moment to people who had no role in the business of entertaining us. Njördur presented Ed with the copy of his book *A History of the Commonwealth of Iceland* and autographed it for him.

"Where did I read . . . " Ed began, "somewhere . . . that Iceland publishes more books per capita than any other country in the world? Is that right?"

"This is true," affirmed Njördur.

"It is because of our language," Bera explained.

"So few people in the world speak it. We must write our own stories, or always read translations."

"You must be a nation of readers," Ed concluded.

"Yes. Yes. The long winter nights," Njördur nodded.

"And a nation of writers," I remarked.

"Since the days of the sagas," said Farley.

"We have been literate for a very long time, yes. Of course, now we worry about the effect of television. So much culture pouring in, not our own culture, so much of it from America."

"Welcome to the club," I said.

"We are concerned about what this will do to our children," added Bera.

Until the arrival of a second commercial station in 1986, Icelandic television was solely a state-owned network like the CBC. Programming began around five o'clock in the afternoon with a news-and-current-events show. This was followed by an hour of dead air when, presumably, all of Iceland sat down to dinner. Later in the evening there were two more hours of programming before the station went off the air around nine o'clock.

During the 1970s, a television station operated by the American military for the servicemen stationed at Keflavik had blanketed Reykjavik as well. During our first visit to Iceland, Njördur and Bera and a group of colleagues had been involved in a struggle to reduce its signal so it could only be received on the base. Believe it or not, they won. With a show of national determination that would be impossible to imagine in Canada, the Icelandic government had forced the American military to limit the range of their transmission to themselves.

The five of us passed a stimulating hour together,

but Lily was nowhere to be seen. Longing for fresh air and exercise she had gone out for a walk earlier. Thelma, hovering off-stage, was anxiously pacing from room to room. Although Lily could don her evening clothes and all the trimmings faster than anyone else I know and emerge looking as polished as if she had spent hours at the task, sometimes she ran the timing a little too close for Thelma's peace of mind. It was a point of honour with Thelma that Lily be perfectly turned out. Lily was the third governor general's wife she had served, and if any of them had ever departed for an event with a run in her stocking, the wrong handbag, or only one earring, I think Thelma would have died of shame.

Lily finally turned up, a bit breathless. After her private tour of the surrounding streets, she had discovered a gift shop in the lobby of our hotel, full of sweaters, jackets, and mitts, a treasure trove of the hand-knitted clothes for which Iceland is world-famous.

"Where did you say it was?" I asked eagerly.

"Show you tomorrow," she called, as Thelma gently herded her away to get dressed. She had exactly nine minutes.

Jason had completely given up attending state dinners by now. He was going to eat dinner in the suite while he watched television. I rather envied him. I am always interested to know what kind of television entertains the people of other countries. He had to wait until seven o'clock for the evening's program to begin, and then he had the dubious pleasure of watching a rerun of "The Muppets" with Icelandic subtitles.

He had ordered spaghetti for dinner. It arrived in a large bowl, without sauce, but mixed with carrots and peas. He said later it looked something like mine-strone soup without the soup. Adaptable, and even adventurous about food, Jason usually ate whatever was served without a fuss, but this time he called room service to ask why there was no sauce with his spaghetti. Aiming to please, the waiter soon returned with another bowl. It was, Jay discovered, a bowl full of ketchup. Icelandic cuisine boasts many specialties but pasta is not one of them.

I was at the head table in the Sulnasalur banquet room that night. Since we were once again in a country without a monarchy, there was more room at the top. As usual I sat between two cabinet ministers, one of whom spoke English well while the other was just capable of explaining that he spoke virtually none. For the first half-hour the bilingual minister was engrossed in a conversation with the lady on his left, which left me with more time than I needed to read the menu card propped against my wineglass. It didn't tell me much. It was in Icelandic, not French. I noted that I was about to dine on *Kjötseydi, Kjúklingur, Lambahryggur*, and finally *Bessastadatriffle*. Luckily I love surprises.

Eventually, after the *Kjötseydi* (which turned out to be a clear soup with one meatball floating in it), the English-speaking minister turned to me.

"And where did your tour begin—New York?"

New York? Did he think that New York was in Canada? Or worse, did he think that Canada had no airports?

"Our flight left from Ottawa," I told him politely, adding, "That's our capital city."

He turned back to his food and evinced no further interest in Canada. The rest of our conversation dealt exclusively with matters Icelandic. I suspect he knew so little about us that he couldn't think of a relevant question. I had bemoaned the people I'd met whose experience with things Canadian was based on a stopover at Gander, but it was worse to find someone who didn't even know that much.

Fortunately conversation can always be generated around the topic of food. As the courses came and went, the shrimp (*Kjúklingur*) led to a discussion about the fishing industry, and the lamb (*Lambahryggur*) to a chat about the economics of raising sheep in a cold climate. Food can bridge the chasm between strangers. In fact, a celebration without food, in my opinion, doesn't qualify as a proper celebration at all. These interminable state banquets were rooted in the ancient practice of sharing food and recognition of the fact that people who eat together are far more likely to harbour friendly attitudes towards one another than those who don't.

This banquet didn't follow the usual form of the Scandinavian countries. Icelanders believe that the longer an event lasts the more successful it has been. As a result, we waited fifteen or twenty minutes between each course. That, I daresay, would be lots of fun if one were among old friends or felt free to move around the room. However, with only the company of one rather glum man who probably believed that Canada was full of log cabins, those interludes seemed endless.

What a relief it was to discover that there would be live entertainment between the second and third courses. A troupe of singers attired in Icelandic national dress filed in and sang three lighthearted folk songs. Just before dessert we were entertained again, this time by a poet who read from his work, first in Icelandic and then in English. It was a nice

296

touch. I cannot imagine a state dinner in our country at which a Canadian poet would be invited to read his work to overseas visitors. Poetry is taken seriously in Iceland which has more published poets per capita than any other country in the world. Statues of the country's most renowned poets dot the parks of Reykjavik. In Canada we have erected statues in honour of the Scots poet, Robbie Burns, but I have yet to hear of a statue of any Canadian literary figure, or even the intention of erecting one.

The final drain on our stamina that evening was the two-hour time difference between Denmark and Iceland. Flying from east to west works against you if you have to be alert the subsequent evening. Midnight in Iceland, when the banquet ended, was actually two o'clock in the morning by our Danish body clocks.

The concluding hour of that banquet felt like the last mile of a pentathalon. We Canadians were all struggling to suppress our yawns and to keep our eyelids from falling to half-mast. Even the old pros were having trouble. Esmond Butler, who has survived as many banquets as your average king, had trouble staying awake. Saucy Captain John, who was seated next to a lady with an ample figure and, fortunately, a sense of humour, asked her if she would mind if he put his head on her shoulder for a snooze. He didn't do it, but by the time we finally got to the dessert course, the same idea must have crossed more than one weary mind. In the final phase of the evening, while the coffee was being served in an adjoining reception room, only our energetic governor general and his sociable wife, inveterate night people, managed to look as bright-eyed as our hosts.

In the Icelandic summer, when there are only a few hours of twilight to delineate day from night, most people tend to sleep less than they do in winter. Children, buoyed by the endless evening, play out-doors until ten or eleven o'clock. So it was second nature for the Icelanders to keep the party going until the sun rose. However, once the president of Iceland made her departure, we exhausted Canadians left too.

The windows in our room were covered with two sets of draperies. Those facing into the room matched the bedspread, but behind them were inner draperies of thick black cotton, a real boon to travellers who had to adjust to the absence of night.

The darkness of that room resulted in an unex-pected side effect. Next morning, for the first time on the tour, we both slept in. The arrival of a waiter just past nine o'clock with a tray of coffee and rolls jolted us into wakefulness. Worse was the arrival of Colin Sangster ten minutes later with news that the day's schedule had been advanced by forty-five minutes. The distances we had to travel had been miscalcu-lated. Most of our destinations lay beyond Reykjavik and could be reached only over gravel roads — an impediment our team had failed to consider when they had organized the schedule two months earlier. So now the Ladies' Party had to be off and running by 9:30.

That left me with barely fifteen minutes to wash and dress. The night before, as I drifted off to sleep, I had imagined that June the fourth, our very last day of fingerbowls and flags, would begin gently with some moments to reflect on all we had seen in the previous weeks. Instead, it was mayhem. Where was my last clean blouse? Where were my navy-blue shoes? Yesterday's black ones would have to do. Even yesterday's pantyhose. No time to select just the right earrings. I struggled into my clothes, grabbed the only bracelet I could find, slapped on a dab of make-up and, with my hair barely combed, dashed for the elevator.

I landed in the hotel lobby at the precise moment Lily emerged from the other elevator. As ever, she looked terrific, her red hair smoothly in place, her clothes in harmony, her smile genuine.

"Claire!" she exclaimed, as glad to see me as I was to see her. "Where are they taking us? I didn't have a chance to look at the book this morning."

"Oh, Lordy, neither did I," I confessed. By then a lady from the protocol office was striding forward, ready to escort us out to the waiting cars. It would have been undiplomatic to haul out the little blue book at that point, so we just smiled, shook hands and remarked on the wonderful weather.

"Let's hope it's a nice surprise," I said *sotto voce*, as Lily and I parted to board separate automobiles.

And it *was* a happy surprise — a fashion show of Icelandic jewellery, a spectator event that didn't tax our endurance. We were taken to a centre in downtown Reykjavik that promoted the work of Icelandic artisans. In a spare, wood-panelled room, we watched while three flashy-looking models strutted in and out. They were dressed entirely in black to better display the unusual jewellery they wore. Much of it looked as if it had originated in central Africa rather than in Iceland. Earrings dangled to the shoulder, necklaces to the waist, and some of the bracelets enveloped the arms up to the elbow. Most of it was crafted from silver and a variety of semi-precious stones. Obviously the creative output of Icelanders ranged far beyond knitting interesting sweaters.

When the show ended, a woman carrying a tray full of pottery mugs appeared and started passing them out. Ahhh, coffee. What could have been more welcome, since I had no time for breakfast. But when I lifted a mug from the tray I discovered it was full of sherry! Sherry at ten o'clock in the morning? I dutifully took one sip to toast the spirit of accord between Iceland and Canada, and then discreetly found a window-sill where I abandoned it.

Knitting is still the backbone of the Icelandic craft industry and there was a display of every kind of cold-weather clothing imaginable, warm, serviceable, and always fashionable. There were sturdy mitts, hats, and jackets as well as some exquisite long evening gowns knitted in woollen lace. In retrospect, I wish I had bought one but that was the penalty one paid for being a visiting panjandrum: there was no time to shop. I suspect that, when a male head of state or government leaves office, one of his wife's first indulgences is to go out shopping without being pressured, watched, guarded, or followed.

Our men had been taken to see a hot-water pumping station somewhere in the Reykjavik suburbs but an hour later we were all reunited far outside the city at Thingvellir, the birthplace of democracy in Iceland. Icelanders are intensely proud of their *Althing*, the oldest parliament in Europe. While other nations endured centuries of serfdom, uprisings, revolts, and wars, the people of Iceland gathered together at Thingvellir once every year to more or less rationally discuss the concerns of their island state. This historic place is a natural amphitheatre, a rift in the rock where two cathedral-sized walls partly enclose a few acres of lichen-covered boulders.

The first Althing at Thingvellir was held in 930 AD. Apart from a period in the early nineteenth century after the Danes seized control of first, trade and, secondly, the government, the people of Iceland have enjoyed over one thousand years of democracy. It all began in this wind-swept place.

There is no architectural monument, or even the remains of one, to admire at Thingvellir. You can see right to the horizon across a silent, barren landscape. The terrain looks vaguely like the interior of Labrador. There are few signs of human habitation nearby, and only one modest plaque to tell visitors that they are standing on a spot revered throughout the nation. While other Europeans endured such miseries as the divine right of kings and the Wars of the Roses, Icelandic communities sent delegates to this undisturbed place. Here the people set up tents and huts, and the yearly gathering grew into a ceremonial festival as well as a forum for every Icelander who could manage to get there. That ancient congress has evolved into the sophisticated democracy Iceland boasts today. Now, of course, they have a permanent (and much warmer) assembly building in Reykjavik, and elections are held every four years.

It would be a rare Icelander whose spirits would not be lifted at Thingvellir. From their early school days, Icelandic children learn they are the heirs to a process that began more than a millennium before. There would surely be a deeper dimension to the Canadian psyche if we were able to pinpoint some rugged spot in our beautiful land and know that that was where the roots of our democracy began. We do have places where our native people used to gather for potlatches and other ceremonies, but they have been largely erased from living history by the invading Europeans. The native people's loss is great, but ours, perhaps, is even greater.

The Very Reverend Erik Eriksson, whose misleading job description in our briefing-book was

301

''National Park Caretaker,'' was actually a Lutheran bishop. He stood in the centre of the Thingvellir amphitheatre and addressed us, just as the people's representatives had done in this place so long ago. He talked at length about the history of Thingvellir —but I confess I didn't pay much attention to him. I had been here once before and I knew what he had to say. Thingvellir was the kind of place in which you could imagine the voices of the past if you were there alone or with only one or two close friends. I distanced myself from the group and gazed out over the lava landscape speculating that the debates of citizens a thousand years earlier were not essentially any different from those we have today.

President Vigdisi, as she is affectionately called by her fellow countrymen, later told me that her most memorable visits to Thingvellir had also been when she was alone. She had been there more times than she could remember, starting in her student years when she worked as a tourist guide. Later she became an actress, the only fragment of her personal history that she has in common with former American President Ronald Reagan. It was her work in helping to found the National Theatre of Iceland that gave her the incentive to run for public office. However, since becoming president she had been unable to indulge in solitary sojourns to Thingvellir. A president rarely goes anywhere alone.

The silence of rural Iceland is uncanny. Traffic is sparse on the two-lane gravel highways. Those few farms that manage to survive on the scattered tracts of fertile soil are a long way from one another. The loneliness is overwhelming, even for Canadians who are accustomed to large, empty landscapes. Actually, the land mass of Iceland is larger than most foreigners realize—about the same size as the island of New-

302

foundland. Urban Icelanders can find their way to a rural retreat more readily than most Canadians.

The Valnoll Resort, a few miles from Thingvellir, is one of the few places outside Reykjavik with a large restaurant. That day it was barely large enough. When we arrived there for lunch we were met by one hundred more people who had arrived from the city just to dine with us. In a small country it is a trickier proposition to organize state celebrations than in a big one. Everyone of any importance and his dog expects to be invited. We sat elbow-to-elbow eating delectable trout caught in a nearby stream, finishing the meal with the traditional *ponnukokur*, Iceland's version of the crêpe suzette. It tasted so good I took a second one.

For the third time in three weeks I dined beside a chief justice. They never disappointed me as dinner companions. This one was wise and unpretentious like his counterparts in Denmark and Finland. I was starting to feel like Hermes bringing greetings from one to the other.

That day I discovered another significant difference between Iceland and the rest of the Nordic countries: the Icelandic irreverence for the almighty schedule. Luncheon seemed to take forever and the troupe of folk dancers who entertained us afterwards danced so many encores that by the time we boarded the bus we were running an unprecedented forty-five minutes behind schedule. If that had happened on the first day of the tour, I suspect that the collective blood pressure of the governor general's household would have soared right off the Richter scale. But this was our last day. The campaign was nearly over and the soldiers were falling out of step. The mood was almost reckless — well, about as reckless as protocol officers ever get. On this day when Lily and I returned from a ladies' room three minutes late, there were no anxious frowns.

The first afternoon event took place miles from anywhere. After leaving the restaurant we drove for a bumpy half-hour before our sturdy bus headed up a steep, stony road in low gear. At the top of a hill was a small white building, surrounded by a serpentine maze of huge pipes and valves. This was the control station of the Hverageroi Geothermal Area where the hot water was channelled from the depths of the earth into buildings throughout the country. We had come to see how it worked.

This was one of the most dramatic natural settings imaginable. Surrounded by gritty lava hills, a barren canyon stretched far below us. Known as a *gja* (pronounced *gyow*), it was the ancient pathway of a mighty glacier which had inched its way to the ocean thousands of years ago. The north Atlantic, in the distance, was as blue as President Vigdisi's eyes. The hilltop was utterly quiet, save for the haunting cries of curlews.

We formed a circle around the director of Hverageroi as he explained how this marvellous operation worked. I listened with one ear. It was more inspiring to watch the birds soaring and swooping down into the ravine. Besides, I have little aptitude for understanding how any machine more complex than a wind-up toy works. But I was impressed by the fact that this incomprehensible maze was tended by just two men. To demonstrate the force of the pressure generated in the hot rock below us, they opened a valve by pulling a lever that looked like the mechanism that opens the St. Lawrence Seaway locks. A sudden Niagara of boiling water shot out of a huge pipe with the force of a cannon. The torrent roared down, down, down into the rocky valley while we watched in fascination. Hot springs must be one of God's compensations to Iceland for her scanty soil, stormy climate, and intermittent volcanic eruptions. The supply of boiling water seems virtually limitless. The only real cost is the construction and maintenance of the system of conduits that carries it to its destination. Rivers of *hot* water are alien to most of us. We are accustomed to rivers that turn to ice for part of the year. Here, in a land of hot mud and smouldering volcanoes, being scalded is as real a hazard as being frost-bitten during a Canadian winter.

While the engineer talked on, I was thinking I ought to compile a compendium of the world's most enviable jobs according to their surroundings. It could be an interesting magazine article. Did those two engineers ever tire of that stupendous hillside? I very much doubt it. For weeks I had been meeting people who laboured inside some of the world's most extravagant buildings amid works of great art. Yet I suspected that, for the people who worked among them, all those tapestries and statues ultimately blended into the woodwork. In time they would become as humdrum as the filing-cabinets. Art is not reality. At times, those two Icelandic engineers might curse the wind and the rain, but I doubt if they ever yawn at their surroundings.

The bus jolted down the hill towards our next event as I dutifully read about it in the briefing-book: *Principal Unnsteinsson will introduce the school's banana cultivation and various other projects.* Bananas? In Iceland? Yes. We were en route to the State Horticultural College at Raykirl, a complex of glass-roofed buildings and a showcase of Icelandic ingenuity. All that hot water didn't merely heat homes and swimming-pools; it was also used to heat acres of greenhouses.

An eloquent Mr. Unnsteinsson led us into a sky-lighted room where trees bearing oranges, lemons, and bananas flourished. We passed into a second room filled with rows of young lettuce plants and then into another big room ablaze with red carnations. Lily was presented with a bouquet of pink roses that had been grown there.

At the rear of Rideau Hall in Ottawa there is a large greenhouse. Amid the sea of flowering plants grown there to beautify grand occasions (as well as daily life) at both Government House and the prime minister's residence are half a dozen orange and lemon trees and one banana tree. Every once in a while the governor general is presented with an orange that has ripened enough to be eaten. At Ray-kirl, in western Iceland, just south of the Arctic Circle, we sipped champagne standing within reach of thousands of bananas, oranges, and lemons being grown in commercial quantities for the Icelandic market.

Because of the Gulf Stream, Icelandic winters are slightly warmer than most of ours. Still, one cannot help but wonder why it is economically feasible for Icelanders to grow commercial quantities of lettuce at the same latitude as the Canadian Arctic and not for someone in Canada to do the same using the energy from local gas wells. Most of the fresh produce that reaches places such as Iqualuit or Inuvik has been grown in California and trucked to Montreal or Edmonton and then flown northward. The few who can afford this wilted produce pay double or treble the price paid in the Canadian south. Hot springs are rare in Canada, but our land abounds in other sources of fuel. I think we have something to learn from a nation with a population no bigger than the city of London, Ontario that has arrived at such rational solutions to the problems of northern living.

Outdoors there wasn't a tree anywhere within sight of the Horticultural College. But if you looked carefully at the ground there were lots of flowers, tiny subarctic flowers no bigger than my smallest fingernail.

When we boarded our bus for the return journey to Reykjavik we were already one hour behind schedule, and by the time we reached our hotel we were an hour and a half late. Our tenth and final state dinner was only thirty minutes away, so there was no time for a relaxing bath or a shampoo. I slithered out of my gabardine suit and into my evening gown. By then I was beginning to be annoyed that all this fuss should be necessary. I had reached the point that comes to all travellers sooner or later: I didn't want to open any more suitcases or unpack any more clothes. As long as I was tidy and presentable would it matter if I, or anyone else, ate dinner in the same clothes I had worn all day?

The answer was, of course, that the clothes you wear to a celebration do make a difference. And that evening the president of Iceland turned my theories about dress protocol upside down. She arrived wearing Icelandic traditional dress. Her outfit consisted of a long black skirt, a black blouse with embroidered flowers, and a tall, conical headdress made of black velvet from the top of which hung a mediaeval white veil. There she was, the most emancipated of women in a very progressive nation, dressed in the formal clothes that her ancestors had worn for centuries. And half a dozen other women were wearing approximately the same thing. The women of a nation that elected a woman as its president and formed the first feminist political party in the world still revered the traditions of their great-grandmothers.

This was a departure in more ways than one. I had been observing all along that, at formal occasions in the culture of the western world, only the men wore identical clothes as a way of making a statement about their brotherhood and their solidarity. Suddenly I was looking at several women, including the president, who were almost identically dressed. They too knew how to make a show of solidarity. I wished we had a costume we could wear to display our bond with one another on Canadian ceremonial occasions. In our country a woman would have to be a Hutterite or a Highland dancer to feel comfortable wearing exactly the same clothes as her peers.

At our very last banquet, I sat in a circle of seven articulate Icelanders: one politician, two academics, and four bureaucrats. Not one of them had been to Canada yet all of them were inveterate travellers. On an individual basis, Icelanders are the most travelled people in the world. Statistically, every second Icelander makes one overseas journey every year. Like Canadians, they usually think in the general direction of south when they plan a journey, so I could understand why Canada was not high on their list of desired destinations.

The one foreign place that all of my dinner companions had visited was, surprisingly, Glasgow. That matter-of-fact Scottish city is, as the jets fly, their nearest metropolis and Icelanders go there a lot. It is both nearer and cheaper than Copenhagen, Oslo, or London. For Icelanders Glasgow has become what Buffalo, New York, used to be for Torontonians in search of the exotic at budget prices.

We chatted about Glasgow and dined on shark.

Shark is one of the national delicacies of Iceland, and the ultimate treat for foreign visitors, which puts it in the same epicurean league as Canadian wild rice. Wild rice was, in fact, served at every one of our reciprocal banquets. Easy to transport, it was an ideal choice. But there was a problem in Iceland. The chef had misunderstood the instructions and he served it cold as a separate side dish. It looked—and tasted—about as inviting as yesterday's porridge. The Icelanders who tried to eat that tasteless, sticky blob must still be wondering why we hold it in high esteem in Canada.

At the conclusion of banquet number ten we listened to the Galliard Ensemble for the last time. Resourceful Robert Bick had unearthed a piece of classical music by an Icelandic composer. He told the audience that he regretted not having heard of the work of Haflidi Hallgrimsson before he prepared for this tour; but I suspect that not too many Icelanders knew of his work either. A composer of contemporary chamber music, he had written one of those dissonant, abrasive pieces that I defy anyone to remember. I listened attentively to *Verk Fryir flautu og sello*, a work for flute and cello, philosophically bearing in mind that Beethoven's Fifth Symphony had been received with unanimous disapproval the first time it was performed. That evening, the chief merit of Hallgrimsson's composition seemed to be its brevity.

At midnight, the Cinderella president was carried away in her limousine. After a while our other guests began to drift away too. It was, after all, a Thursday night and they doubtless had to get on with their workaday lives the next morning. But we didn't.

You wouldn't think that a group of people who had attended so many extravagant events would want to gather for yet another party, but we did. This was the very last night of the very last day. Knowing that within twenty-four hours we too would be returning to our own mundane orbits gave us a final burst of energy. We were now veterans of a strenuous campaign and, like every good team, we had grown fond of one another. Only a handful of us was likely to meet again after the flight home, and even if we did, the circumstances would never again be quite like this. So it was that majors and musicians, accountants and aides-de-camp, secretaries and speech-writers all ended up in a convention-room in the hotel basement that the management had hastily provided, fearing our spontaneous celebration might disturb the other guests. After weeks of being punctual and predictable we were about to throw off our watches along with our collar studs.

Lily came to this impromptu party in her favourite flowered dressing-gown. Jason wore jeans. Commodore Gordon Edwards arrived in his plaid bathrobe. I never did find out where Farley found a Marimekko patio gown that had not been designed for male proportions, but that was what he was wearing. No one looked funnier than Robert, Joe, Doug, and Paul of the Galliard Ensemble. They arrived dressed in their bathing trunks — topped with white tie and formal jackets. Thus attired they started the party with a lively little piece by Mozart, while we all broke up laughing. Mozart could never have imagined that his music would one day be performed by four semi-clad Canadians with hairy legs, on a night in Iceland when the sun didn't set. It was a scene from *A Midsummer Night's Dream* as filmed by Fellini.

If I had written our final crazy episode into a novel, no one would have believed me. Yet if anyone had predicted that I would one day take on the role of a lady-in-waiting, I would never have believed that. Had any of us—Ed, Lily, Jason, Esmond, Léopold, Colin, Bernie, Dave, Farley, and all the others —ever pictured ourselves dining with kings in our fantasies about the future?

Ed didn't attend our final, frivolous gathering. He is a convivial, warmhearted man yet he kept part of himself in reserve during his years as governor general. The dignity of the office never left him. Though Farley—who was the only one who dared—went up to his suite and tried to coax him to join us, he declined. By then he was in his bed with a good book, *A History of the Commonwealth of Iceland*, by Njördur Njardvik.

On the morning of June 5 our Canadian Forces 707 stood on the tarmac at Keflavik waiting for us to board for the flight to Ottawa. Near the ramp stood the serene President Vigdisi Finnbogadottir and her ministers, lined up to say goodbye. I shook her hand and said "Bless." It is the Icelandic way of saying goodbye, a word which has the same meaning as it does in English.

"Bless," she replied and then I boarded the plane for the last time. On this final glorious morning I felt just that. Blessed.

And here, as the old Scandinavian story-tellers used to say, this saga ends.

About the Author

Born and educated in Toronto, Claire Wheeler Mowat has pursued various careers including graphic designer, housewife and writer. With her husband, Farley Mowat, she has lived in Newfoundland, the Magdalen Islands, Cape Breton Island and Ontario. She has had a lifelong interest in remote, northerly places and has travelled widely in Siberia, Scandinavia and the Canadian Arctic. Her first book, *The Outport People*, was the story of her years in a small community in Newfoundland.